HITLER'S
GULF WAR

Also by Barrie G. James

The Little Black Book of Pharma Marketing

Trojan Horse: The Ultimate Challenge to Western Industry

Business Wargames

The Marketing of Generic Drugs

The Future of the Multinational Pharmaceutical Industry

HITLER'S GULF WAR

The Fight for Iraq, 1941

by

Barrie G. James

Pen & Sword
AVIATION

First published in Great Britain in 2009 by
Pen & Sword Aviation
an imprint of
Pen & Sword Books Ltd
47 Church Street
Barnsley
South Yorkshire
S70 2AS

ISBN 978 1 84884 090 4

Typeset in Sabon by
Phoenix Typesetting, Auldgirth, Dumfriesshire

Printed and bound in the UK by
the MPG Books Group

Pen & Sword Books Ltd incorporates the Imprints of Pen & Sword Aviation,
Pen & Sword Maritime, Pen & Sword Military, Wharncliffe Local History,
Pen & Sword Select, Pen & Sword Military Classics and Leo Cooper.

For a complete list of Pen & Sword titles please contact
PEN & SWORD BOOKS LIMITED
47 Church Street, Barnsley, South Yorkshire, S70 2AS, England
E-mail: enquiries@pen-and-sword.co.uk
Website: www.pen-and-sword.co.uk

Previews of Hitler's Gulf War

"What a fantastic and enjoyable book, fast moving, entertaining and exciting. I read this in a single dose and loved it. It reads like a thriller yet is a tale of courage, bluff and daring the like of which is rarely seen anymore. The characters that populate the tale are really from another era of heroes from a desperate yet more noble age and the daring of senior leaders causes me to reflect that we have few like this, if any, nowadays. I found it special as I was in Habbaniya often, the last time being March 2008. I was aware of the incident but not the details. I look forward to returning and telling anyone who will stop and listen – read *Hitler's Gulf War!*"

Colonel Tim Collins OBE, Gulf War 2003 (the inspirational *Eve of Battle* speech in Kuwait in 2003, a copy of which reputedly hung on the wall of the Oval Office in the Bush White House.)

"Twice in the last twenty years, British troops have been active in a Gulf war. I was Prime Minister during the first war in 1991. I saw events as they unfolded and marvelled at the skill and courage shown by our armed forces. Barrie James reverts to an earlier conflict against a more deadly enemy. It is a stirring story of courage against the odds that would grace the pages of any work of fiction – yet this is all fact. It tells the story of a forgotten war that deserves to be remembered and hopefully, through these pages, it now will be. I thoroughly enjoyed it."

The Rt. Hon. Sir John Major KG, CH Gulf War 1991

"Intrigue, politics, compelling characters, chaos and courage. Barrie James brings Iraq's history alive, revealing the best and worst of human nature and how individual acts of heroism and bluff combined with tenacious spirit and individual choice determine international events. James is Hercule Poirot in a murder mystery. He deconstructs the whole to make us realise the significance of each clue, each individual foible, each decision demanding us towards the conclusion, compelling us to understand how it all fits together. I read this story in one day and if you want to understand how wars are won and lost, how impossible it is to predict outcomes and gain a personal insight into how timing and one human choice really can tip the balance of history, then read this book. Iraq is still the world's stage and we are all merely players."

Squadron Leader John Peters, Gulf War 1991 (co-author of *Tornado Down*)

"In the spring of 1941 I was a subaltern in the Royal Horse Guards (The Blues) and a member of 'A' Squadron of the Household Cavalry Regiment which in turn was part of the 4th Cavalry Brigade in Palestine, together with the Wiltshire and Warwickshire Yeomanry. In May 1941 the Brigade, christened 'Habforce', together with the Arab Legion from Jordan and a Battalion of the Essex Regiment, was despatched across the desert between Palestine and Iraq to relieve the siege of the RAF base at Habbaniya. The siege had resulted from a coup by a pro German faction in Iraq under the leadership of Raschid Ali. The story of that siege and that of the British Embassy in Baghdad is recounted in fascinating detail in Dr. James' book. In the course of the relief of both Habbaniya and the British Embassy, two regular divisions of the Iraqi army were defeated by the Brigade group and the valiant efforts of the RAF. I am proud to have taken a small part in the 'Fight for Iraq 1941' and would like to pay tribute to Dr. James for the research he has undertaken to bring a little known but successful conflict to the knowledge of a wider world than that of those who took part in it."

His Grace The Duke of Wellington KG, LVO, OBE, MC, DL, Gulf War 1941

"The British operation in Iraq in 1941 is one of the most interesting and yet least known episodes of the Second World War. It is an extraordinary story of audacity and courage that prompted even Churchill to get excited about 'the arrival of His Majesty's Life Guards and Royal Horse Guards, in armoured cars, across many hundreds of miles of desert'. Barrie James' well-researched account now tells this intriguing story, and he tells it very well, so that this book reads as much like a thriller as it does the very important historical contribution that it undoubtedly is. I enjoyed the book greatly'.

Major General Barney White-Spunner CBE Iraq 2008, GOC HQ, Multinational Division [South East], Basra

Contents

Preface

Hitler's Gulf War is set around the epic story of one of the most remarkable examples of daring in military history and the first real German defeat in the Second World War.

On an isolated, indefensible airfield fifty-five miles from Baghdad a group of poorly armed and outnumbered RAF airmen equipped with obsolete aircraft, together with a few soldiers, outfought the much larger and better-equipped Iraqi forces aided by the Germans and Italians.

It also tells the story of how trucks, taxis, buses and antiquated armoured cars were commandeered to move a small, hastily assembled relief column of cavalry, infantry and Bedouins. They accomplished what no conquering army in history had done. They fought their way across a 500-mile barren, unmapped desert, enduring temperatures approaching 120 degrees to reach the airfield.

In a gigantic game of bluff, fewer than fifteen hundred soldiers, supported by the RAF in their obsolete aircraft, against odds of twenty to one went on to take Baghdad. They foiled a coup, returned a king to his throne and destroyed Axis aspirations in the Middle East.

Following German successes in Greece and the Western Desert in 1941, a defeat in Iraq would have rolled-up Britain's position in the Middle East, lost her the Suez Canal and her independent oil supplies and threatened India. This would have provided the Axis with the opportunity to create a land bridge between Europe and Asia. A mortally wounded Britain would no longer have had the capacity to continue her sole resistance against Germany, making it impossible to free mainland Europe from the Nazis.

A strong German presence in Iraq and Iran would have brought Turkey into the Axis camp, enabling Germany to finish off Russia at her leisure. The spectre of an Axis-dominated region running from the Atlantic to the Pacific would have provided the isolationists in the United States with enough ammunition to persuade Roosevelt to abandon Britain as a lost cause.

History has overlooked the strategic implications of this isolated battle. The victors and the vanquished were buried where they fell. No monuments exist and no awards were made to commemorate the immense personal courage and the ultimate sacrifices made by many of all races, religions and nationalities.

ix

Hitler's Gulf War is based on a wide range of official, academic and public sources. The book uses reported American, British, German, Italian, Iraqi and Saudi dialogue, and personal reminiscences, to add richness to give what is, to the best of my knowledge, the first full account of the events precipitating the thirty-one-day war in Iraq in 1941. *Hitler's Gulf War* covers the interplay between individuals and countries which reordered the landscape of Iraq, it describes how the war played out and how it set the scene for Iraq's turbulent future which has come to haunt the West.

Acknowledgements

I am breaking with tradition to start by thanking my wife. Mary is my soul mate, best friend and encourager, whose patience, enthusiasm and support have seen me through five previous books, a Master's and a PhD, and have effortlessly handled several very disruptive country-to-country moves.

Mary makes everything possible in my life.

I also need to thank my late parents. My father Ivor was a man with a deep sense of right and personal honour. His tales of travels in the Middle East, including a hilarious trip across the Iraqi desert in a Nairn Brothers bus from Haifa to Baghdad, on his way to work for the Anglo-Persian Oil Company in Abadan in 1943, gave me the wanderlust and a consuming passion to find out why things happened the way that they did. Both of these have driven my life. My mother Dora nursed me back to life on so many occasions, supported me in everything that I wanted to do and gave me the will to succeed.

The genesis of *Hitler's Gulf War* was a Starbucks in the Barnes & Noble bookshop in the Menlo Park Mall in New Jersey in early September 2000. In between cappuccinos while skimming through a number of military history books, I became fascinated reading a few snippets about the events in Iraq in 1941, and the idea emerged for a book. However, things only began to get serious in November 2005, following my relocation from Switzerland to the UK.

I had chosen by accident to live in East Anglia, which put me among not only a number of RAF stations but, more importantly, residing in my village and the next, a number of retired RAF officers who willingly gave me their time and experience.

My neighbour, Gp Capt Steve Lloyd, is the Deputy Director of the Air Historic Branch of the RAF. Steve kindly started me off with a trawl through their files. I was also very fortunate to have AVM Warwick Pike brief me on combat medicine, Air Cdre David Bywater related his experiences in flying the Shuttleworth Trust's biplane fighters and Gp Capt Brian Lee gave me a run-down on photo-reconnaissance. By the greatest of coincidences I also found Wg Cdr Alan Robertson in the next village, who told me about his fascinating visit to Habbaniya in 1988.

Any researched work depends on assistance and advice to help to fill in the inevitable blank spaces, tease out long-forgotten gems of information and broaden the work by suggesting new directions.

The regimental museums – the Essex Regiment (Ian and Keith Hook), the Green Howards (Sarah Taylor), the Household Cavalry (John Lange) and the King's Own Royal Regiment (Peter Donnelly) – helped to add both depth and balance to what has been largely written about as solely an RAF victory rather than the first true British use of combined operations.

Catherine Morris (*The Times*), Julia Burgess (RAF Disclosures) *Fregatenkapitan* Dr Jorg Hillmar (*Militargeschichtliches Forschungsamt*), Herr Betten (*Deutsche Dienstelle*), John Rolph (RAF Armoured Car Association) and Arnaldo Minuti (Italian Foreign Ministry) were kind enough to provide me with obituaries from their files, enabling me to complete a further dimension by featuring the post-1941 lives of the key characters involved in those thirty-one days in May.

Wg Cdr Martin Hooker of the RAF Regiment Association was even kind enough to recommend a publisher.

I was also very fortunate to be able to use the formidable resources of three of the world's greatest archives – the British Library, the Imperial War Museum and the National Archives.

However, I would not have been able to source the bulk of my research without the considerable help of Huntingdon Library staff: Sue Booker, Kathryn Bottomley, Michelle Clark, Joy Glazier, Manju Mathew, Elaine Mountfort, Sharon Reed, Lynn Reynolds, Laura Southgate, Moira Storey, Ann Teal and Lesley Wood with great kindness, enthusiasm and understanding, obtained all manner of difficult-to-source books and journal articles; nothing was too much trouble.

Motorbooks in London, probably the best military bookshop in the world, located some obscure books for my research, accompanied by some mean rockabilly from Wanda Jackson.

Two old friends were of immense help. Michael Fenwick made a crucial introduction at Jak's Black Pudding Luncheon Club, and military historian Guy di Carlo in Florida cast his critical eye over the work and made some important suggestions which transformed the work.

I thank you all.

Prologue

The make-believe country

The very name Iraq conjures up notions of intrigue, passion, obsession, war and wanton violence – in almost equal measures.

These perceptions are rooted in the way in which Iraq was created out of the complex past of Mesopotamia, the influence of seminal events – the disintegration of the Ottoman Empire and two world wars – and the forces that they unleashed, nationalism, ethnic feuds and religious intolerance.

Iraq is pure invention, the result of diplomatic gerrymandering.

Iraq only became a country in the aftermath of the Great War with the fateful Ottoman decision to ally itself with Germany and the equally fateful British decision to stay after the Turkish defeat and carve out a subservient nation in the heart of the volatile Middle East. Iraq, based loosely around the ancient land of Mesopotamia, encompassed Basra, Baghdad and later Mosul – three previously quite separate and disparate *Vilayets*, or provinces, at the eastern edge of the Ottoman Empire.

A continued and controlling British presence in Iraq was seen as crucial to Imperial communications. The central concern was a secure route to India, and Iraq offered an air and land bridge across the Middle East shortening both time and distance. The proximity of Iraq to Britain's growing investments in oil-rich southern Persia and the discover of oil at Kirkuk in 1927 made the justification, retrospectively, even more compelling.

Control was legitimized by having the League of Nations grant Britain a Mandate over Iraq in 1920.

From the very start things went wrong, as the British completely underestimated their task. The *Vilayets* had never experienced democracy or produced a society not dominated by oppression, autocracy or mayhem. Among Iraq's two million people there was no national unity, and the predominant influences were family, blood, tribe and religion, and where all else failed, and even if it did not, brutal violence.

The British found Iraq virtually ungovernable, and faced a continual round of uprisings, massacres of their troops and officials, widespread brigandage and incursions across Iraq's porous borders by the Turks

1

from the north and Ibn Saud's militant Wahhabi *Ikhwan* from the south and west.

A widespread and ferocious series of revolts that broke out in 1920 from Shia and Sunni clergy opposed to rule by non-Muslims, Kurds who refused to submit to an Anglo-Arab authority ruling from Baghdad and tribes resistant to paying taxes brought the British face-to-face with 130,000 mobilized and armed Iraquis. It took until late February 1921 to regain full control of what became known as the *Ath Thawra al Iraqiyya al Kubra* (The Great Iraqi Revolution), at the cost of the lives of 6,000 Iraqis, 500 Imperial troops and £40 million.

The large army needed to police Iraq, as well as simultaneously fighting an insurrection in Ireland, manning a stand-off with Russia over Persia and containing growing problems in India, caused increasing domestic difficulties in Britain. Compulsory military service abroad and the fact that many soldiers were serving when they should have been demobilized at the end of the Great War caused widespread unrest. Britain was going through an industrial class struggle supported by the emerging power of the trades union movement and the growth of the Labour Party, which gave a sharp political edge to government concerns over stability in Britain.

The continued unrest in Iraq was also an unacceptable financial strain on a Britain which was struggling to come to terms with the crippling economic costs of the Great War. Cutting government spending in order to restore an overstretched Britain's declining economic position and to reduce the vast debt accumulated during the First World War became a political necessity.

However, cutting the cost of the large garrison in Iraq called for radical political and military remedies other than direct military occupation.

The solution adopted was indirect rule, using a surrogate ruling through a strong centralized government beholding to the British. This approach had worked successfully in both the Indian and Malay states, and there was every indication that this would apply in Iraq.

The British arranged for Feisal, the third son of Sharif Hussein of Mecca, to be enthroned as King in 1921. This also helped to mollify his father, to whom the British had promised an independent Arab state as payment for his support against the Ottomans, as well as assuage the ambitious and power-hungry Hashemite dynasty. Although acclaimed in a one-question plebiscite as the people's choice, which gave him a ridiculous 96% of the vote, Feisal was elected by ballot-rigging by the British on a monumental scale. Feisal, from the Hejaz and a Sunni, relied on his descent from the Prophet Mohammed's family as his

Islamic credentials to appeal to Muslims. While Feisal looked like a king – slim, bearded and aquiline nosed – and acted the part with regal dignity, he, like others uncertain about where their best interests lay, intrigued with his subjects and dissembled his patrons. He was a slippery customer and few believed a word he said, with the result that everyone distrusted him.

Feisal depended on British political and military support, but to cultivate popularity and enhance his legitimacy he needed to appease anti-British sentiment by obtaining concessions from the British. Convinced of the advantages of indirect rule, the British went along with Feisal's demands for the growing transfer of power to the Iraqi government.

In an attempt to reduce the size of their garrison and the crippling costs of Imperialism, the British hit on the novel idea of using air power to control the country. Air power with its speed of application, geographic reach and economy far outweighed the value of ground troops, and, applied by the Royal Air Force, air power quickly became the major instrument for maintaining order.

As part of the policy of indirect rule and to create stability and stem the outflow of money, the British later formed and financed an Iraqi army to take over from Imperial troops, using the RAF in a supporting role. However, this was one more factor in the uneasy relationship between Britain and the regime she had created in Iraq. The British visualized an Iraqi army as a small voluntary force to maintain internal security, while the Iraqi nationalists visualized a large conscript army to unite the disparate communities in a cohesive national institution.

To their credit the British spent millions to vastly improve the lot of Iraqis. They rebuilt roads, canals and bridges, repaired the railways and established clinics and hospitals, and provided Iraq with a revenue department, a judiciary, medical and education systems and a police force, and put in place an elected government.

The British finally gave Iraq its formal independence in 1932, and Iraq joined the League of Nations.

Nevertheless, Britain still maintained a level of indirect control. The Anglo-Iraqi Treaty signed in 1930, which was to run for twenty-five years, guaranteed Iraqi assistance to Britain in time of war and allowed the passage of British troops through Iraq. A British Military Mission remained with the Iraqi Army, and the RAF retained two bases – Habbaniya, fifty-five miles west of Baghdad, and at Shaiba, near Basra.

On the surface Iraq seemed to be moving towards a prosperous future. Beneath the surface, however, the country was in turmoil. This was not surprising, as Iraq, in many ways, was a make-believe kingdom built on false pretence with a monarchy that lacked legitimacy with the majority of its subjects. Iraq had an imposed king, in a country where monarchy was an alien concept. Feisal, a Sunni from the Hejaz, was an outsider in a country with a Shia majority. He spoke an Arab dialect barely intelligible to most of his subjects, and had no sense of connection with Iraq's ancient past. Iraq was kept going by a government designed and sponsored by the British for British purposes, communications and oil, and its elaborate and expensive administration was never asked for nor wanted by Iraqis.

Britain's policy of indirect control carried with it the seeds of its own destruction. Running a country on the cheap inevitably produces massive risks. By ridding themselves of the immediate responsibility of direct government, the British, in the interests of saving money and tying this neatly together with Hashemite ambitions, conceded their influence in the country. Ever greater concessions to the Iraqis to prop-up Feisal's legitimacy, and giving Iraq its own army, contributed to the emergence of a powerful military that was hostile to both the British and civilian political control.

Internal dissent

There were constant problems among Iraq's heterogeneous population.

The Sunni minority, who owed their allegiance to Mecca, were concentrated in the centre and west of Iraq and made up around a quarter of the population. They were exposed to education and urbanization and were inclined to support nationalism, and resented even surrogate British rule. The Shia majority, around half the population, lived mainly in the south, followed tribal and Sharia law and looked towards Persia. The Shia were suspicious of any government control, particularly because of their experience under the Ottomans of Sunni autocracy. The Kurds, although Sunni Muslims, were not Arabs. They represented about a fifth of the population, lived mainly in the north and had more in common with Kurds living in Turkey and Persia than they did with their fellow Iraqis. Then there were scattered communities of Assyrians, Armenians, Turkomans and Yazidis, together with Jewish and a number of Christian minorities in the towns.

Added to this volatile mix were endemic conflicts between the tribes and the cities, the landowners and the peasants, the merchants and the bazaaris, Iraqi nationalists and pan-Arabists, and the urban Effendi, who had served under the Ottomans, and young Army officers. These disparate groups were all fighting for a place in the emerging state structure.

Feisal was forced continuously to maintain a balance between these competing interests in a country lacking both internal cohesion and unity.

Parliamentary democracy under Feisal became a façade, with cabinets formed and forced to resign by direct intervention of the King. Iraq was a parliamentary state where parliament had no effective power and where political opportunism, greed, corruption, blood feuds and personal rivalries flourished, leading to continuous changes of government. In fact, between 1922 and 1936 there was not even a pretence of constitutional rule: military power, not the electorate, determined who had the right to rule.

There was no universal suffrage in Iraq, and few except the wealthy and the powerful played any part in the political process. The political process itself failed to develop procedures for resolving internal conflicts other than rule by decree and the frequent use of repression.

More problematic was the fact that fifty families, largely wealthy Sunni, governed the destiny of Iraq, as parliament primarily represented their interests. The ruling élite consisted of fourteen people who frequently changed cabinet posts and were trying to get into the government if they happened to be out. A popular joke in Baghdad in the 1930s was that the *Ins* were trying to keep the *Outs* out while the *Outs* were trying to get in and get the *Ins* out.

Shortly before his death Feisal said, rather tellingly, of the people over whom he ruled, that they were 'unimaginable masses of human beings devoid of any patriotic idea, imbued with religious traditions and absurdities, connected by no common tie, prone to anarchy and perpetually ready to rise against any government whatever'.

Feisal had hoped that once independence was achieved the politicians would close ranks and would devote their efforts to internal reform.

Nuri al Said, a former Ottoman officer and the then Prime Minister, with a pro-British stance, resigned, and the King invited Rashid Ali al Gailani, a shrewd, industrious and ambitious lawyer and a political pragmatist, as well as a passionate nationalist, to form a new government.

The Christian Assyrians rebelled in 1933 as the government would not provide them with assurances of security as had been guaranteed by the British and Iraqis under the Mandate. Rashid Ali wanted to impress the public with a tough policy towards the Assyrians to demonstrate that the government could keep the many minorities in Iraq in line. Feisal was in Europe when he heard of the Iraqi Army's brutal massacre of 300 Assyrian women and children. Facing mounting criticism from the League of Nations, he replaced Rashid Ali with a more moderate government.

Feisal died in 1933 and was succeeded by his son. Ghazi, a 25-year-old playboy, was a wayward, immature and self-willed young man, ignorant of state affairs and unequipped by training for his duty of king-ship. His main pursuits in life had been motor-car racing, flying, horse riding and the cinema.

Not surprisingly Ghazi was unable to keep the fragile balance his father had struggled, often successfully, to maintain between competing interests. Politicians took advantage of his inexperience and the flimsy political order to compete for power. Between 1932 and 1934 five more changes of government occurred as politicians embarrassed each other with press attacks, palace intrigues and incidents. Politicians also incited the tribes, habitually opposed to any central authority, to rebel. This caused the fall of a further three governments between 1934 and 1935.

From the early 1930s the Iraqi government became utterly dependent on the Army to maintain authority and unity to such an extent that the Iraqi Army became the *de facto* arbiter of political power. The Army, disillusioned with chronic and unresolved instability due to the failure of the politicians to manage Iraq, eventually took matters into its own hands and moved into the power vacuum. Iraq suffered its first military intervention, the Bakr Sidqi coup, in 1936. Until parliamentary democracy, of a sort, was restored in mid-1941 all governments in Iraq were either run directly by the military or functioned only at the pleasure of the Army, with cabinets heavily staffed by Army officers.

However, even in the military there were differences of opinion and jealousy. The 'old guard' of Sharifian veterans, predominantly Sunnis, who had fought with Feisal and Hussein against the Turks, were increasingly challenged by the ex-Ottoman officers, who were often from urban and lower-middle-class Sunni and Kurdish families. The result was that Iraq suffered a series of coups and counter-coups as the two military factions divided by networks of patronage built around religion, sect, ethnicity, regional affinity or ideology jockeyed for power, with each faction supporting a different set of civilian leaders.

Exacerbating the praetorianization of Iraqi politics was the rise of pan-Arabism and the Palestine Question.

Arab nationalism

The defeat of Turkey in 1918 and the abolition of the Ottoman Empire in 1922 created an ideological tidal wave among its subjugated people of nationalism – the desire of people to run their own affairs.

The failure of the British in Palestine and the French in Syria to fulfil their mandates and to create independent Arab states stoked the fire of nationalism among both Arab intellectuals and Army officers. This intensified as the prestige of Britain and France declined in the late 1930s, resulting from their repeated appeasement in the face of German and Italian aggression. The impression of weakness that this created fanned the flames of pan-Arabism throughout the Middle East.

In Iraq leading nationalists saw an emerging opportunity to create a much larger state centred on Iraq, encompassing Palestine, Syria and Transjordan. From the beginning of the 1930s Iraq became steadily more nationalistic and more anti-British.

German nationalism, with its emphasis on language and history as unifying factors, and the efficiency of Hitler's totalitarian state, which seemed to offer a more effective way of governing in a fragmented society with endemic political instability, was seen as the perfect role model by many Iraqi nationalists and Army officers.

The primary purpose of the Iraqi education policy from 1930, under the influence of Sati al Husri, the Director-General of Education, and his successor Sami Shawkat, was to overcome the difficulties of forging a nation-state out of the diverse and conflict-ridden social structures, as well as transform parochial loyalties – tribal, ethnic and religious – into a national identity. To inculcate a national ideology and strengthen patriotism among the young, government schools quickly degenerated into political seminaries to impart *Husriyya* – political extremism and xenophobia. Military training became a compulsory subject at the Teachers' Training College, technical schools and all government schools, and a paramilitary youth movement, the *Futuwwah*, was formed. Following the German and Japanese militaristic models of the 1930s, the *Futuwwah* had enforced codes of conduct, its members drilled military style and wore uniforms, complete with ranks and insignia.

A vision of Iraq as an autocratic, Prussian-style, highly centralized state which could eventually engulf its neighbours began to capture the imagination of the nationalist intellectuals and the Army officers like Taha al Hashimi. This clashed with ex-Sharifians like Nuri Said, who saw Iraq's future in a Hashemite federation with Transjordan.

Clubs like the *al-Muthanna* and leading newspapers, such as *Al Alam Al Arabi*, were used as conduits for promoting a national ideology and shaping anti-British feeling to further develop nationalism.

Under Feisal Iraq was not over-concerned with Zionism. Feisal believed that an accommodation could be reached between the Arabs and the Jews. The situation changed radically under Ghazi. Ghazi listened to neither Iraqis nor the British, and proved to be an ineffective ruler easily manipulated by politicians. Despite his failings be began to be seen as a national hero following his demands for the annexation of Kuwait and his support for the Palestinians Arabs during their 1936–1939 revolt.

On his death in 1939, in a road accident, Ghazi became revered as an Iraqi martyr. Opportunistically the nationalist movement was able to convince a substantial part of the population that Ghazi had been killed by the British, who opposed his policies.

Ghazi's son, King Feisal II, ascended to the throne, but as he was only four years of age his pro-British uncle, Emir Abdul Ilah, was appointed Regent.

Religious zealotry

The catalyst moving forward both Iraqi nationalism and pan-Arabism was the arrival in Baghdad in October 1939 of the Mufti of Jerusalem, Haj Amin al Husaini.

Haj Amin, a former artillery officer in the Turkish Army, was a powerful combination of a Palestinian Arab from a leading family, a fervent nationalist and a Muslim religious leader. At the end of the First World War Haj Amin agitated for the creation of an Arabic state in the Middle East comprising Palestine, Syria, Lebanon, Jordan, Iraq and even Cyprus and parts of Turkey. When this failed he created an anti-Jewish party, *El Nadi al-Arabi*, and fomented the murderous riots in Jerusalem in 1920. He fled to Damascus but was sentenced to 10 years imprisonment *in absentia* by the outraged British Colonial Administration. The British, in a mistaken gesture of lenience, pardoned Haj Amin. Fooled by his soft-spoken, mild manner and dignified exterior, which concealed burning Arab nationalism and a violent non-compromising nature, the British committed an even bigger error in 1921. The British agreed to Haj Amin's appointment to the post of Mufti, which his family had held almost unbroken since the seventeenth century, and a role that usually went to jurists who arbitrated disputes by interpreting Koranic law.

As Mufti he began to work behind the scenes, playing a major role in the anti-Jewish violence in Palestine in the late 1920s, and he was a major force behind the Palestine Arab revolt of 1936–1939. Assassinating moderate Arabs in the cities, who supported the British and urged compromise, and attacks orchestrated by the Mufti on Jewish settlements and British installations became the norm.

Haj Amin fled to Beirut in October 1937, one step ahead of the British, who were seeking him for complicity in the murder of Lewis

Andrews, the British Commissioner in the Northern District of Galilee. The Mufti eventually fell foul of the French, due to his involvement in nationalist politics in Syria. He again fled, this time to Baghdad, in 1939.

The Iraqi parliament offered sanctuary, welcoming Haj Amin with open arms as a Palestinian hero, and they and the Iraqi government and the public helped finance the Mufti and his cause. Haj Amin was not short of funds, as money was also supplied by other Arab countries, like Egypt and Saudi Arabia, as well as Germany and Italy. All saw the potential for the Mufti to ferment trouble for the British.

The Mufti established his headquarters in Baghdad with his Chief of Staff, Jamal al Hussaini, his Islamic religious adviser Sheik Musa al Alami, as well as his military commander, the ruthless Syrian-born guerrilla leader Fawzi al Qawujki, who had been trained at St Cyr, the French military academy.

The Mufti began to spread a malevolent influence throughout Iraq. He started his own newspaper, *Istiqal,* which was subsidized by the Germans and Italians. More pointedly, Haj Amin proposed Palestinian and Syrian refugees to fill essential government positions which the state of illiteracy in Iraq prevented its own subjects from assuming. Rapidly key posts in the administration and in the professions – engineers, doctors, lawyers, teachers and, importantly, the police – were filled by Palestinians and Syrians who owed allegiance to the Mufti.

Haj Amin quickly established a broad range of relationships with the leading politicians, the important merchants and the Army leaders, and became the guest of honour at many government functions. Against a background of general unrest created by the war, the Mufti became the focal point of nationalist aspirations among the Army leaders and younger politicians.

In this safe haven, leadership of Arab nationalism throughout the Middle East quickly began to coalesce around Haj Amin. On a pan-Arab level he became the spokesman of a secret committee of leaders from Syria, Iraq, Palestine and Transjordan, as well as the leader of the Palestine nationalists.

However, the Mufti came into his own in Iraq as the leader of the *Committee of Seven* – a cabal of influential Army officers and politicians – who increasingly made the political decisions in Iraq.

German Aspiration

Germany had had designs on the Middle East, and particularly on Iraq, since the 1890s, driven by the Kaiser's jealousy of Britain's commercial empire in the East. His obsession, the Berlin–Baghdad railway, reached the Turkey-Iraq border in 1913 and was only halted by the outbreak of the Great War

The Arabists at the *Auswartiges Amt*, the German Foreign Ministry, in Berlin kept the idea of German influence in the Middle East alive through the Weimar period, and made an astute choice in selecting Dr Fritz Grobba as the *Chargé d'affaires* of the German Mission in Baghdad in 1932.

Grobba was the central figure in Germany's Middle East policy in the 1930s and early 1940s. Although being a member neither of the Nazi Party nor of the aristocracy that traditionally ran foreign policy, he was, nevertheless, a highly able and influential German agent.

Grobba, who spoke fluent Arabic, Persian and Turkish, had served with the German Military Mission to the Turkish Army in Palestine during the Great War, and knew the people and the mentality of the Middle East. While he found an increasing radicalization of Iraqi politics and a country simmering with resentment towards the British, he also found people who were impressed by Germany's strong leadership and militarism and inspired by the resurgence of German power and by its intimidation of Europe.

Grobba was very ambitious, some say unscrupulously so, and many thought that he had 'Lawrentian dreams'. Grobba saw that bringing Iraq into the German camp could provide him with a springboard into a major career at the *Auswartiges Amt*.

Grobba was egalitarian and a very active and highly personable diplomat, and he and his charming wife worked diligently to create a wide range of relationships embracing leading political, religious, military and economic leaders in Iraq. He was very successful in promoting German trade, but his role changed after 1935 and he became much more political.

Although the Iraqi Army, and later the Mufti, had continuously requested German arms, Grobba, while sympathetic to the nationalist cause and to the trouble that the Mufti wanted to create for the British in Palestine, was caught in a policy trap.

Between 1933 and 1939 Hitler's *England Politik* was designed to strike an alliance with England, which meant that Grobba was unable to be seen to support radical anti-British nationalists. Complicating the issue was the 1936 Rome-Berlin Axis agreement, where the Eastern Mediterranean was deemed to be within the scope of the Italians, who were already trying to undermine the British funding newspapers like *Saut al Shab*.

Grobba believed that these factors, together with Hitler's anti-

Semitic and racial doctrine, the *Weltanschauung*, which excluded Arabs, and the *Auswartiges Amt*, with a greater interest in Europe, all contributed to underestimating the value of Arab nationalism. This compromised Germany's Middle East policy, which Grobba had helped to both design and implement, and undermined his mission in Iraq.

Attitudes towards the Middle East policy in Germany were diverse. The *Aussenpolitisches Amt*, the Office for Foreign Policy of the Nazi Party, and the German military intelligence organization, the *Abwehr*, were interested in expanding Germany's influence. In the *Auswartiges Amt* only a few people valued the Arab nationalist movements positively, and the prevailing view was that they were not to be taken seriously. The *Wehrmacht*, the German armed forces, felt that Iraq was too far away and too difficult to reach to support an armed insurrection.

Grobba also felt that Italian involvement was an embarrassment, as many Arabs viewed Italy as a colonial power with imperial ambitions in the Middle East.

As a consequence a frustrated Grobba could provide only financial support and personal encouragement rather than public displays of support, overt propaganda and arms shipments.

Nevertheless, Grobba decided to continue 'his' policy in a covert fashion. He intrigued with Iraqi Army officers, exploiting their Anglophobic and Germanophilic sentiments through dinners, parties and film shows, and financed pro-fascist groups and cells. From the mid-1930s his house was a central meeting point for Iraqi nationalists. He subsidized newspapers to run pro-German and anti-British propaganda as well as the serialization of Hitler's *Mein Kampf* in Arabic in *Al Alam, Al Arabi* in 1933, and negotiated successfully for German to replace French as the second language in Iraqi schools. Grobba also began to subsidize the creation of clubs promoting Iraqi-German friendship in Baghdad, as well as reciprocal visits by politicians of the two countries. In 1937 he arranged for the Hitler Youth leader Baldur von Schirach to visit Baghdad with a delegation, and financed representatives of the paramilitary *Futuwwah* to attend the Nuremberg Rally in 1938.

After Munich, Germany paid less attention to appearances, and in 1938 followed Italy's lead by broadcasting anti-British propaganda in Arabic from Radio Zessen, near Berlin, using an Iraqi announcer, Yunis al Bahri.

With high levels of illiteracy throughout the Middle East, the radio was an ideal instrument for spreading propaganda. As early as 1934 the Italians had launched an Arabic-language service from Radio Bari, glorifying Italy and its achievements and supporting the Arab nationalist cause against the British and French. The Italians provided radio sets at nominal prices throughout the Middle East, which was extremely popular with the owners of Arab cafés, the centre of social life, who installed the sets for their patrons.

British indifference

Strange as it may seem, the British in Iraq did little to counter the Mufti, nationalism, anti-British propaganda and growing German and Italian intrigue. In particular there was a lack of perception of the symbiotic relationship between nationalism, the Army and public education created by *Husriyya*. The Military Mission was marginalized by nationalist officers who shared little with their British counterparts, and frequent staff changes and the lack of interest that many, if not most, British diplomats had in Iraq contributed to the problem.

The lack of action had become a hallmark of a British diplomatic service, with a culture steeped in decades of languid appeasement.

The ambassador, Sir Basil Newton, did not speak Arabic and had little direct contact with community leaders except those who were pro-British. He was disinclined to listen to anything which challenged the conventional wisdom that the country was unstable but manageable with 'our' Iraqis, and he dismissed everything else as rumour and speculation. He even obstructed countermeasures by refusing to have intelligence operatives join his staff to conduct covert propaganda and political subversion.

Surprisingly, things did not change when the British declared war on Germany in 1939.

Declaring war on Germany, as the Anglo-Iraqi Treaty required, created controversy among Iraq's leaders. The Army officers opposed, while the pro-British politicians like Nuri supported, a declaration of war. Others, like Rashid Ali, saw opportunities for gaining concessions on Palestine and Syria as the price for Iraq's entry into the war. Major opposition in both September 1939 and again in February 1940 to a declaration of war resulted in merely a break in diplomatic relations between Iraq and Germany.

While Grobba was declared *person non grata* and had to leave Iraq, and German citizens were deported to India for internment, the nationalists and the Mufti continued to communicate with Germany through the radio of Lugi Gabrelli, the *Chargé d'affaires* in the Italian Legation.

As the war intensified and the Germans scored victory after victory, Nuri's position worsened and the pro-British group became isolated. Rashid Ali again took office in March 1940.

The second testing time came in June 1940, when Italy declared war on Britain and France. The Iraqi government not only refused to declare war on Italy but also would not break off diplomatic relations, despite intense pressure from the British Ambassador.

Perceptions of weakness

The fall of France in May 1940 changed the Iraqi cabinet's attitude towards Britain. The view prevailed, even among the pro-British faction, that a British defeat was inevitable and that the best course of action was to adopt a strictly neutral stance and limit the fulfilment of treaty obligations towards Britain to a minimum.

When the Ambassador requested Iraqi agreement to land British troops in Basra to proceed to Haifa across Iraq in June, the government responded by limiting the number of troops and imposing a fixed time for their presence on Iraqi soil. Although there were intense negotiations between the British and the Iraqis, particularly over changes in policy in Palestine, the British rejected the Baghdad proposals.

This inevitably led to the Iraqis' increasingly turning towards Germany. Several visits were made by Iraqi government ministers and by the Mufti's private secretary, Osman Kemal Haddad, in June and July 1940 to Fritz von Papen, the German Ambassador in Ankara, to discuss opportunities for collaboration with Germany.

In September 1940 Haddad travelled to Berlin to see Grobba, Otto-Werner von Hentig, the Head of *Pol VII*, the section of the political department of the *Auswartiges Amt* responsible for the Middle East, Dr Ernst Woermann, the Under-Secretary of State and Ernst von Weizsacher, the Secretary of State.

Haddad's visit was designed to solicit German support in the form of an immediate formal statement guaranteeing Iraq's independence.

The Germans were cautious, and while agreeing in principle, were unwilling to make a public commitment, and Haddad returned to Baghdad with vague promises rather than firm undertakings. The Germans also requested that the Iraqis should not act militarily against the British without German agreement, or encourage the British to occupy Iraq.

However, the Mufti and Rashid Ali continued to pressure the Germans, and finally, in October 1940, the Germans, together with the Italians, issued a joint communiqué which, while expressing sympathy with Arab aspirations, was more aimed at anti-British propaganda than a full statement of support.

Anglo-Iraqi relations deteriorated further, and despite Nuri's attempt at conciliation Rashid Ali refused to change his stance. Although the majority in the government rejected Nuri's viewpoint that Britain would prevail, and felt that Britain was now isolated and on the brink of ruin, many in parliament were pro-British and favoured cooperation with Britain. When the Italian forces under *Maresciallo d'Italia* Graziani took a beating from the British in the Western Desert in March 1941, neutrality had an aura of safety about it. The majority feeling in the country was that Iraqi neutrality was essential: if Britain were to win, Iraq would be safe anyway, and if the Germans won, Iraq's best hope was to do nothing to offend them.

Haddad undertook a second visit to Berlin in December 1940 with the specific objective of securing economic and military aid, in particular captured British weapons. As increasing political tension in Baghdad was weakening Rashid Ali's position, he became desperate to clarify the attitude of the Axis towards Iraq and to obtain arms.

This time Rashid Ali's requests fell on sympathetic ears, as Germany needed to put pressure on Britain to counteract her successes against the Italians in Cyrenaica. Creating a new battleground in the rear would distract the British.

Despite the fall of Rashid Ali's government in January 1941 in response to his ongoing dispute with the British and the Regent, the Germans were well advanced in their plan to ship weapons to Iraq. The Germans correctly believed that the new regime of Taha al Hashimi was an extension of previous nationalist governments. al Hashimi was a known admirer of Germany and of the *Golden Square*, a cadre of four extreme nationalist Iraqi colonels – Salah el Din al Sabbagh, Fahmi Said, Mahmud Salman and Kamil Shabib – whom he regarded as his protégés.

With the promise of German arms on the way and a Britain becoming increasingly weaker, the Mufti, the *Golden Square* and Rashid Ali and his cabinet of ultra-nationalists began to plan their coup.

Chapter One

Slippery Slope to War

Baghdad, 28 February 1941

Outwardly the white villa with its green window shades in a quiet palm-lined street looked nothing more than the home of a wealthy Iraqi merchant or leading civil servant.

In fact, the large, two-storey structure, with big airy rooms, complete with a garden shaded by nebk trees and surrounded by a 2 m high wall, had been built in the early 1900s as the city residence of a leading *pasha* in the Ottoman administration.

Since October 1939 the villa in Zahawi Street provided by the Iraqi government was the official residence of Haj Amin, the Mufti of Jerusalem.

The only thing out of the ordinary on that late February day was the succession of unmarked cars that drew up to the entrance to the villa around 10 o'clock that morning.

The first car, a highly polished black Studebaker, arrived at ten minutes to ten and deposited three men outside the villa. All three had a military bearing and looked uncomfortable wearing civilian clothes. A few minutes later, from the direction of central Baghdad, a grey Mercedes drew up to the main gate, and a small man in a white suit and a red fez, carrying a black briefcase, hurried past the guards into the villa. At two minutes past ten o'clock a dark blue, dust-covered Wolseley with a dented wing stopped outside the villa. The two men inside had driven themselves, and a guard slipped behind the wheel and drove off as the two men walked down into the sunken garden, designed like most Baghdad suburban gardens for watering, and mounted the steps to the villa.

Once assembled in one of the larger downstairs rooms, the six guests were joined by their host, the Mufti.

Haj Amin, a tall man, surveyed the gathering. The Mufti's delicate features and gentle manner, accentuated by his unusually bright, deep blue eyes, trimmed and hennaed goatee, which gave him his nickname,

15

'The Red Fox'. His calm voice belied his zealousness and his malevolent and violent nature. He was ruthless, humourless and of the authentic stuff of which dictators are made. He emitted, as Freya Stark noted, 'a radiance of a just-fallen Lucifer'.

The two young boys in white skull caps and green and white striped robes who had been serving bitter Arabic coffee from long-necked copper pots to the guests were dismissed. Haj Amin then closed the double doors to the room and indicated to the group that they should take their seats at the large table.

The Mufti in his black gold-trimmed robe, wearing a white turban around a scarlet *tarbush*, took his place at the head of the table on a throne-like chair of the kind peculiar to the Orient – plenty of gold and tinsel, with its back upholstered in a vivid green.

'To bind us to our purpose we must swear our allegiance to our duty on the Koran', said Haj Amin.

Following Haj Amin's lead, Rashid Ali, Naji Shawkat the Minister of Defence, al Sabbagh, Yunis al Sabawi the Minister of Economics, Fahmi Said and Mahmud Salman all swore allegiance

The Mufti, to the irritation of Rashid Ali, was chosen as the leader of the group as much for his closeness to the *Golden Square* as for his link between Rashid Ali and the nationalist politicians.

'My friends,' the Mufti began, 'Britain is finished. She has been defeated at Dunkirk and is now isolated from mainland Europe. A few days ago the Germans began to attack the British in Libya. Britain is already stretched fighting the Italians in East Africa. Malta is under siege. Palestine is an armed camp and the Vichy French are already working with the Italians in Syria. German and Italian radio propaganda is working in our favour. Arabs all over the Middle East now see the British as the vanquished. The British are surrounded by enemies and they are vulnerable. Now is the time for us to move decisively against them.

'We need to take the initiative in defining our own future. If we allow the Germans or the Italians to clear away the British we will be merely substituting one master for another as we have done with the British for the Turk. First we must show the British that we will not tolerate one more concession which undermines our independence. This means that we must refuse all and any attempts to land more British troops in Basra or have any of their troops transit Iraq. We must also continue to refuse to break off diplomatic relations with Italy.'

'We must be careful', interjected Rashid Ali. 'If we stick rigidly to the terms of the Anglo-Iraqi Agreement of 1930 we will give the British no reason to act against us. This will also give us the breathing space to arm ourselves with more modern weapons from the Germans and prepare for German military help.'

'No!' said al Sabbagh, 'The time has come to show our resolve. Arguing the legalities has brought us nothing!'

'It has prevented the British from moving against us until we are ready', Rashid Ali responded angrily.

'Friends, we must speak with one voice', soothed the Mufti. 'We must not fall into the common trap in Iraqi politics of arguing among ourselves. This only destroys our ability to fulfil our destiny.'

'We must also remember that we need to move decisively against pro-British elements in politics, the armed forces and in the administration', pointed out Salman.

'That means that we need a new government,' added Shawkat, 'and we must neutralize the Regent. Why not appoint Sharif Sharaf, who is a distant relative of Abdul Ilah, so that there is a bloodline? He is a bit gaga, but he is someone who will do what he is told. We also have to make our government appear to be a unifying agent for the country, and at the same time have a semblance of legality about it. Sharif Sharaf offers us a way out of a constitutional crisis.'

'Why don't we call it a Government of National Defence? This would imply that our actions are being taken in the public interest', added Said

'But,' said al Sabbagh, 'it must not appear that the Army is controlling the government, so we will need a civilian prime minister to give the government a semblance of legality.'

'Precisely! I nominate Rashid Ali,' Haj Amin said, 'to head our new revolutionary government.'

While Rashid Ali smiled, acknowledging the agreement of the others, he was under no illusion that the Mufti would be the power behind the throne of any new Iraqi government.

'We should establish a date for our assumption of control', suggested Said.

'We need enough time to get our forces, their equipment and supplies into position without arousing the suspicions of the British', rejoined al Sabbagh.

'But above all, we must not lose the initiative, and we need to move soon', added Haj Amin.

al Sabawi, who had remained quiet throughout the discussion, said, 'The perfect time would be March 31st, the day of the closing session of parliament. All the politicians will be in Baghdad, enabling us to pick up the pro-British elements and capture the Regent with ease.' He added, 'March 31st will give us enough time to complete our military preparations and for the German and Italian aid to reach us.'

'Good, then it is agreed', said the Mufti. 'Now we need to decide upon our individual responsibilities and set up a timetable for action.'

Throughout March 1941, planning for the *coup d'état* progressed. However, the plotters faced a challenge. The Regent, together with the British Ambassador, pressured al Hashimi to move members of the *Golden Square* out of Baghdad to provincial garrisons to reduce their influence. While the Regent did order the transfer of the least influential of the *Golden Square*, Kamel Shabib, to a remote post, the Colonels managed to get the order reversed. Realizing that they could no longer count on al Hashimi's support, and that the Regent was their enemy, they planned to neutralize both problems.

The British, who knew of al Hashimi's friendship with the pro-British Nuri, invited al Hashimi's Foreign Minister, Tawfik al Suwaidi, to meet Anthony Eden, the British Foreign Minister, in Cairo to discuss Anglo-Iraqi relations.

Cairo, 6 March 1941

Anthony Eden, a handsome, patrician figure, motioned al Suwaidi to sit down at the lunch table set for two on the columned verandah of the large, two-storey, colonial-style villa which housed the British Embassy in Cairo.

The view from the veranda of the magnificent lawns and gardens that spilled down almost to the Nile did what it was supposed to do – impress visitors of Britain's Imperial power.

When the lunch was finished, the coffee served and the small talk ended, Eden rose and asked al Suwaidi to follow him down the steps into the garden so that they could walk down to the low wall which bordered on the corniche and be alone for a private discussion.

'Minister,' Eden began, 'Britain's problem is that we have endured a lack of cooperation with Iraq since the war began which is in conflict with our 1930 Treaty. I realize that your government has inherited this situation, and my reason for inviting you to Cairo is to suggest how we may resolve this together.

I have a number of recommendations which I feel your government would be wise to consider. First you must sever diplomatic relations with Italy. Neither you nor we can tolerate an enemy presence which poisons our relationship. Secondly, British troops must occupy a number of areas in Iraq.'

'But, Sir Anthony, that would cause considerable unrest', interjected al Suwaidi for the first time.

'You need to sell this both as a build-up to liberating your brother Arabs, as we will need to move against the Vichy French in Syria, as well as protect the oil wells and pipelines from sabotage to ensure that Iraq receives an uninterrupted flow of revenue from the sale of its oil.

Thirdly, there is a strong anti-British clique centred on the Army and some leading politicians. It is probably wise that you retire these senior officers and replace the politicians with a pro-British cabinet.'

The Foreign Minister considered Eden's remarks carefully before responding. 'Everything that you have mentioned, Sir Anthony, depends on overcoming the considerable opposition of the Army commanders. This is not something that we can achieve quickly. We need time.'

'Minister,' Eden said as he turned and led al Suwaidi back towards the villa, 'we both know that neither Iraq nor Britain has time. We must do this together, now, before events spiral out of control and we have no way to resolve this problem as friends.'

They mounted the steps to the veranda and strolled in silence through the villa to the lobby, with its antique Chinese chests and chairs.

al Suwaidi collected his Homburg and briefcase from the servant waiting in the lobby, and the two men walked together down the short stairway flanked by two stone lions towards the Rolls Royce waiting in the driveway.

al Suwaidi paused, and Eden stopped and turned. 'Perhaps, Sir Anthony, it would be easier for the Iraqi public to accept these concessions if Britain implements the 1939 White Paper on Palestine and let the Palestinian leaders return.'

'Minister,' responded Eden sharply, 'I cannot implement such sweeping changes in the middle of a war. As we discussed, we need to focus on resolving our mutual problem in Iraq before we even begin to think about problems which do not affect your country.'

Eden quickly changed his tone and smiled at the Iraqi minister, who was now looking glum. They shook hands. al Suwaidi entered the car, and as the door closed Eden lent forward and spoke to him through the open window: 'Minister, I am glad that we had this opportunity to discuss our mutual problem. I know that you will present our recommendations to Prime Minister al Hashimi. I look forward to receiving your agreement to resolve the problem and the steps you will take so that we may put this matter behind us and work together for a better future.

As the car pulled away from the villa, al Suwaidi sat back and reflected that Eden had given al Hashimi little more than an ultimatum. Either you fix the problem in Iraq or we shall do it for you. He knew that whatever al Hashimi felt, implementing these recommendations would be virtually impossible, given the certain opposition of the *Golden Square* and the Mufti.

Cairo in early 1941 was a nest of spies. Within twenty-four hours Eden's 'recommendations' were in front of the Mufti and the Colonels in Baghdad, and on the desks of Joachim von Ribbentrop at the *Auswartiges Amt* on Wilhelmstrasse, in Berlin, Count Ciano the Italian Foreign Minister at the Palazzo Chigi in Rome and Cordell Hull the Secretary of State at the State Department in Washington.

In Baghdad the conspirators realized that if al Hashimi capitulated to the British they would be sidelined and would lose a golden opportunity to rid themselves of the British. If anything, Eden's 'recommendations' spurred them past the point of no return.

Baghdad, 1 April 1941

On the night of 1 April 1941 the plotters seized power. Truck-loads of troops were ferried into Baghdad to secure the radio station, the telegraph office, the three main railway stations, the bridges across the Tigris, the airport, the palace and the main roads into the city.

The doctor who had signed, under duress, a certificate of the Regent's death from coronary thrombosis, managed to smuggle a copy to the Regent through the palace cook.

The Regent spirited himself away to the house of an aunt, Princess Salha, who lived in an old building on the east bank of the river. They, together with the Queen Mother and Princess Badiya, asked Dr Harry 'Sinbad' Sinderson,the palace physician and royal confidant, to come to the Princess's house to discuss what they should do. Sinderson, after a roundabout journey to avoid the growing military presence on the streets, managed to persuade the Regent that he should dress as a woman and make his way by horse cab to the American Legation rather than to the British Embassy, which was on the other side of the Tigris and bound to be guarded by the plotters.

Dressed in a woman's *abba*, veil and shoes, the Regent arrived at the American Legation in the early hours of the next morning. As an unknown 'woman' he had difficulty in gaining admittance to see the Minister, Paul Knabenshue. Eventually he managed to see the Minister's wife, Olive, who, realizing it was the Regent, quickly admitted him

Transferring the Regent safely to the protection of the British Embassy across the river would be impossible, and it was decided that he would leave Baghdad with the Knabenshues. They were due to welcome the new British Ambassador, Sir Kinahan Cornwallis, who was flying into RAF Habbaniya, some fifty-five miles due west of the city, later in the day. If they could get the Regent to Habbaniya he could be flown to safety.

Concealed in the Ambassador's white Buick under a rug which covered the legs of the Minister and his wife, the Regent left the American Legation on his way to Habbaniya.

As the car approached the King Feisal bridge across the Tigris, it was flagged down at an Iraqi Army roadblock.

The soldiers raised their rifles, pointing them at the car, and a captain from the 3rd Division strode forward and peered into the vehicle. Knabenshue rolled down the window. 'This is an official car from the American Legation and I am the accredited Minister. Please let this car pass', he said authoritatively.

He rolled up the window quickly and sat back as if to signify that this was all he needed to say to be allowed through the roadblock.

The captain stood back, clearly puzzled, as he had been ordered to detain all Europeans.

Olive Knabenshue looked on in alarm as the Minister, out of sight underneath the window, drew back the slide cocking his Colt 45 automatic, and she saw the end of the Regent's pistol sticking out from under the rug.

The captain conferred with another officer and returned to the car. The flag of the United States on the bonnet of the car seemed to have done the trick, and the captain stood back, smiled, gestured for his troops to raise the barrier and waved the Buick through the roadblock.

Just over an hour and forty minutes later the Buick entered the gates of RAF Habbaniya.

Across Baghdad the hunt was under way by the conspirators for the Regent, Nuri Pasha and other pro-British politicians.

Also forewarned, Nuri Pasha had called Sqn Ldr Patrick Domvile, the British Air Liaison Officer with the Iraqi Air Force. Domvile met Nuri at a mutual friend's house and had him dress in one of his spare RAF uniforms before driving out to Habbaniya. They had a close call at the Falluja bridge, fifteen miles from Habbaniya, when they were stopped by an Iraqi Army roadblock.

With hats pulled down over their eyes and collars turned up to hide Nuri's well-known face, they eventually managed to convince the lieutenant in charge that they were just a couple of RAF officers returning from a weekend leave in Baghdad. After a few minutes' deliberation, the barrier across the road was raised and they were allowed to proceed to Habbaniya.

Later that evening the Regent and Nuri Pasha, as well as three other politicians, a senior member of the Royal bodyguard,Ubaid bin Abdulla, and another member of the Royal family, all of whom were able to make their way to Habbaniya, were flown out to Amman in Transjordan, and then on to Jerusalem.

Habbaniya and Baghdad, 2 April 1941

After inspecting the RAF honour guard at Habbaniya, Sir Kinahan 'Ken' Cornwallis, the incoming British Ambassador, met Paul Knabenshue in one of the Air Headquarters block's small conference rooms.

Knabenshue, who had been the American Minister in Baghdad since 1932, quickly brought Cornwallis up to date with the current situation. Rashid Ali's intrigues, the malevolent influence of the Mufti on Iraqi affairs, the coup engineered by the *Golden Square* and the flight of the Regent and the pro-British faction led by Nuri Said had combined to create a very unstable situation.

Knabenshue and Cornwallis quickly put together a joint programme of evacuation of both countries' citizens, should the need arise, calling the plan Operation *Concentrate*, and agreed to meet at the British Embassy the following afternoon to finalize their positions.

'What are you going to do about presenting your credentials to Rashid Ali?', Knabenshue asked as they emerged out of the cool of the admistration block into the blazing sun and walked towards Cornwallis's cars.

'I think that my best move is to withhold the presentation as long as possible. Rashid Ali expects me to present my credentials, which is an endorsement by the British government legitimizing his illegal coup. My strategy is to make Rashid Ali work for our endorsement', Cornwallis replied.

Cornwallis, a giant of a man well over six feet tall, with a distin-guishingly large nose, needed time to think. He had his wife travel in his deputy, Adrian Holman's, car, and Cornwallis now sat silently in the back of his Daimler as it took him from Habbaniya towards the Embassy.

An Arabist, Cornwallis had first arrived in Baghdad in 1921 and had worked diligently to help King Feisal create the new state of Iraq. Those had been heady days, he remembered with fondness, building a modern state out a group of warring tribes and religious factions. Although they had had their setbacks they had steadily developed a form of democ-racy and the infrastructure to support a state.

However, his closeness to King Feisal had been resented by the ambitious Rashid Ali. Following Feisal's death, Rashid Ali, then Minister of the Interior, had conspired to have Cornwallis recalled to the Foreign Office in London. This was Cornwallis's first visit to Iraq since 1935 and he steadfastly resolved to put his animosity towards Rashid Ali behind him in the interests of stabilizing the current state of unrest. He hoped that Rashid Ali would also put aside his resentment.

As the car neared Baghdad Cornwallis could see the tops of palm trees poking over the walls surrounding houses and the sand-coloured minarets hidden in dark green palm groves. Over to his left, some five miles or so in the distance, he could see the sun reflecting off the twin golden domes of the Khadimain mosque with its four minarets looking like soldiers protecting one of the most holy Shia shrines. To his right was a large date orchard and, just beyond, he could see a bund with a line of gum trees which marked a bend in the Tigris.

As the car moved past Baghdad West station nothing much appeared to have changed in the fabled city of 'One Thousand and One Nights'. However romantic the images that Baghdad conjured up, it had not been a true capital city since the seventh century, and in many respects it was just another hot, dusty city on the way to somewhere else.

Little had happened since the time of the caliphs, and most of the old houses with their white or ochre-painted mud, brick or plaster walls had been rebuilt, refaced and reroofed. Cornwallis remembered that when he had left Baghdad in 1935 the city boasted only a few modern houses. A group of wealthy merchants had been roundly criticized when they built several villas in colonial style, complete with balconies, along Haifa Street

As the car entered the city proper he could see the houses in the Salhya district. With grated windows and intricately carved wooden shutters on the first floor, wooden balconies that jutted out into the street and nail-studded wooden doors, the houses gave out an aura of timelessness. Interspersed between the houses were twisted and dusty alleyways so narrow that donkeys with their panniers could fill them from side to side. Even quite wide streets radiating off the main thoroughfares like King Feisal Avenue, along which he was travelling, were still unpaved and became virtually impassable in a rain storm and contained any amount of dust in the summer.

None the less, Baghdad had a certain charm, and Cornwallis looked forward to meeting the many people who had befriended him and with whom he formed close relationships in the fourteen years he had spent among the Iraqis.

April 1941 was a tense time for both Iraqis and the British. Political and military reverses for the British mounted. Bengazi fell to Rommel's *Afrika Korps* on 4 April, and by the 10th German tanks were on the Egyptian border at Sollum. Within twelve days Rommel had regained the ground that had taken Wavell fifty days to win against the Italians.

Yugoslavia capitulated on the 17th and the Greeks on 24 April, and the remnants of Wavell's battered force, sent to support the Greeks at Churchill's insistence, were digging in on Crete awaiting a German assault.

In Iraq the plotters consolidated their position. They forced al Hashimi's government to formally resign, and they arrested pro-British politicians, including the Governor of Basra. The King, his mother and other members of the Royal family were exiled to Kurdistan.

The new government was quick to manage the flow of news, and jammed the Regent's broadcasts from Jerusalem. The tone of the press changed and became vitriolic. The Arab-language broadcasts of Radio Zessen and the Italian station, Radio Bari, contributed to the propaganda by claiming that the British had poisoned King Feisal and murdered King Ghazi.

But the Germans and the Italians were still a long way from Iraq, and Rashid Ali needed an excuse to keep the British talking until Axis arms arrived and the Germans could intervene directly. Cornwallis correctly assumed that Rashid Ali was playing for time, and withheld presenting his credentials to the new government to indicate Britain's refusal to accept the new regime. With the Regent in Jerusalem preparing to form a new Iraqi government to challenge the legitimacy of his regime, Rashid Ali was forced to solicit recognition from the British and the Americans.

Rashid Ali had publicly declared on 3 April that his government would respect all its international obligations. This made it difficult for the regime to prohibit the landing and transit of British troops, and Rashid Ali sought a compromise with Cornwallis.

However, in Iraq the pressure on the British began to increase. Following the banning of British military personnel from travelling between Baghdad and Habbaniya, and the seizure of the radios from the British Military Mission on 6 April, AVM Harry Smart, the AOC RAF Habbaniya, lobbied Cairo for both air and land reinforcements. AVM Arthur Longmore, Wavell's AOC Middle East, responded that due to the gravity of the situation in North Africa, the German campaign in the Balkans and Greece, the considered view was that Iraq's priority was too low and nothing could be spared.

The next day Wavell advised the Foreign Office that any support for Iraq was beyond his means.

A frustrated Churchill contacted Gen Claude Auchinleck, the C-in-C India, who agreed to spare an infantry brigade and an artillery regiment intended for Malaya. Convoy BP7, supported by the aircraft carrier HMS *Hermes*, the cruiser HMS *Emerald* and a few small warships, set sail for Basra from Bombay on 12 April.

Baghdad, 16 April 1941

It had taken Cornwallis less than twenty minutes to drive the two miles from the Embassy, cross the new King Ghazi bridge and arrive at the Serai government building which housed the Council of Ministers and Rashid Ali's office. In 1935 it would have taken him almost two hours to cross the wide river by ferry and then pass through streets thronged with people.

Cornwallis had a fascination for the streets of Baghdad and its cosmopolitan inhabitants, who could be distinguished by their bewildering array of headgear and clothes. All of which seemed to Cornwallis to be an attempt to resist assimilation.

The wealthy, educated and employed Iraqis wore western dress topped with black *sidora* caps. The *Effendis* wore red *fezzes*, the Kurds in their sheepskin coats had black felt pot-caps perched on their heads and the *Mujtahids*, the elders, wore black turbans. The *burnoosed* marsh Arabs in their *gallabeahs* and the Bedouins from the desert in camel-hair cloaks topped by *agals* and *keffiyehs* mixed with Sikhs in khaki and white turbans, Baktiaris in their brimless top hats, Bengalis in *dhotis* and Europeans in tropical suits topped by straw hats or topees. They were only part of the rich pageant of styles, colours and materials. Moving among them were Persian pilgrims on their way to and from the Shia holy places in black and brown *abbas*, Sunni and Shia mullahs, priests from the Orthodox faiths and rabbis and Arab, Armenian, Christian and Jewish merchants and the odd Parsee in a hat like a cow's foot.

Here and there were story tellers and scribes, money lenders and carpet sellers and the tea and water carriers, and weaving among them would be donkeys, camels, horses, oxen and even barefoot children pulling carts loaded with all sorts of imaginable, and even unimaginable goods. Everywhere were *fellahin* and the ubiquitous beggars all wearing once-white *dishdash*. Gliding amost silently, and virtually unnoticed, through the melée were women in black *abbas* and veils.

Baghdad's miles of covered bazaars were interconnected with vaulted passageways crammed with a bewildering array of stalls piled high with bananas and dates, manna and fish and grain and nuts. Inside was a riot of smells of dung and wood smoke mixed with incense and spices and a cacophony of sound, as people haggled in Arabic, Armenian, Farsi, Greek, Hebrew, Hindi, Turkish, Syriac and English amid the incessant barking of dogs and the braying of donkeys.

Cornwallis could see that since the *coup d'état* things had changed. The city was now strangely silent. The soldiers on every street in dark khaki topees or *fezzes*, wearing khaki shirts and shorts, with rifles slung over their shoulders, watching the few people that ventured into the streets, created an air of menace.

As Cornwallis's car drove down Raschid Street he saw that Dellal's department store was closed, as were the banks – The Eastern, The Ottoman and The Rafidan – while shutters covered the store fronts of Bata Shoes, Loya Brothers American Watch Company, Abu Maurice's ice-cream parlour and the cinema that showed Egyptian films. Even those fixtures of Baghdad street life – the outdoor cafes with customers smoking their *nargilehs* and the hawkers, peddlers and street vendors – were all gone. The wise Baghdadis stayed at home, fearful that they could be part of any further round-up of people who could possibly challenge the new regime.

Cornwallis's journey had not been without incident. Twice when the Daimler, flying the Union pennant, had slowed down to turn a corner people on the pavement had spat at the car, confirming to Cornwallis that if he had arrived sooner things might now have been different.

Cornwallis was responding to an invitation from Rashid Ali to meet to discuss, as it was delicately phrased, 'matters of mutual interest'.

He had no intention of letting the meeting become a negotiation session or of being ambushed by a group of people from the new regime and harangued, and he had stipulated that they meet alone for an hour.

Leaving his companion, Adrian Holman, the Councillor and Cornwallis's deputy, in the anteroom, Cornwallis entered Rashid Ali's office. The Prime Minister rose from his desk smiling and indicated that they should sit at a group of comfortable chairs.

'Thank you for coming, Sir Kinahan,' Rashid Ali, a small bespectacled man, began in Arabic as they shook hands, 'it is nice to see you again despite the circumstances under which we meet. My government is concerned about the poor feelings that the British have about our new regime. I have been instructed to find a way in which we can quickly reach a mutually beneficial agreement so we can normalize relations between our countries.'

Cornwallis was too old a hand to be drawn into an endless discussion in flowery Arabic. Exaggerations, implied meanings and false perceptions of wounded pride were widely used in Arabic as bargaining points throughout the Middle East.

'Rashid Ali', he responded in English in his slow, deep, husky voice, to convey a simple but one meaning message. He was also careful not to use the title of Prime Minister, which could be taken as an indication that the British government accepted the legitimacy of his office and his regime. 'I would like your permission in accordance with the Anglo-Iraqi Treaty of 1930 to land additional troops at Basra and to have them transit the country. You have confirmed on 3 April that your regime intends to honour its obligations, and, given the situation in Iraq, we consider that the presence of British troops can hardy fail to act as a stabilizing factor. Consequently this would be to our mutual benefit.'

He waited a few seconds for the message to sink in. 'Furthermore, when we receive your unconditional approval to establish our communication route through Iraq from Basra, the British government will immediately extend informal relations, and after a while we will fully recognize your government.'

Rashid Ali, unused to such directness, was momentarily taken aback. 'Naturally I will need to discuss this with my cabinet before I can give you a definitive answer,' he responded. 'I have a number of other issues, Sir Kinahan, which we should also discuss, which concern propaganda, gaining public support for the rupture of diplomatic relations with Italy, the White Paper on Palestine, as well as problems of interpretation of the Anglo-Iraqi Treaty. I would like these to be linked to your request for landing additional troops and diplomatic recognition so that we have a comprehensive agreement.'

'No', said Cornwallis, sidestepping Rashid Ali's attempt to broaden the discussions to drag out their resolution, so giving time for help to arrive from the Axis. 'We have to handle each issue separately, and begin with a simple permission to land and transit our troops in accordance with our agreement. As a gesture of good faith we will then immediately resume informal relations with your government. You will now have to excuse me', he said as he stood up. 'I have a prior engagement and I was only just able to fit in our discussion among my other meetings today.'

He shook hands with Rashid Ali, and as they walked together towards the large double doors he added, 'I very much look forward to receiving your agreement at the earliest possible time so that I may initiate the process of resuming informal relations.'

While Cornwallis kept his silence until he was safely back in his office in the Embassy, Rashid Ali was immediately on the telephone, arranging a meeting with his fellow conspirators to discuss the British offer.

Baghdad, 17 April 1941

At ten o'clock in the morning the Mufti, three of the four Colonels of the *Golden Square* and Yunis al Sabawi met with Rashid Ali in al Sabbagh's office in the Citadel.

The Citadel was where the Ottoman governors of the *Vilayet* of Baghdad had lived and where Feisal had stayed during the early part of his reign. It now formed part of the complex which housed the head-quarters of the Iraqi armed forces.

Rashid Ali quickly outlined Cornwallis's offer and his acceptance, but minimized his failure to broaden the discussions.

'This is treason to the nationalist cause!' shouted Kamil Shabib, a small, obstinate and arrogant colonel who commanded the 1st Division. Salah al Din al Sabbagh, a tall sallow man with a reputation of being a careerist with ambition, who commanded the 3rd Division, added in a quiet yet forceful way, 'Rashid Ali, the Army opposes your undertaking with the British. This is just a tactic to stall for time until they are strong enough to move against us.'

'You have to understand, Rashid Ali, that a war with Britain is neces-sary – if not immediately, then within a matter of days or weeks', said al Sabawi.

'There can be no compromises', Colonel Mahmud Salman, the head of the Royal Iraqi Air Force, added.

The Mufti contemplated the position before raising his hand to stop the diatribe against Rashid Ali. 'On the one hand we must not do anything to provoke the British to occupy Iraq before the delivery of weapons from our allies. On the other hand if we allow the British to land troops and transit them through Iraq we give them the opportu-nity to occupy us.

The Germans and Italians will not be pleased if we allow British troops to enter the country in force as it would compromise any mili-tary action that they will take to support us. They are unlikely to help us if they are convinced that we are an occupied country. There is also the need to manage the public perception that we are capitulating to the British, which could lose us popular support.

I recommend', said Haj Amin, 'that we accept the British request. However, we need to stipulate that this is acceptable only if it is limited to 3,000 troops in Iraq at any one time, and under the condition that they proceed as rapidly as possible from Basra to Rutba Wells. This way we can limit their size and presence while still fulfilling our legal obligations.'

The Colonels, Rashid Ali and al Sabawi nodded their agreement, and the Mufti suggested that Rashid Ali meet Luigi Gabrielli to advise him of their planned action.

Baghdad, 19 April 1941

Five significant events occurred that day.

Rashid Ali sent a message to Cornwallis at the Embassy. While confirming the Iraqi government's agreement to the landing of British troops in Basra, it had three conditions. Firstly, that all troops must proceed as rapidly as possible to Rutba Wells. Secondly, that the British government must announce well in advance any intention to ship any more detachments of troops to Iraq. Finally, British troops must not exceed at any one time the strength of one mixed brigade, and that no more units should land at Basra as long as there were still some British troops in the country. Cornwallis pointedly sent no reply.

The 20th Indian Infantry Brigade, the 3rd Field Regiment RA and the Headquarters of the 10th Indian Division began their disembarkation from Convoy BP7 at Maqil docks, Basra, and Maj Gen William Fraser assumed command of all British Army forces in Iraq.

Rashid Ali met the Italian Minister at his office. 'This is to advise you of the decisions taken by the National Defence Council yesterday.' He went on to outline that the Iraqi response to the British landing was a way of stalling for time. 'However, Minister, we need to know as quickly as possible from the governments of Italy and Germany whether we can count on support from the air forces of the Axis. Naturally our airfields will be placed at your disposal. We also need to know whether you can send our orders for weapons by air. I would also like to reiterate our request of 25 March that all the arms requested and the financial support promised be sent as soon as possible.'

Iraqi hostility began to show itself. One of two 31 Squadron old biplane Valentias carrying troops from Shaiba to Habbaniya was forced to put down at Pumping Station K-4 on the Tripoli pipeline, and it was immediately attacked by Iraqi troops. The crew and the fifteen soldiers on board were captured and the Valentia was set on fire. The other Valentia attempted to land but was driven off by Iraqi ground fire, which wounded two of the crew.

A change in AOC in Cairo to AVM Arthur Tedder brought re-inforcements in the shape of six obsolete and worn-out Gloster Gladiator biplane fighters. They were flown in to Habbaniya from storage in Cairo. A request from AVM Harry Smart commanding RAF Habbaniya to retain the motley collection of ferry pilots – two Free

French, one Pole, a Yugoslav and two Britons – to fly the aircraft was overruled by Tedder, and the pilots were flown back to Cairo.

Habbaniya, 20 April 1941

Smart realized that there was little, if anything, that could be sent in terms of reinforcements in the short term. Habbaniya was on its own. Although he had every confidence in Cornwallis, Rashid Ali did not seem to be interested in negotiation.

RAF Habbaniya had been designed from the outset as a peacetime flying school, and was indefensible against a ground attack. While Smart agonized over the outcome of negotiations and what might happen to his command should it be attacked, a meeting was taking place in the nearby office of the Commander of No. 4 Service Flying Training School, Gp Capt William Savile.

Larry Ling, a young wing commander and chief flying instructor, had approached Savile with one of his flying instructors, Sqn Ldr Tony Dudgeon, with ideas about what could be done to protect Habbaniya in the case of an attack.

Savile, a non-flying officer, was regulation and discipline bound. He was more interested in keeping up the flying programme to meet Habbaniya's quota of pilots than in doing anything which could inter-rupt the programme.

'Sir, I think that you will be interested in Tony's ideas, which have relevance as they come from one of the few pilots at Habbaniya with recent air combat experience', Ling began.

Savile nodded his approval with a frown. He did not like his officers referring to their subordinates by their Christian names, believing this to led to poor discipline.

'Sir,' began Dudgeon, 'all of our aircraft are obsolete and are not designed for modern warfare. However, I have done some checking. I believe that with a little imagination we could make what we have into a potent strike force.

'We have nine Gladiators, our three plus the six which arrived from Cairo yesterday. Although they are pretty clapped-out we can still turn these into useful fighters. Our only problem is belted ammunition for their four Brownings. We do have a slow hand-cranked belt filler in the armoury, together with belts and .303 ammunition. If we run the machine around the clock in shifts we can get sufficient ammunition to arm the Gladiators. We need to run the belt filler around the clock as a ten-second burst from the four Brownings will fire off an hour's work, and we will need as many belts as we can get our hands on.

'Our Fairey Gordon biplane bombers date back to 1931, and we now use them to tow targets. But they still have their bomb-release gear, and if we fit Universal racks they can handle two 250 lb bombs. This will give us seven bombers.

'We have thirty Hawker Audax biplane trainers which are rigged to carry eight 20 lb practice bombs. With the bomb-release gear already in place all we have to do is fit Universal racks, and again we have bombers that can handle a useful load of two 250 lb bombs.'

Savile interrupted. 'But the Audax were Army cooperation aircraft and not bombers like the twenty five Hawker Harts that we have on strength?'

'Yes,' replied Dudgeon, 'but the Harts have been stripped of their mountings, cables and levers for practice bombing so there is little that we can do with them. The Audax is essential a Hart. I have flown them in India with a load of over 1,000 lb, so we should be able to convert the Audax to a bomber, as it has all the equipment excepting the Universal racks.

'We have only nineteen sets of Universal racks in the stores, so with the seven for the Gordons we can create another twelve bombers with 500 lb bomb-loads out of the thirty Audaxes we have on strength. The remaining eighteen Audaxes can carry the eight 20 lb bomb-loads.

'Finally we have twenty-seven Airspeed Oxfords which we use for advanced and photographic training. They are rigged to carry eight 9 lb practice smoke-bombs. The airframe is largely wood and is not strong enough to handle 250 lb bombs. But if we cut some holes in the bottom of the fuselage and bolt two plates onto the plywood fuselage and mount bomb-racks on the plates, we can carry a useful eight 20 lb bombs.

Dudgeon and Ling sat back waiting for Savile's reply.

Savile readily agreed to the Gladiators and that they be commanded by Flt Lt Dicky Cleaver, and to the modifications to the Gordons and to their command by Flt Lt David Evans. However, when the conversation turned to the Audax and the Oxford the air turned purple. Savile turned around and took two weighty volumes off the shelving behind his desk and placed them in front of Ling and Dudgeon. 'There is no standard bomb-load quoted for either the Audax or the Oxford in the manufacturers' manuals. No quotation means no modification.'

Ling argued tenaciously, citing Dudgeon's experience with the Audax, and finally had Savile, more to get them out of his office, agreeing to Ling and Dudgeon talking to the Engineers.

The Engineers were even more straight laced, and would not countenance any modifications. Through his continuing tenacity, Ling got the matter referred to the Operating Air Staff. While they did see the point, it was not authorized. Again Ling's tenacity got authorization for the Engineers to contact the Air Ministry in London.

Habbaniya, 21 April 1941

The Habbaniya Engineers, allowed to draft the signal to London, asked what the bomb-load was for the Audax. The obvious reply was eight 9 lb practice smoke-bombs, which ruled out authorization for the modification.

While the Engineers were happy, Ling and Dudgeon, over several beers in the officers' mess, decided on a new tack. Ling went back alone to Savile. 'Sir, out of courtesy I am advising you that we are going ahead and fitting the Universal racks to an Audax and taking it up for a test flight.'

'Absolutely No!' spluttered Savile.

'I know the problem, but we potentially face a much bigger problem. Unless we defend ourselves we are going to have to surrender. This will be the only RAF station in history to give in to an enemy without firing a shot in its defence. We have the opportunity. All I want is to seize that opportunity. It will not look good in the official enquiry that we did nothing to defend ourselves.'

Savile thought for a moment, realizing the implications. 'All right, I want a written note from you, or Dudgeon, that the test flight is being made on your sole responsibility and in the full knowledge that this is against my wish and my advice.'

'No, Sir,' Ling replied, furious at the buck-passing, 'I will not write such a note. We are all in this together and I plan to take this action on behalf of the station.'

Within one hour the Audax had the racks fitted and had made its successful test flight.

The Oxford proved to be a bigger problem. Dudgeon went to the Station Workshops to use their cutting and drilling machines to make the hundred or so metal strips to fix to the bottom of the Oxford's fuselage as the base on which to bolt the light series bomb-racks.

The Workshops flatly refused to make the strips unless Headquarters accepted all responsibility for the change of aircraft load and to its flying characteristics, to be responsible for whatever might happen and to supply an official set of blueprints for the modifications.

The Engineering staff officers were also against any 'unauthorized modification', which could only be agreed by the Air Ministry in London after discussions with Airspeed, the designers and manufacturers, of the Oxford.

Smart got wind of the situation, and to make sure that there was no repetition of the unauthorized Audax flight issued written orders to Ling, forbidding a test flight.

Ling and Dudgeon sat in the mess. 'Tony. I am not showing you Smart's orders, so you don't know its content. The only way we can do this is for you to do it alone. You have not seen this order and you are not to involve anyone else.'

Dudgeon borrowed a drill, bits, punch, hammer, hacksaw, files and a work-bench, plus some strip steel that someone purloined for him. He set to work in the back of Hangar Six, creating the plates on which to bolt the bomb-racks.

Nothing can be kept quiet on an RAF station, and word soon reached Smart that Dudgeon was hard at work in Hangar Six.

Smart sent for Ling, as Dudgeon's direct superior, together with Savile. 'Ling, by not stopping Dudgeon at the outset you have conspicuously failed in your duty. This is a gross breach of Good Order and of Air Force Discipline. Clear and specific orders in writing have been issued and are being flagrantly disobeyed. If we lose a valuable aircraft or a pilot you will be held fully and personally to blame. Now I am issuing you with a clear order. Find Dudgeon and stop him. Arrest him if necessary!'

By luck Dudgeon had already taken off with eight 20 lb bombs in the racks bolted on to the bottom of the Oxford. Dudgeon had made a successful landing by the time that a very slow-walking Ling arrived at the hangar.

Within a few days of the incident all was forgotten, Ling and Dudgeon were forgiven and the Workshops were instructed to make and fit the plates to each of the remaining Oxfords

Berlin, 27 April 1941

Woermann sat in front of Ribbentrop's massive oak desk in his opulent office at the *Auswartiges Amt* on the Wilhelmstrasse. 'I thought, Woermann, that you should be aware of my letter to the *Fuhrer* which endorses action in Iraq.

'I have pointed out that the movement of British troops through Iraqi territory might turn the scales in North Africa and that Britain's real aim is to gain a jumping-off position against the Vichy in Syria and to exert pressure on Turkey. The ultimate success of British policy in Turkey might have a major influence on the situation of German troops should they fight the Red Army.

'I have also added that the scepticism shown by the *Luftwaffe* and

Wehrmacht is unfounded as the information they submit on the number of enemy troops is too high. We know this because we have penetrated the US Embassy in Cairo and we are able to read the dispatches sent by their Legation in Baghdad, which is based on British-supplied information.

'We are also now in a position to pressure the Vichy French so that our planes can refuel in Syria on their way to Iraq. Is there anything I should add?'

'I would impress on the *Fuhrer, Herr Reichsaussenminister*', said Woermann, 'that we need to act quickly in providing both materiél and a military presence. The longer we delay, the more chance there is for the British to reinforce Iraq and for the Iraqis to lose the initiative and their nerve.'

Baghdad, 28 April 1941

At three o'clock in the afternoon Cornwallis met Rashid Ali at the latter's office at the Seria government building.

'Rashid Ali, the British government requests the Iraqi government's agreement to the landing of a further 3,500 troops at Basra in the next few days.'

'Ambassador, we had an agreement to limit the number of troops, the transitory nature of their stay and no retention of troops to create a base in Basra. Any deviation is a gross breach of the treaty.'

'Rashid Ali, we need to take a much broader interpretation of the treaty. We cannot obviously give you prior notification in wartime for security reasons. We also need to safeguard the Imperial lines of communication which transverse Iraq. Consequently we need more troops, and some will have to stay in the country.'

'No, No, No! We have an agreement which you are now seeking to change. This is something neither I nor my government can countenance.'

'Rashid Ali, the landing of these additional forces will nevertheless take place, and the consequences of opposing these landings will be serious.'

'Ambassador, let me also make myself perfectly clear. If these additional troops disembark before the dispatch of those already in Basra I will broadcast a denunciation of British action. I cannot and will not be responsible for the consequences which might follow an outburst of popular feeling!'

'From your response, Rashid Ali, I have grave concerns about the safety of British women and children in Iraq, and I need to send them outside the country at once. I would appreciate your giving the women and children safe-conduct.'

'Ambassador, the Iraqi government has no quarrel with women and children, and you should feel free to move them outside Iraq should you feel the necessity. As we cannot seem to make progress, I suggest that we call a halt to this meeting to give you and your government time to reflect on your position.'

The meeting with Rashid Ali had been deeply disconcerting for Cornwallis. With the Iraqis' uncompromising position, no doubt bolstered by British losses in Greece and North Africa, it seemed almost impossible to patch up the difficulties between the two countries.

Immediately on his return to the Embassy, Cornwallis sent a cipher telegram to Smart at Habbaniya initiating Operation *Concentrate*. Thirty RAF buses and trucks, together with a requisitioned Harrington-Marmon 38-seater from the Nairn Brothers' Baghdad-Damascus desert bus service, were to arrive at Baghdad's civil airport starting at 2.30 p.m. the next day. They were to begin to evacuate the women and children to Habbaniya, from where they would be flown to Basra. Next he called in Adrian Holman to initiate the phone calls to the Alwiyah Club, British companies with offices in Iraq and to the group of Embassy wives who would begin to call their lists of expatriates to have their wives and children assemble at the airport late the next morning.

Warning notices were also prepared and delivered to the district wardens and to the Vice-Consul for delivery on the other side of the Tigris, where the bulk of the British community lived. Finally he called Paul Knabenshue at the American Legation on the east bank of the Tigris. 'Paul, this is Ken. I have had a very unsatisfactory time today which has left me no option but to initiate our agreement. Operation *Concentrate* starts at eight tomorrow morning.'

Knabenshue called in his secretary and asked her to begin to call the small number of Americans in Baghdad, to have them assemble at the Legation the following morning. Cornwallis and Knabenshue had agreed on an Anglo-American plan where the citizens of either country, and any other friendly neutrals or allies, could seek refuge in the British Embassy or American Legation, whichever was closer, with the RAF transporting all British and American wives and their children to Habbaniya.

Luigi Gabrielli, the Minister at the Italian Legation, looked through the list which had been given to him by Rashid Ali. The Iraqi requests were becoming more detailed, and the tone more urgent. He wondered how long he could continue to stall Rashid Ali until Rome and Berlin agreed between themselves what they were going to do.

The Iraqis wanted large sums of money to offset the costs of their war – not only for military operations, but also to bribe the tribes for support and to compensate for the loss of Iraq's income from customs revenues and oil royalties. They also wanted Axis aircraft to bomb British naval units in the Gulf and the bases at Habbaniya and Shaiba, and offered the use of airfields at Baghdad, Mosul and Mikdadia, as well as Iraqi petrol stocks.

Rashid Ali had also requested the Axis to supply large quantities of aircraft, armoured cars, armour-piercing guns and ammunition, grenades and machine-guns. The Iraqis were particularly anxious, he noted, to obtain captured British infantry weapons with which they were familiar.

While the Iraqis were no longer insisting on a declaration from the Axis on the future independence of Arab countries, the list was long and extensive.

Gabrielli feared that Rome and Berlin would again ask him to stall, at a time when it looked as if war between Iraq and the British was inevitable, compromising his position with the Iraqi leaders.

Back in his office in the Serai building, Rashid Ali contemplated his future as Iraq drifted towards war with Britain. Throughout his political life he had changed cliques with the tide, always one step ahead in picking the winning side. His own personal pique had forced him to turn to the Mufti and the Colonels and the Axis. He had played both the Germans and the British in an attempt to maintain neutrality in a war which did not concern Iraq, while veering to support the Axis as insurance in case they, rather than the British, won.

Now the Colonels and the Mufti had made the decision to go to war, shattering the delicate balance he had created and striven to maintain. Iraq's only hope was urgent support from the Germans and Italians, not only in terms of money and equipment but also in the form of a military mission, complete with ground troops and airmen to stiffen the Iraqi armed forces.

Ling and Dudgeon's request to Savile to prepare the polo field and the golf course as an additional landing and parking area was finally approved. Both had argued that the airfield alone was not large enough to support the Habbaniya Striking Force, and they needed an alternative. Although opposed by some of the senior officers, Savile, much to the surprise of Larry and Tony, had fought tenaciously and won permission from Smart. Two steamrollers had been pushed into service, and with floodlights would finish the make-shift runway before midnight that day.

Baghdad, 29 April 1941

Just after ten that morning, buses and cars began to arrive at the British Embassy and the American Legation, and started to ferry the women and children to Baghdad's civil airport. Only a few women chose to stay behind. The wives of the British Ambassador and the US Minister remained, together with two Consulate wives, one typist and the Matron and nursing sisters from the hospital.

Masked by the loading of the women and children, two covered RAF trucks pulled up outside the Chancellery of the British Embassy. Airmen began to unload sandbags, rolls of barbed wire, several cases of rifles, ammunition and a few tear-gas bombs, which were labelled variously 'stationery' and 'garden tools', together with cardboard boxes full of tinned goods. All of these were hurried out of sight into the ballroom for storage.

By the end of the day 132 women and ninety-nine children had been registered and packed aboard a convoy of buses and lorries at the airport. Twenty minutes later the convoy completing Operation *Concentrate* moved off in the direction of Habbaniya.

An emergency cabinet meeting was held at al Sabbagh's office in the Citadel at eleven in the morning with Rashid Ali, the four Colonels and the Mufti.

Rashid Ali summed up the situation. 'The British action clearly signals that the British have decided to pay no attention to their agreement and that they plan not only to station more troops on our soil, but to occupy the whole of Iraq. I believe that we have no choice now but to resist the British with the full force of our Army.'

'Are we all in agreement?' asked Rashid Ali.

'I think that this is an opportune time', said al Sabbagh. 'The British are isolated and in an indefensible position at Habbaniya. If we breach the bunds in the south and cut the railway and telegraph links between Basra and Baghdad, we prevent their troops, three hundred miles away, from coming to their aid. Habbaniya gives us a bargaining chip should the British try to force the issue.'

'I agree', said Salman. 'Our Air Force is numerically larger and our planes are more modern than those the British have in Iraq. With all their other commitments I do not see them reinforcing Habbaniya before we overwhelm them.'

'They have no armour and no artillery and are not a match for my Mechanized Force', added Fahmi Said.

'It is time we showed the British that we are not a vassal state', added Kamil Shabib.

'Naturally I will send a note of protest to the British Embassy rejecting their demand to land more troops, and our objections against any further landings.'

'We also need to send a further note to Gabrielli at the Italian Legation, advising him of our plans and requesting immediate military and financial support from Italy and Germany', suggested the Mufti.

'That is under way, Haj Amin,' confirmed Rashid Ali.

'Well, gentlemen,' said the Mufti, rising from his seat, 'the situation has developed much better than I could have hoped for. If the British stand and fight we will win. If they do not fight we will starve them out of their airfield. Whatever the outcome we will humiliate the British.

They will be forced to seek an agreement on our terms. This will mean the end of British involvement in Iraq and a just settlement for Palestine. Britain's loss of face will have profound effects throughout the Middle East and will make their position in both Egypt and Palestine impossible. Our victory will also send shock waves through their other possessions, like India and Burma, where they also face unrest.

I will leave you to plan for our victory!'

At the time of the meeting of the *Golden Square*, men of the King's Own Royal Regiment began to arrive at Habbaniya from Shaiba in an airlift by 31 Squadron's old Vickers Valentia troop carriers. By the end of the day 364 officers and men of the 1st Battalion, with their twelve light and six heavy Vickers machine-guns and two Boys anti-tank rifles, were reinforcing RAF Habbaniya.

In the late afternoon additional elements of 20th Indian Brigade landed at Basra from Convoy BP1 without incident, despite the Iraqi government's refusal of permission to land.

Both the British and the Germans failed to exploit their opportunities, and as a result a war started which could either have been easily averted or quickly won.

Inaction by the British in nipping the problem 'in the bud', and the snail-like pace of the Germans in taking advantage of Britain's vulnerability, appears strange in hindsight. However, this was due to competing sets of interests on both sides, which coloured their perceptions of the value of Iraq and the urgency of their responses.

In the British camp there were vastly different views held about the evolving problem. The men on the spot, Wavell in Cairo and Cornwallis in Baghdad, understood the issues of Arab nationalism, and with the lack of British resources saw armed intervention as both provocative and risky, believing diplomacy and conciliation were sound roads to take. This position was supported by AVM Smart, who commanded RAF Habbaniya, who saw conciliation as a way to avoid armed confrontation on the ground which he would lose.

Wavell's position was understandable. He was already fighting for his life in North Africa against Rommel and in East Africa against the Italians. He was awaiting an air assault on Crete on his battered forces that had been evacuated from Greece. He was also unsure of the intentions of the well-armed Vichy French in Syria, who could invade Palestine at their choosing. With too many demands on his few troops and limited equipment, Wavell was reluctant to assume more commitments.

In contrast, Churchill in London and Claude Auchinleck, the C-in-C India, favoured rapid armed intervention, not only to safeguard oil supplies and the quickest way to India by air and land, but to avoid undermining the British position in the Middle East as a whole. Both men feared that conciliation, together with Britain's lackustre performance against the Germans, could signal weakness and incite unrest throughout the region.

Churchill, the strategist, saw the British position in the Middle East as a house of cards held in place by Egypt. Already pressured in the Western Desert by Rommel and in Abyssinia by the Duke of Aosta ,and the possible loss of Crete, would make it easy for Axis forces to take Cyprus and to then threaten Egypt from the north, west and south. A German bridgehead in Iraq, together with the Vichy French in Syria, would enable the Axis to complete their encirclement of Egypt, forcing the collapse of Britain's position in the Middle East and cutting Britain off from India, Australia and New Zealand.

Both Churchill and Wavell realized that they were fighting a global conflict which demanded difficult strategic choices, each had a powerful intellect and was an aristocrat and scholar, and each was attracted to unorthodox solutions. However, there the similarities ended.

Wavell was one of the British Army's great trainers of men, a meticulous planner with a talent for administrative detail who was attuned to the complexities of operation rather than the strategic implications. Wavell was an altogether too simple, too straight and too decent a person to survive in the muddy waters of politics where the intriguers laid traps and the sharks hunted. However, Wavell lacked the imagination, the decisiveness and the speed of action which are the hall-marks of successful military leadership. In contrast Churchill had strategic vision and demanded from his commanders an enthusiasm that bordered on zealotry, and took it upon himself to meddle in campaigns from a distance, often in excruciating detail.

Wavell's resentment of Churchill's constant meddling led him to shield information from Churchill. This lack of transparency and Wavell's caution, bordering on inaction, only increased Churchill's distrust of his C-in-C Middle East.

Things were no better in Berlin. Advocates of support for Iraq were primarily driven by two different factions in the *Auswartiges Amt.* Grobba and Woermann were concerned with exploiting their carefully built relationships in Iraq to strengthen Germany's position while weakening that of a vulnerable Britain. However, Von Hentig and Von Weiszacher were more interested in using Iraq to deflect Hitler from prosecuting Operation *Barbarossa*, the attack on Russia, which they felt was the wrong fight for Germany at the wrong time.

Hitler was totally focused on *Barbarossa*. believing that Iraq was a side show. His racial theories about Semites, which equated Arab with Jew, provided a stumbling block to overcome before support could be given to Iraq. Adding to these problems was the *Luftwaffe*, which felt that Iraq was too far away to provide meaningful help. The *Wehrmacht*, with its hands full in Greece and Crete and with Rommel in Africa, did not want to get involved in another 'adventure', given the pending attack on Russia.

Complicating the matter further was an agreement with Mussolini which gave Italy a free hand in the Middle East to create a new colonial empire. With the need to keep Italy firmly in the Axis fold, both Hitler and Ribbentrop were reluctant to take any action which would compromise their relationship with Mussolini.

These perceptions and the delayed responses by both sides not only caused the crisis but dictated how it would play out and when and how it would end.

Chapter Two

Target Habbaniya

Baghdad, 30 April 1941

A little after three in the morning Pat Domvile, the Air Liason Officer, gently shook awake Maj Gen George Waterhouse, Head of the British Military Mission, who was asleep on a camp bed in his office in the Embassy.

'Sir, we have company', he said to a sleepy-eyed Waterhouse. 'The guards woke me about half an hour ago. They thought that we were being surrounded by the whole Iraqi Army. I took a shufti along the river bank. There are trucks filled with troops, towed artillery, tanks and armoured cars heading west across the King Feisal Bridge. It looks to me that they are moving out of the Raschid Camp. They have not come our way, and as the only possible target to the west is Habbaniya my chaps could be in for a spot of trouble.'

'You had better let them know', said Waterhouse.

'I have already sent a cipher telegram to the Air Vice-Marshal,' Domvile said, 'but I wanted you to be aware of events.'

'Good thinking, Domvile. Now that I'm up I need a cup of tea!'

Habbaniya

It took twenty-eight minutes for the cipher telegram to reach Smart. Sending the cipher took seconds. The rest of the time was spent in decryption by the Duty Officer, verification by the Chief Signals Officer, a dispatch rider to take the message to Smart's quarters and for his batman to wake him.

Quickly reading the message, Smart had his batman contact his ADC to arrange an emergency meeting in the conference room adjacent to his office on the top floor of the Air Headquarters block at 04.00. The summons went to Savile, Wg Cdr Paul Holder, the Senior Administration Officer, Lt Col Alastair Brawn commanding the RAF Levies, and Lt Col Edward Everett of the King's Own Royal Regiment.

41

At precisely 04.00 Smart, a small, dapper man, walked into his conference room where those summoned to the meeting waited.

'As you all know, the situation over the last month in Iraq has been very tense. Domvile at the Embassy sent me a cipher at 03.00 which suggests that Iraqi troops, guns and armour are headed in our direction. Whether this is fact or surmise by Domvile I just don't know. However, we need to be prepared for any outcome. Bill,' to Savile, 'at first light, which should be in about an hour, I want you to get an Audax up and take a shufti to see what, if anything, the Iraqis are up to.

'I am going to sound a General Alarm and I want you all back here at 07.00, together with Page who runs the Armoured Car Company and the Chief Flying Instructor. I would like the Levies, the Army and the Armoured Car unit to give me a ground defence plan. Bill, I want you and Ling to brief us on the air striking component, and Paul, I would like you to let us know our supplies situation.'

After sounding the General Alarm, Smart went to his office and sat quietly contemplating his two predicaments.

Firstly, RAF Habbaniya, while in many ways a perfect posting, was almost defenceless. The station, situated on a bend on the Euphrates, embraced RAF Headquarters Iraq, No. 4 Service Flying Training School, six large hangars, an aircraft depot with repair and workshops, a hospital, a meteorological station, administration and barrack blocks and an airfield with two intersecting runways of packed sand. Complicating things was the fact that Habbaniya was home to some 9,000 people – Arabs, Armenians, Assyrians, Indians and Kurds and their families – who worked at the station.

The base, built in 1937, contained all the amenities of a peacetime station. RAF Habbaniya boasted a social club, a swimming pool, a polo ground, riding stables, thirty-six tennis courts, rugby, soccer, and hockey fields, a cricket ground, a gymnasium, a golf course and the Astra cinema with its outdoor and indoor facilities. Incongruously it also had horses and a pack of hounds known as the Royal Exodus Hunt managed by Lt Alistair Graham of the Levies, and a Yacht Club, based on the other side of the plateau, on Lake Habbaniya.

Lines of eucalyptus trees were planted along all twenty-eight miles of the camp's paved roads to give shade. Hibiscus and oleander shrubs, green lawns and carefully tended vegetable gardens were dotted around the station. The camp had its own water supplies contained in a single, high tower, and an electric power station provided all the camp's power, while three churches catered for the Anglican, the Armenian and the Assyrian communities.

RAF Habbaniya was not built with war in mind, and had none of the usual defences of dispersal areas, bomb-proof shelters, redoubts and anti-aircraft positions that an operational station would contain in a war zone.

The only protection for the camp's five hundred acres was a seven-mile-long, ten-foot-high steel perimeter fence, curved outwards to keep the *kleptiwallahs* at bay. The fence was interspersed, every 300 yards or so, by one of fourteen twenty-foot-high brick blockhouses. However, the airfield was outside the perimeter fence. The Air Ministry had considered that expanding the perimeter fence was too expensive to protect an airfield of packed sand which sat in a boiling desert miles from anywhere in a friendly country.

On the camp's southern and western flanks the station was dominated by a plateau some one hundred and fifty feet high, while to the north and east the Euphrates contained the station. Beyond the plateau to the south was Lake Habbaniya used by RAF and BOAC flying-boats. RAF Habbaniya was a very soft target for both ground and air attack.

Secondly, the senior officers, including Smart, reflected the ambience of Habbaniya. They had been selected on the basis of suitability for managing training. Their rules, regulations, targets, timetables and patterns of work were designed solely for the production of an efficient, effective and regular flow of trained aircrew. Anything that interfered with this process could not, and would not, be tolerated.

AVM Harry 'Reggie' Smart was a very brave man who had served his country with distinction in both war and peace, in the air and on the ground. But he knew that both he and his senior officers lacked the leadership qualities, the flexibility in thinking, the sense of urgency and the combat experience demanded in a modern war to turn the adversity they faced into success. Smart dreaded the coming meeting.

Half an hour after first light, Colonel Fahmi Said, commander of the Mechanized Force and a key member of the *Golden Square*, stood at the edge of the escarpment looking down on RAF Habbaniya.

From his vantage point the camp and its airfield were spread out before him, like a toy village, with the Euphrates like a silver snake coiled at its back. The hangars, the barrack blocks and the playing fields all dominated by the water tower seemed so close in the sharp early morning sunlight that Said felt he could reach out and touch them.

As the single Audax landed back at the camp, Said smiled, knowing that the British would be aware that his armour and guns now totally dominated their base and that more troops were on the way to support him.

Now was the time to challenge the British. He signalled to his ADC, Major Hussain Najib, that it was time to take the message to Habbaniya.

The Ford staff car carrying a white flag passed by the signpost with RAF Habbaniya in English and Arabic topped by the little direction board pointing to London, a long 3,287 miles away, and Baghdad, now an uncomfortable fifty-five miles near.

To Najib the sign seemed to amplify Habbaniya's isolation and vulnerability, and to reinforce the Iraqi Army's dominance over the British.

At precisely 6 am Najib's car pulled up at the guardhouse at the main gate. Najib, immaculately dressed in his cavalry uniform complete with gleaming riding-boots, got out carrying a white flag and walked over to the duty officer who was just emerging from the guardroom.

'I have an urgent message for your commanding officer', Najib stated, dispensing with a salute and looking contemptuously at the young pilot officer wearing a khaki shirt and shorts and an RAF Police arm band.

The pilot officer snapped off a salute and the guard detail came to attention. 'I will have you taken to his office, sir. But first you must wear a blindfold.'

The pilot officer motioned to a burly flight sergeant to fix the blindfold, and Najib was then led back to the car. A grinning sergeant from the Levies, immaculate in a pale blue open-necked shirt, khaki shorts and puttees and a dark brown felt hat turned up at the side, Australian style, climbed onto the running board to direct the driver to the two-storey Air Headquarters block a mile away.

Twenty minutes later Smart contemplated Said's message:

For the purposes of training we have occupied the Habbaniya hills. Please make no flying or the going out of any force or persons from the cantonment. If any aircraft or armoured car attempts to go out it will be shelled by our batteries, and we will not be responsible for it.

Smart realized that he could not comply, yet had no orders to take things further, and decided to bluff it out replying:

Any interference with training flights will be considered an 'act of war' and will be met by immediate counter-offensive action. We demand the withdrawal of the Iraqi forces from positions which are clearly hostile and must place my camp at their mercy.

When Najib had left with the reply to Said, Smart immediately signalled Cornwallis in Baghdad, Fraser in Basra and Tedder in Cairo with Said's message and his reply. He asked Cornwallis to arrange for the immediate withdrawal of the Iraqi forces from Habbaniya, adding that any increase in Iraqi forces would compel him to take air action.

Punctually at seven, Smart entered the conference room adjacent to his office and gestured to the participants to bring their coffee and take their places at the table.

'As you probably know, I received an envoy from the Iraqis, who told us to stop flying. I told him that we will continue to fly and any action that they may take will be considered as an act of war. I regret having to force the issue but I had no choice. Right. Bill, why don't you bring us up to date on the Iraqis' deployment?'

'Ling here', said Savile, 'conducted the air reconnaissance.'

'Things do not look good. I flew across the plateau and then carried on to Khan Nuqta, half way between Falluja and Baghdad, before looping back across Lake Habbaniya, and then flew at low level over the plateau for a closer look. There are about 2,000 Iraqi troops on the plateau busy digging-in. There are a number of gun batteries and machine-gun positions already in place, plus some tanks and armoured cars. All of which are protected by anti-aircraft guns including some 20 mm cannon.

'If you look out of the window you can see them for yourself. Some of the heavy guns are sited less than 2,000 feet from our perimeter, and cover the camp at point-blank range. The road from the plateau back past Falluja towards Baghdad is jam-packed with troops in trucks, towed artillery, armoured cars and some of their new light tanks. I estimate that by the middle of tomorrow there will be between 8,000 and 9,000 Iraqi troops up there on the plateau.

'Coming back over Lake Habbaniya, I saw two of the big Empire flying-boats sitting on the water. There were no Iraqi military formations on their way, but I suspect that a visit to BOAC is only a matter of time. I took photos of the Iraqi positions on the plateau, as well as along the Falluja road, which we can use to both verify the number of troops we face and map out their positions on the plateau.'

Smart was clearly shocked. 'This is a gigantic bluff! They are just throwing their weight about to see if we will crack. Bill, I want you to get every airman to start digging trenches. Commandeer all the airmen, all the pupils and junior officers and get them to start digging defence trenches around the camp.'

'Why don't we hear from the land forces to ensure that we work in concert on our defences?' responded Savile, taken aback by Smart's outburst.

'A good idea, Bill. Why don't you start, Col Brawn, and let me know how you plan to deploy the land forces?'

'The overall plan for ground defence has been a joint undertaking with the King's Own and the Armoured Car unit, so I will just elaborate on the deployment of the Levies. We have a strength of 1,199 officers and other ranks composed of five companies of Assyrians, one company of Kurds, together totalling 750 men, plus a headquarters company. Each of the blockhouses along the perimeter fence will contain two NCOs and six troopers. I have divided the camp into three sectors, each covered by one company with two companies in a mobile reserve.'

'The Levies are Iraqis and have never been in combat, Colonel. What is their reliability and capability?' questioned Smart.

'The Assyrians are Christians and the Kurds, although Muslim, are not Arabs. Both have recently suffered very badly at the hands of the Iraqis, so I am sure that we can count on their support. They have been well trained and are very enthusiastic, and I am sure that they will acquit themselves well. However, the Levies are lightly armed. We have one machine-gun section armed with some ancient Hotchkiss and Lewis guns, a 3-inch mortar section and one Boys anti-tank rifle.'

'Col Everett, what can the King's Own do to help out?' asked Smart.

'We have 364 officers and men. Given the size of the base, it would be best to split my force into two. Half of the King's Own will be involved in point defence around the key installations like the Air Headquarters block, the power station, the hospital, the fuel store and the water tower. The other half will join the Levies' mobile reserve. We have a few Vickers heavy machine-guns and some Boys anti-tank rifles.'

Smart turned to the camp's youngest 'military man', Sqn Ldr John Page, who commanded No. 1 Armoured Car Company RAF.

'How are you fixed, Page?' questioned Smart.

'I have eighteen armoured cars. These were originally built for the Royal Navy in 1915 on Silver Spirit chassis. They are thin skinned and no match in a confrontation with the modern Crossley armoured cars or the FIAT light tanks operated by the Iraqis. The Colonels and I agree that our best bet is to use these with their heavy Vickers machine-guns as part of the mobile reserve to break up infantry ground attacks and to carry the fight to the enemy at night. We have also given some of the cars a Boys anti-tank rifle to give us a bit more punch if we come up against Iraqi armour.'

'Bill, you have command of the Air Striking Force. What do you plan?'

'We have divided our forces in two. The Audaxes will be in two squadrons under the overall command of Ling, here. One squadron of twelve aircraft with two 250 lb bombs will be run by Wg Cdr John Hawtrey. The second squadron of nine Audaxes carrying eight 20 lb bombs will be headed by Wg Cdr Glynn Silyn-Roberts. Paul Holder, here, will have a roving commission to fly Audaxes for anyone. Ling's force will fly out of the converted polo field, which is out of sight of the gunners on the plateau. The rest of the aircraft, under the overall command of Sqn Ldr Tony Dudgeon, will fly out of the main airfield. Dudgeon will have the nine Gladiators for airfield defence under Flt Lt Dicky Cleaver. The seven Gordons with their two 250 lb bomb-loads will be run by Flt Lt David Evans, while Dudgeon will command all twenty-seven Oxfords with their eight 20 lb bomb-loads. While we can field sixty-four aircraft out of the eighty-nine airframes we have on station, we have a shortage of pilots. We have no pilots classed as both medically fit and operationally experienced for combat. Most are instructors who have never fired a bullet or dropped a bomb in anger. Some are pilots who have been classed as 'unsuitable' for operational flying, others are woefully short of productive flying training or recent practice. Three, including Dudgeon, have been sent here for a rest following extended combat tours. We also have some pilots from the Royal Hellenic Air Force, whose command of the English language is limited, to say the least.

'All told, we have nineteen pilots for the twenty-one Audaxes and twenty pilots for Dudgeon's forty-three aircraft. So our true operating strength is thirty-nine aircraft. On the aircrew side the situation is worse. We have split the two experienced bomb aimers and four part-time air gunners equally between Ling and Dudgeon. So we have had to revert to asking pupils and ground-crew to volunteer to fill the vacant aircrew seats.'

Smart, growing more despondent, asked his Senior Administration Officer, Paul Holder, to bring the meeting up to speed on the supply situation.

'We have food and supplies for the RAF, the Levies and the King's Own for twelve days and four days for the 9,000 civilians in the cantonment. I plan to fly down to Shaiba and buy supplies to supplement our food stocks, so we should be able to keep up the level of our stores. We have three months' supply of 100-octane aviation-grade petrol stored in "A" and "B" dumps, so we will have adequate supplies through the short to mid-term.'

'Good, Paul. Now does anyone else have anything to add?' asked Smart, looking around the room. Two hands were raised, Everett and Ling. Smart gestured to Everett.

'Sir, this camp is vulnerable not only to Iraqi guns. We have no defences against their armour. The temperatures are rising in the day. If the water tower or the electric power station are put out of action our capability to fight stops. The camp is also situated on low ground and the Euphrates runs for about ten miles behind us at ten feet or so above the surrounding land protected by artificial embankments, bunds. If these are breached by Iraqi shellfire Habbaniya could be flooded out. Again this would curtail our capability to resist.'

'Your point, Colonel? a clearly annoyed Smart asked.

'We have no military option other than to take the fight to the enemy, and to do it first', said Everett.

Smart cut Everett off and gestured to Ling.

'The Iraqi Air Force is larger and better equipped than our own here at Habbaniya. They have over seventy operational aircraft, including Savoia Marchetti bombers and Northrop and Breda fighters that are all faster than anything we have. Even their version of the Audax, the Nisr, has a more powerful engine. We have also trained many of their pilots. While I agree that the clapped-out Gladiators are better than nothing, we need to take the fight to the Iraqis. We need to hit them on their airfields before they come here and take us out.'

Smart went apoplectic as the murmurs of general assent followed Everett's and Ling's remarks. 'What you two are advocating is for me to start my own private war against the Iraqis! We have a treaty with the Iraqis, and while things do look a little dicey I am sure that these problems things can be resolved diplomatically. In the absence of any directives from higher authority no immediate defensive or offensive action will be taken in spite of the risk of not taking such a course involves. I have already contacted Basra, Cairo and New Delhi, so we will just have to sit tight until we hear from them. In the meantime we need to get cracking with our defences. Bill, I would like you to keep an Oxford up, performing continuous reconnaissance, so that we are up to date with developments. You also need to get started on trench building. Thank you all. I will advise you as and when the situation develops.

Smart went back to his office, and after shutting the door sat pensively at his desk, staring out at the plateau, where he could see, in the distance, figures moving about. He did not want to make a decision to attack the Iraqis without provocation, and even if he did there was no guarantee of success. However, if the Iraqis struck first, Habbaniya could be lost. Either way his decision would bring death and destruction to the people and equipment under his charge. Habbaniya was completely vulnerable to attack and there were 9,000 civilians in the cantonment at the mercy of the Iraqis. The longer he waited, the more vulnerable the camp became as the initiative shifted in favour of the Iraqis.

Alex Thompson, the BOAC Manager at Lake Habbaniya, was not expecting a call before eight o'clock in the morning, and just managed to pick up the telephone at the third ring.

'Hello Alex, it's Paul Holder at the camp.'

'I hope that you got some personal mail in the sacks I sent up on Wednesday', Thompson said.

'Alex, we don't have much time,' Paul replied, cutting through the pleasantries, 'and I want you to listen very carefully as time is of the essence. The Iraqis have turned funny and they have invested the plateau looking down on the station. I flew over earlier and saw the two Empire boats on the lake. How quickly can you get them off?'

'We fuel at dawn in the cool to minimize fuel evaporation. The passengers and crew are just sitting down for breakfast. By the time they have finished it will be a couple of hours, so we will meet our 9.30 take-off time. One 'boat is on its way to Bahrain and the other is going to Tiberius', answered Thompson.

'Alex, forget breakfast. Have them load up now, and get Doris and the children off as well as anyone else who is non-essential. There is nothing we can do to help you out. Your best bet is to get out now, while you can, as the Iraqis will be coming around to see you later today. Best of luck', said Paul, breaking the connection.

Thompson, still holding the phone, dialled his bungalow. 'Doris. Listen to me. Pack two suitcases for you and the children and get down to the jetty in half an hour. The Iraqis are being very difficult and the RAF suggests women and children leave as a precautionary measure. There is no real danger, it's more a move to avoid provoking the Iraqis. I will tell Stan what is happening, and you tell Maggie to pack right away.'

He walked out of the BOAC Manager's office and gazed out at the two big silver Short S23C Empire-class flying-boats gently bobbing at their moorings, looking like two contented whales. BOAC, and its predecessor Imperial Airways, had not seen fit to invest in pontoons at Habbaniya, so everything had to be ferried out by launch. Luckily the time-consuming and messy process of refuelling was completed, and all that remained was to load the crew, passengers and their baggage and the aircraft could be on their way. A quick word to his radio operator and deputy, Stan Freeman, and he would walk over to the Airways Guest House and break the bad news to the two captains, and give them the job of telling the passengers.

Thompson knew that he should not enjoy the passengers' discomfort, but wealth and privilege often seemed to bring out the worst in people. He could just imagine the scene as the two captains had to face the angry reactions of the passengers. That insufferable countess, the arrogant politician who owed his junior cabinet position to the fact that his betters had gone off to fight, the pushy self-made millionaire with those awful teeth who had found that money was not enough and wanted power and public recognition, and the fading actor given a new lease of life entertaining the troops, who was deeply in love with himself and wanted everyone to share his fascination.

Just after nine in the morning, Smart sent off another signal to Cornwallis, Fraser and Tedder, adding the Air Ministry in London. This time Smart reported on the steady increase in Iraqi strength and that heavy artillery was now trained on the camp. Smart added that air action might have to be taken that day if the Iraqi forces did not withdraw, as the risk of night attack would be unacceptable. Again, Smart requested assistance to be sent by air that day. A few minutes later Cornwallis replied, endorsing Smart's action in reply to the Iraqi message.

The very air seemed to sweat. As the sun rose higher in the clear sky the temperature began to move past 104°F, and perspiration began to roll down the bodies of the airmen digging trenches all over the camp.

When the temperature rose above blood heat, prolonged human activity became difficult, and to avoid heat stroke the men were forced to wear their shirts and topees and to stop frequently to drink water to avoid dehydration.

The airmen were not used to being out in the sun. At Habbaniya flying began at dawn and ended at eleven in the morning. After midday, with the mercury rising, you either stayed in the shade or indoors until nightfall, when the temperature fell sharply.

Major Najib returned to RAF Habbaniya half an hour before noon with a second message, and again demanded to see Smart. This time the pilot officer asked Najib if he would care to wait in the guardhouse or in his car, as it would take a little time to contact the Air Vice-Marshal.

Najib elected to sit in his car for twenty minutes. By the time that Najib reached Smart's office, his once immaculate uniform was drenched in sweat and he looked less the martinet and more the drowned rat.

Smart looked at Said's second message:

The British have broken the Anglo-Iraqi Treaty. The Iraqi Commander will not allow any training or anything else to be carried out as long as the Treaty is not respected.

This placed Smart in a precarious position, but he decided to stall for time, sending Said an ambiguous reply:

You have raised a political question which neither you nor I can answer. I suggest that you and I refer this to our respective Ministers to come to an agreement.

In the meantime I would recommend that you remove your forces from the plateau to avoid the occurrence of any accidental problems.

Smart immediately sent the gist of this second Iraqi demand and his reply by signal to Cornwallis, Fraser and Tedder, as well as the Air Ministry in London. Smart also stated that he would continue to avoid offensive action until the Iraqis opened fire. He asked for an immediate directive as well as the status on reinforcements.

Ling and Dudgeon left Savile's office in a state of shock. While Savile had agreed to Ling's suggestion of Savile setting up his 'operations room' in the back of Hangar Six, the furthest away from the plateau, and to Dudgeon's recommendation to take up an Oxford and photograph the whole plateau and the surrounding areas to create photo-mosaic maps on which to pinpoint Iraqi positions for targeting, he would not countenance relieving the ground-crews from trench digging.

'Sir, if the Iraqis start something, the trenches and our few machine-guns, with the best will in the world, are not going to stop their tanks. However, a determined attack from the air with everything that we could put up might hold them off until such time as we can be reinforced. The problem is that all the essential people – the armourers, the electricians, the mechanics and the riggers – have been spread all over the camp. We don't know where they are so we cannot find them in a hurry if the balloon goes up.'

'I understand your position but the AOC has given explicit orders', replied Savile.

'Sir, you cannot expect the few pilots that we have to fuel and service the aircraft and find and load the bombs and ammunition, get briefed and start the aircraft all on their own. Just as an example, the Audax, Gladiator and the Gordon all need a second person to hand-crank to get the engine going!'

'Dudgeon, until the AOC countermands the order it stands', Savile replied frostily.

Later in the officers' mess Ling turned to Dudgeon. 'We cannot get caught again disobeying orders, so we have to find away around this absurdity.'

'We will have to get the pilots to walk around the trenches now and tell the individual ground-crews their assembly points – behind the hangers or on the polo field – when we get the call to go into action. While this is not perfect, at least it will give them a rallying point and stop them running around like headless chickens', suggested Dudgeon.

'You're right. We have to avoid a repetition of Smart's General Alarm this morning. No one knew what was up, where to go or what to do, and it took hours to get some sort of order in place. The last thing we need when we have to go into action is confusion', agreed Ling.

Smart looked unhappily at the copy of a fence-sitting signal he had just received from Cornwallis to the Foreign Office in London. Cornwallis agreed that Smart should use force to restore the situation, indicating that the Iraqi threats were acts of war justifying immediate air action. While he awaited a Foreign Office directive to force the issue, Cornwallis was trying to get the Iraqi government to withdraw their forces

Smart, watching the continual build-up of Iraqi forces on the plateau, sent a signal in frustration to Cornwallis. Smart wanted to know if Cornwallis agreed with his replies to the Iraqi commander and whether Cornwallis would have preferred that Smart had sent an ultimatum and, if necessary, an air attack against the steadily increasing forces threatening Habbaniya.

A strict system of rationing was introduced that morning to preserve food supplies. It became increasingly common to see both RAF and Army officers sit down in the mess to a table complete with a peace-time setting of silver and crockery and staff, but precious little food.

During the late afternoon Alistair Thompson and five other BOAC employees were rounded up by the Iraqi police and taken to a civilian jail in Baghdad, and remained there for the duration.

That evening Smart received a signal from AM Tedder in Cairo. Ten Vickers Wellington bombers would be sent to Basra immediately, and another ten would be on stand-by in Palestine. If the Ambassador agreed, they could be used immediately should the Iraqis open fire on Habbaniya.

To Smart these 'reinforcements' were virtually useless. To get the Wellingtons, from either Shaiba three hundred miles south or Aqir in

Palestine five hundred and fifty miles to the west, bombed-up and fuelled and over Habbaniya would take at least five hours, by which time the Iraqis could have completely overrun the camp.

Habbaniya, 1 May 1941

Smart had taken to sleeping in a camp bed in his office – partly to be available for any eventuality and partly to avoid waking his wife.

A flurry of messages arrived for him after midnight, which all gave moral support but were short on both directive and reinforcements. Both Cornwallis and Auchinleck supported immediate action. Fraser in Basra was unable to support Habbaniya due to the extensive flooding, and suggested that he seek help from Middle East Command in Cairo. The breakfast-time signal from the Foreign Office in London received by Cornwallis was also copied to Smart. It stated that the position must be restored and Iraqi troops withdrawn without delay, giving Cornwallis, and by implication Smart, full authority for taking any steps necessary to ensure this, including air attack. For Smart it was no longer *if* but *when*.

Smart contemplated issuing an immediate ultimatum to the Iraqi commander to withdraw his troops. However, he knew that the commander on the spot would have to consult Baghdad before making a move. Reasonably this would take a minimum of three hours, bringing them up to noon. If there was no withdrawal, Smart would then have to attack.

However, a noon attack would leave only half a day for air operations before nightfall. Smart would need the maximum amount of daylight to mount a heavy first strike, which would hopefully dissuade the Iraqis from a night attack. Smart signalled Cornwallis to issue an ultimatum to the Iraqi government at 05.00 hours on 2 May, which would run to 08.00, giving Habbaniya the whole day from 08.00 to attack if the ultimatum was unsuccessful.

Smart was incensed when he saw his copy of Cornwallis's lunchtime signal to the Foreign Office in which the Ambassador stated that he had asked Smart to attack that very day. Smart quickly fired back that he would not attack that day given the few remaining hours of daylight, and that he would attack the next morning. However, Smart also changed the delivery of the ultimatum. It would now be given to the Iraqi commander at 05.45, with thirty minutes' grace to observe movement, otherwise air action would be taken.

Tedder's advice, which followed at the end of the afternoon, added nothing, and if followed could have had a disastrous effect on the situation. Tedder gave Smart the choice of telling the Iraqis either that he was continuing his flying training programme or that he was giving them an ultimatum to remove their forces surrounding Habbaniya. If they opened fire or refused to accept the ultimatum he should attack the Iraqi government offices and their Raschid barracks. Either course would have left Habbaniya wide open for an unstoppable ground assault on the camp

Smart knew that the time had come for him make a decision. He could no longer wait for reinforcements that might or might not come, nor could he wait for the Iraqis to make the first strike.

Attacking well-dug-in armour, artillery and troops exclusively from the air had never been achieved in warfare. If he failed he would personally carry the blame both for wrecking any chance to negotiate their way out of the problem and for the civilian and military casualties. If he succeeded he could still face censure for making an attack on a friendly nation where a peaceful solution could have been negotiated.

Smart now knew what the *loneliness of command* really meant. The chips were down. He was out on a limb with no directives and no help. He called Savile and asked him to assemble the Air Striking Force commanders and the ground force commanders for a meeting in his conference room at 20.00.

Arriving at the designated time, Smart found Savile waiting to introduce him to Col Ouvry Roberts, chief of staff of 10th Indian Division. Roberts had flown in that morning from Shaiba on a 31 Squadron DC-2 to take a look at the situation. As Roberts was the senior Army officer, Savile had requested that Roberts stay and take over command of the land forces at Habbaniya.

Smart, Savile and Roberts moved over to where Dudgeon had laid a photo-mosaic map across the conference table, where the other participants were crowding around. They all looked up as Smart walked over. He turned to Dudgeon and said, in a subdued voice, 'Why don't you bring us up to date with the Iraqi investment?'

'The photos, taken just before dusk, show that the Iraqis now have at least twenty-eight field guns and howitzers and up to 9,000 troops dug in on the escarpment. Vehicles are dispersed here, and here, and armoured cars there, there and near our main gate,. Iraqi troops have also occupied Humfriya and Sin el Dhibban, the little villages on the outskirts of the cantonment. The Iraqis have also ferried two howitzers and some machine-guns across the Euphrates so that they are now in a position to shell us from both sides. Troops and supplies are still coming down the Falluja road to reinforce their positions. I also took a shufti at Ramadi. I estimate that the Iraqis are there in brigade strength. This is probably insurance in case someone comes to our aid from Palestine', Dudgeon said, looking up from the map table.

Turning to Roberts, Brawn, Everett and Page, Smart asked whether they had finished their preparations. 'Yes, speaking on behalf of the ground forces', said Roberts. 'We are all in place and have already initiated fighting patrols along the perimeter fence this evening to deter the Iraqis from mounting night attacks.'

'Bill, how are the trench defences coming along?'

'They were completed late this afternoon', he replied. 'We also found a half-a-dozen more Lewis guns with anti-aircraft pedestal mountings tucked away in the stores. We have set these up, together with the other 34 Lewis guns, in sandbagged emplacements around the vulnerable targets to give us some protection from attacks by the Iraqi Air Force.'

'Gentlemen,' began Smart, 'I think that we no longer have the option to wait, and if the Iraqis are still up on the plateau I am ordering an air attack at first light tomorrow morning.'

One could almost sense the feeling of relief which swept through the conference room.

'I want you to get every aircraft we can get into the air before dawn so that we can commence bombing and strafing the Iraqis as soon as you can distinguish ground targets', Smart went on. 'Our strategy is concentrated, continuous bombing without warning to demoralize the Iraqis. We should have them in full flight within about three hours. Air Marshall Tedder has sent ten Wellingtons of 37 and 70 Squadrons from Cairo to Shaiba to help out. They carry a useful bomb-load of four and a half tons each, so that should augment our striking power.

'Just before the meeting I received a signal from the Prime Minister which I think you all should hear, as it sums up what we are about to do.

If you have to strike, strike hard. Use all necessary force.

'I think that you have all a lot of things to do and you face a busy night ahead. But before I let you go are there any things that we need to finalize?'

'Yes, sir', said Ling, raising his hand. 'There are a number of practical issues that we need to resolve. For example, the lack of facilities at the polo ground for rapid resupply of fuel, ammunition and bombs. We also need to release ground-crew from the trenches so that we can get ready for our pre-dawn take-off.'

'Wing Commander, we cannot let any one leave the trenches: they are our only form of ground defence, I repeat our only defence, so they must stay! Gentlemen, do the best you can', Smart said as he concluded the meeting.

Smart went back to his office to draft a signal to Cornwallis, Tedder, Fraser and the Air Ministry in London, explaining the deterioration in the situation, which now made it necessary to attack the next morning without warning

Leaving the meeting, Larry motioned to Dudgeon, Hawtrey, Holder and Silyn-Roberts, as well as the two flight lieutenants, Cleaver and Evans, to follow him into an empty office on the ground floor of the administration block.

'You all know where your ground-crews are, so get them out of their trenches and round up your pilots. You need to name your air-crews and allocate their tasks for tomorrow morning. We all need to be fuelled and bombed-up ready to go by 04.30 latest to get us over the plateau to start action at 05.00. See you at your aircraft at 03.00 hours.'

'Just one thing,' Ling continued as they moved towards the door, 'for God's sake keep this quiet from Headquarters and from Savile. What they don't know about, they can't stop!'

None of the 'Habbaniya Striking Force' commanders got to bed much before midnight, and the last pilot was back at his aircraft by 03.15 the next morning.

Chapter Three

Strike Hard, First

Habbaniya and Baghdad, 2 May 1941

As the first molten rays of the coming dawn spread like a halo around the plateau, all thirty-nine aircraft started their engines. They moved into position on both the main airfield and on the converted polo ground for take-off, guided by airmen with hooded torches.

In a combat situation no flare-path or navigation lights could be used, and it had been reluctantly decided that those pupil pilots with no night-flying experience would be excluded.

Dudgeon in an Oxford led the rest of the aircraft allocated to the main airfield out of the gate. He pointed the nose at the black mass of the plateau framed against the lightening sky in front of him and opened up the throttles wide, remembering to pull back the stick as soon as he possibly could to miss the casuarina and pepper trees at the far end of the runway.

Dudgeon's aircraft led the Oxfords and the Gordons, followed by the Audaxes, into a climbing turn to form a huge circle which wheeled over Habbaniya.

The air above the plateau seemed to be filled with aircraft as the ten Wellingtons from RAF Shaiba joined up with the Habbaniya fleet. Now aircraft of five different types, sizes and speeds were all jockeying for space in an area not much bigger than a medium-size golf course.

At 05.00 hours, when it became possible to distinguish objects on the ground, Dudgeon led the attack on the plateau, dropping the first bomb-load at 1,000 feet from his 'training' aircraft.

As Dudgeon banked away from the plateau he saw the rest of the Oxfords painted in 'trainer' yellow follow in at 1,000 feet, the camou-flaged Wellingtons start to bomb from 5,000 feet, while the silver Audaxes and Gordons began to dive-bomb the Iraqi positions. Patrolling at 10,000 feet like protective eagles were the silver-painted Gladiators.

Quickly overcoming their initial surprise, the Iraqis began to retaliate immediately. They opened up with anti-aircraft fire from machine-guns and 20 mm cannon, while their batteries of 18-pounder field guns and 4.5-inch howitzers began to shell RAF Habbaniya.

One of the first Iraqi shells fell on the square, killing Privates Adshead and Rooney of B Company of the King's Own, and badly wounding several others, while other salvoes fell all around D Company, with near-misses throwing up fountains of earth covering the troops in their slit-trenches.

Baghdad

Freya Stark arrived at the British Embassy just after seven in the morning in style, sitting in a horse-drawn ghary, holding a parasol and wearing one of her eccentric hats. She was a small woman who wore her hair looped over one ear to hide a deformity caused by a childhood accident. Her dazzling career as an explorer, writer, photographer and Arabist had been achieved through a combination of audacity and charisma. However, her driven personality and extravagance could exasperate both her friends and her detractors.

Her command of Arabic and her personality helped her to success-fully create the anti-fascist Brotherhood of Freedom in Aden and Egypt for the Ministry of Information, and this had led to her secondment to Baghdad to help counter Axis propaganda.

Freya was on a train on the one-metre-gauge line from the Persian border at Khanikin to Baghdad when the RAF bombs began to fall on the plateau.

It had taken some time to get transport from Baghdad North station to the Embassy.

The early hour, the general surliness of the people at the station and the quiet streets with their windows tightly shuttered in a normally vibrant city created a sense of unease in Freya.

Past the Munahiya and Haidar-Khana Mosques, along al Raschid Street lined with the shops of merchants selling brocade, velvet and silks, past Armenian dentists, Muslim photographers, Jewish jewellers, Christian booksellers, past the Bank of Cairo, the three-storey Orozdibak department store and the Lowel Brothers' Buick and Chrysler agency and over the King Ghazi Bridge, the story was the same: a few, sullen people and a large number of troops on the streets.

Arriving at the Embassy, Freya was confronted by a police cordon and had to wait outside the small wooden postern gate until Leslie Potts, the Consul, identified her before the police let her and her two suitcases through the gate.

The sight inside the Embassy confirmed Freya's worst fears: they were under siege. Three large incinerators in the Chancery courtyard were being fed by staff, while others carried out boxes full of secret files and archives and most of the cyphers to feed the fires. Two Bedford light trucks were parked on the drive and a few cars were on the lawn, petrol tins full of sand were strategically placed to put out fires and a large 'V' of white sheets was spread out on the lawn to warn RAF planes of their position.

The faces of the people Freya passed were pale from sleepless nights, and bore out the general air of uncertainty and even fear. The British looked hot and pensive, the Middle Easterners who had taken refuge in the Embassy looked gloomy, the Indians deeply unsettled, and the Iraqis who had stayed on looked resigned to their fate.

Freya walked into the large hall at the main entrance, where the blue-tiled fountain still played, up the circular staircase and along the passage to the Ambassador's office. Freya knocked on the open door, and Cornwallis, sitting at his desk, looked up and smiled, waving Freya to come in. 'Freya! What a pleasant surprise. I thought that you might have heard and would keep a discreet distance until all this unpleasantness has been resolved', he said, walking around the desk to embrace her.

'How are things, Ken?', asked Freya.

'Not good. Rashid Ali's blind ambition has trapped him between the Mufti, the *Golden Square* and the Axis on one side and us on the other – and he had no way out. The RAF started bombing at five this morning and I am worried that the Iraqis will take revenge on the people here at the Embassy', he said as he walked out onto the balcony overlooking the courtyard and the lawn.

'The RAF buses and trucks which took the women and children out to Habbaniya on the 29th also brought in some Lee Enfield rifles, sandbags and barbed wire. George Waterhouse is having the time of his life drilling men and siting the sandbags and barbed wire', he said, pointing to activity in front of the main gate; 'I just hope to God that it does not come to that.'

'We also have to contend with overcrowding. We now have three hundred and sixty-six men as well as nineteen women – Armenians, Indians, Jews, Poles and Yugoslavs – with no papers which disqualified them from the evacuation. Unfortunately we have toilet facilities for only ten, so Pat Domvile has got some men over there by the west wall,' he gestured, 'digging latrines and wastewater sumps. So far the telephones still work and the electricity and water are running, and we do have enough food stores for about a week. At the moment there is little more we can do.'

Freya tried to look out at the city beyond the walls of the Embassy, but the pall of smoke now hanging over the garden, and the black ash swirling around from the bonfire, which made her eyes smart, seemed to be imprisoning her.

Habbaniya

The RAF aircraft attacking the plateau soon established a routine to maintain their strategy of continuous bombing. After dropping their bomb-loads they would return to their landing grounds to rearm and refuel and then take off again for another bombing run.

Shells from the Iraqi guns were falling all over the camp, making take-offs and landings a hazardous operation. The Audaxes based on the polo field were fortunate as they were screened by a row of trees, which hid not only the parked aircraft but much of the landing and take-off run from the Iraqi gunners. However, the Gladiators, Gordons and Oxfords based on the main airfield were fully exposed to the guns on the plateau.

Dudgeon's flights devised both take-off and landing patterns to reduce their vulnerability to ground fire. Engines were started in the lee of hangars, and after an airman based at the corner of a hangar gave the all-clear if there were no aircraft landing, the pilot would juggle with the throttles and brakes as the aircraft swept out from behind the hangar and opened-up the engine. As soon as the pilot had achieved flying speed and sufficient height he would drop a wing and pull the aircraft to starboard away from the plateau, and then climb to his bombing height before turning and heading back towards the plateau for his next run over the target.

On landing, the aircraft would swing away over the Euphrates on the far side of the camp and then fly in very low, getting the best cover from buildings and trees, and then turn in between the hangars, landing on the taxi way by the airfield fence before swinging through the gate and back between the hangars.

As soon as the aircraft parked, one of the crew would report to Savile in the operations centre on the result of the mission. Savile would mark this on the photo-mosaic map and then assign a new target for the next mission. While this was going on, the other crew member would help the ground-crew to rearm and refuel the aircraft and check for battle damage.

David Evans, commanding the Gordon flight, had picked up several wounds in the first day but kept flying. He experimented and came up with a way of destroying pin-point targets on the plateau. The 250 lb bombs were fitted with safety devices to ensure that the bombs fell at least two hundred feet before exploding, to avoid blowing up the plane from below. Before take-off Evans removed the safety device and had the bombs fitted with fuses to give a 7-second delay between impact and explosion. Climbing to 3,000 feet, he would pick out a target on the plateau and go into a near-vertical dive at a lunatic speed for a Gordon of 200 mph. Pulling out, Evans would lay his bomb at between eight and ten feet above the target, and with his speed and the 7-second delay would get just far enough away before the bomb exploded. The Iraqis soon got the point, and refused to come out and fire at Evans when he started his dive-bombing attacks.

Baghdad

Rashid Ali and Haj Amin sat opposite Luigi Gabrielli, the head of the Italian Legation, in the library in the Mufti's house in Zahawi Street.

'Minister,' Rashid Ali began, 'as you know, we have been attacked by the British without warning early this morning and are fighting back. We have breached the dams on the lower Euphrates and Tigris and have destroyed railway tracks and the telegraph to the north of Basra, preventing the British from moving to support their airfield at Habbaniya. I would like you to convey to Rome and Berlin that we are counting on military aid, and we are relying on your promises as we have been forced to make a stand on Britain's unacceptable demands.

'Mr Gabrielli,' repeating the Minister's name to reflect the gravity of his message, 'we want a prompt reply and emphasize that we need immediate shipments of aircraft, and arms, a military mission and financial aid. If we do not receive this assistance without delay our only hope is to gain time through negotiation. However, I see little chance that this would work, as the British seem bent on occupying Iraq.'

'Minister,' the Mufti added in a quiet, measured tone, 'as soon as we receive aid from your governments I will direct my supporters to begin subversion in Palestine and Transjordan which will help to pin down the British.'

Gabrielli promised to convey the Iraqi message urgently to Rome and Berlin, and left hurriedly for his Legation.

Haj Amin turned to Rashid Ali. 'al Sabbagh made a serious miscalculation by expecting the British to negotiate and not fight. Everything now depends upon Iraq's ability to hold on – the longer that we resist the greater the chance of serious German and Italian support. We need to stall for time. Contact the Turkish Embassy and ask for an urgent meeting with their Ambassador. If we can get the Turks to mediate with the British on our behalf it may weaken British determination and delay further armed clashes.'

Rashid Ali bitterly resented being ordered around by the Mufti. However, Haj Amin's instruction made sense, and this was not the time or the place to risk a confrontation with the Mufti.

Habbaniya

By mid-morning the attackers were experiencing intense, accurate anti-aircraft fire from the plateau.

With the Oxfords cruising at 1,000 feet and the Audaxes and Gordons sweeping even lower as they dive-bombed, they were hard targets to miss, even for the most inexperienced Iraqi gunner. Flg Off Walsh's Oxford was shot down in flames and Plt Off Gillespie's Audax failed to return.

For most of the pilots the tracers floating up gently from below seemed at first to be just pretty lights. When they saw bullet holes being punched through their fabric-covered wings, and bullet strikes through their cockpits and windscreens, the realization set in that this was a fight to the death, and that their flimsy machines with a lack of protective armour plate were virtual death traps.

After a sortie each aircraft was checked for additional battle damage. If it was superficial – it seemed to have passed through the aircraft without hitting anything vital like a fuel line, a spar or control wires – it was patched up with the engine running.

However, within a few hours every aircraft was damaged. The record was held by Flt Lt Dan Cremin, who brought his Audax back after one ten-minute sortie with fifty-two new bullet holes.

As the day grew longer, the human casualties began to grow. Aircrew with minor wounds which were not incapacitating were returned to the attack as soon as the planes could be rearmed. Those with flesh wounds were bundled off to the hospital, often to return in a few hours or the next day, stitched, bandaged and plastered for another sortie.

The example of Wad Taylor, a part-time air gunner, was typical. Wad, because he always took a large sandwich aloft, was in a Gordon when a bullet came up through the floor, went through his eyebrow, scarred his forehead, entered his leather helmet and went out through the top. He covered his blood-filled eye with one hand and used the other hand to fire his Lewis gun. He was rushed to hospital when the Gordon landed, and an hour and a half later, stitched and wrapped in bandages, he took his place in another Gordon and went back into action.

However, the number of seriously injured aircrew began to mount. Flt Lt Jimmy Page, an Audax pilot, was shot through the jaw but managed to land safely on the polo field despite being in great pain and barely able to see. Another Audax pilot hit by three bullets through the lung and shoulder collapsed over his stick, causing his aircraft to go into a steep dive. His pupil gunner, also wounded, was able to pull the pilot back and hold him there until he recovered enough to pull the aircraft out of the drive and land it semi-consciously on the polo field with his one good arm. A Gordon pilot shot in the thigh by a burst of ground fire was able to land. The same burst had hit his oil cooler, and as the oil pressure fell the plane limped to a halt just outside the airfield fence as the engine seized. The pilot and his gunner only just made the safety of the hangar before Iraqi gunfire bracketed the Gordon and then scored a direct hit.

Cairo

GHQ Middle East Command was located in a sprawling warren of offices in a modern five-storey Art Nouveau apartment block dubbed 'Grey Pillars' in Tonbalat Street. This was located at the southern end of Garden City, one of the better residential suburbs of Cairo.

Lt-Gen Henry 'Jumbo' Wilson, an enormous bald man, surprisingly light on his feet for such bulk, alighted from the Humber staff car as it drew to a halt outside GHQ, After showing his pass to the Military Police sergeant at the guardhouse, he quickly passed through the barbed-wire fence.

Wavell, deep in thought, did not hear the first knock of his ADC on the main door to his office. The second, louder and more insistent knock, penetrated Wavell's thoughts and he looked up from his desk.

'Sir, General Wilson is here to see you.'

'Thank you', replied Wavell to his senior ADC, Peter Coates. 'Give me a few minutes to clear my thoughts and then send him in.'

Wavell's responsibility was vast. Geographically, Middle East Command stretched from the Tunisian border with Libya in the west, to Transjordan's border with Iraq in the east and from Greece in the north to Madagascar in the south. No commander in the history of warfare had to deal with an area covering three million square miles, over one million people or with so many countries, cultures, religions, climates, or allies or enemies.

In early May he faced an array of problems. ULTRA intercepts indicated that an airborne assault by *Generalleutnant* Kurt Student on Crete was imminent. Rommel had Tobruk under siege, and advance elements of the *Afrika Korps* were on the Egyptian border at Sollum. The sea lanes across the Mediterranean were in danger of being cut, and Malta was under continuous aerial bombardment. In East Africa his forces engaged in a major battle at Amba Alagi in Eritrea were outnumbered five to one, and intelligence reports indicated that Axis agents were at work throughout the Middle East fomenting unrest.

Worse, Wavell was at war with Churchill. Churchill's distrust of generals was matched by Wavell's doubts about politicians.

Wilson strode into the office and sat down when Wavell indicated a chair. Jumbo was Wavell's right-hand man, 'a man who got things done' – a situation that worked well probably because they were so different.

Wavell, a muscular, bull-necked man with an eye blinded in the First World War, was possibly the best-educated soldier of his generation. He appeared distant, detached and even remote. Celebrated for his unexpected silences and his prolific memory, his reputation was built on hard work and integrity. Wavell attracted loyalty and affection as few others, not least for his personal bravery.

In contrast, Jumbo was a solid and dependable but aggressive man, some said a bully, who was not universally liked by either peers or subordinates. He resembled a benevolent uncle, but looks were deceptive, as few experienced the benevolence he appeared to exude.

'Jumbo,' Wavell began, 'I want you to put together a plan with George Clark in Jerusalem to relieve Habbaniya.'

Discussions with Wavell always contained long silences and Wilson waited patiently for Wavell to continue.

'As you know, I have fought this, but it is now a directive from the Chiefs of Staff, so we have to get on with it', Wavell finally added.

'I know the position, sir, but we face enemy pressures throughout the Middle East and we have serious manpower and equipment shortages. We lost half of our equipment when we had to evacuate Greece, and some of our best troops, the Australians and New Zealanders, are tied up in Crete waiting for Student to attack. Where do I get the resources?' asked Wilson.

Wavell responded enigmatically with, 'That is your affair', and rose to indicate the end of the meeting.

Habbaniya

By noon three of the four flight commanders flying Audaxes were out of the fight. Ling was wounded in the air by ground fire before lunch and out of commission for the rest of the campaign, and Silyn-Roberts was rushed to the hospital for an emergency appendectomy.

Paul Holder's Audax was hit, wounding his air gunner Aircraftman Wad Taylor, and his engine stopped. Holder was able to glide in over the perimeter fence and land. As he and Taylor ran for the nearest trench an Iraqi shell blew up the Audax

All ten Wellingtons from 37 and 70 Squadrons were also out of the fight. The big Wellingtons were nice juicy targets, and on return to Shaiba nine were found to be unserviceable due to battle damage The tenth Wellington, piloted by Flg Off Anstey, made a forced landing at Habbaniya after sustaining serious flak damage to its engines before it had even dropped its bombs.

The large aircraft sitting on the main airfield acted as a magnate for the Iraqi guns, and the aircrew made for the hangars with machine-gun bullets kicking up the sand around their feet as they sprinted to safety.

The Habbaniya ground-crews, although lacking any Wellington equipment, tried desperately to save the aircraft, and a tractor was driven out boxed in by RAF armoured cars on all sides to screen the unprotected driver from the Iraqi bullets. Before the tailwheel of the Wellington could be attached to the tractor the Iraqi howitzers had bracketed the aircraft and scored a direct hit, which also put the tractor out of action.

The tractor driver, Aircraftman Kevin O'Reilly, was unhurt but left wandering around in the open, dazed by the exploding shells. One of the armoured-car commanders, Flt Lt Pyne, saw O'Reilly and had the driver, LAC Tait, drive back, and Pyne and LAC McLennan hauled him into the vehicle in the face of intensive fire before heading back to the comparative safety of the lee of the hangars. Halfway across the airfield, Pyne's armoured car was almost blown over by a huge blast wave as the full 4,500 lb bomb-load and fuel in the burning Wellington detonated.

Just before noon the Iraqi Air Force began a series of attacks on Habbaniya. The Bredas, Gladiators, Nisrs, Northrops and Savoias of the numerically stronger and more modern Iraqi Air Force made a number of sorties, bombing and strafing the camp. As most of these attacks were made with low-level, high-speed runs, they were fairly inaccurate, although the RAF did lose three aircraft on the ground.

While Habbaniya did mount combat air patrols with the Gladiators to counter Iraqi air raids, they had no radar or radio control. This, together with operating worn-out aircraft which could not match the speed of the enemy aircraft, allowed the Iraqis to bomb and strafe the camp with impunity. Probably the only value in the Gladiator standing patrols were that they deterred the Iraqi Air Force from pressing home more determined attacks.

The oxygen-equipped Savoias flew over at high level, well above the operating ceiling of the RAF Gladiators. Dicky Cleaver saw one at around 20,000 feet, and reckoned that he could reach it before he lost consciousness from oxygen starvation or the Mercury engine's carburettor iced up. The Gladiators in the Middle East were usually flown with the canopy slid back to give a better view and fresh air. With no heated suit, Dicky wound the sliding canopy closed and used full throttle to provide the boost to get a full-power ascent. It took almost ten minutes for Dicky to climb to 20,000 feet and get behind the Savoia. Perfectly placed, Dicky took careful aim and pressed the gun button on the top of the control column. However, he did not reckon on the cold at that altitude or the lack of anti-freeze oil at Habbaniya, and all four Browning .303 machine-guns iced up. Helplessly Dicky watched the Savoia fly safely away.

Getting food to the defenders was a difficult and even hazardous job. With the King's Own and the Levies dispersed around the camp, a large part of the RAF personnel manning slit-trenches and the aircrews in continuous combat, the only feasible way to feed the defenders was for the mess staff to bring sandwiches and dixies of tea to them. Many of those shuttling food, tea and water to the troops, airmen and aircrews were locally recruited Iraqi cooks, kitchen staff and barmen who loyally remained on duty throughout the siege.

However, the officers' mess was still functioning, and the senior officers, none of whom had volunteered to fly or fight, were continuing to use the mess, oblivious to the battle ranging around them, much to the annoyance of their younger, fighting subordinates. When disturbed by Iraqi machine-gun bullets through the corrugated asbestos roof and splinters from exploding bombs through the walls, they made vigorous complaints in the Mess Suggestion Book.

To the delight of the defenders, six Iraqi Gladiators strafed the officers' mess, and a number of elderly and portly senior officers were seen to be hastily diving for cover under tables and chairs as the Iraqis roared a few feet over the building.

Early in the afternoon LAC Arthur Briggs, with a nose for business, opened a book and began taking bets on how long it would take for the water tower to catch a direct hit from an Iraqi shell. With his position in a slit-trench directly outside the Air Headquarters block, the large amount of traffic to and from the command centre provided him with the perfect cover to receive bets and pass betting slips across the camp.

Throughout the day the blockhouses along the perimeter fence, and especially those facing the plateau, had been taking sustained fire from the well-dug-in Iraqi positions. Although none of the blockhouses were put out of action, No. 8 was under continuous heavy fire and an Iraqi shell knocked in the front of No. 9.

However, the blockhouses kept up constant return fire on the Iraqi positions, and No. 10, with a field of fire across the Falluja–Ramadi road, shot up Iraqi traffic throughout the day. Four Iraqi officers in a staff car were believed wounded, and an Iraqi dispatch rider was shot off his motor-bike and killed.

Roberts from the outset believed that their best ground defence was in the attack. While Brawn and Everett had planned their defences by meticulously dividing the perimeters into sectors of responsibility, with the blockhouses being supported by communications trenches, Roberts believed that their key objective was to seek out and destroy the Iraqis.

Both the King's Own and the Levies began ground offensives against the Iraqis.

An Assyrian company, using its Boys anti-tank rifles, successfully repelled the only armoured foray towards the camp from the south by eight Crossley armoured cars supported by three FIAT light tanks from the Iraqi Mechanized Brigade.

The two Iraqi 3.7-inch howitzers across the Euphrates to the north began to pour accurate fire into the camp. A Levy platoon from the Kurdish company crossed the wide, fast-flowing river in an old motor-boat supported by small-arms fire from the nearest blockhouse. They were forced to advance across open and partly flooded ground, but were able to inflict over thirty casualties among the Iraqi gun crews before heavy machine-gun fire and a lack of ammunition drove them back.

Later in the day Audax dive-bombing was used to silence the guns.

Under cover of night Roberts planned to use fighting patrols of Brawn's Levies to harass the Iraqi forward positions and to deter enemy patrols from penetrating the camp.

By the end of the day the growing list of casualties from Iraqi shell and sniper fire and bombing strafing raids had taught everyone that digging slit-trenches was more than a necessary fatigue.

Baghdad

As the day began to draw to a close, Adrian Holman found Cornwallis in conversation with Edmund Loftman, one of the leading lights of the British community in Baghdad, in the courtyard of the Embassy, and coughed discreetly to get his attention.

'Adrian, you need me?' said Cornwallis.

'Sorry to disturb you, sir, but I have a pressing problem.'

Cornwallis, sensing Adrian's discomfort in speaking in front of Loftman, excused himself and drew Adrian away. 'My thanks to you, Adrian, in getting me away from that bore. Now what can I do for you?'

'I have an Iraqi captain at the postern gate with about a dozen armed soldiers. He has cut off our telephones and wants us to hand over all our radio transmitters and wants to search the Chancery buildings. What do you want me to do?' asked Adrian.

'I will protest in the strongest possible terms about the violation of our diplomatic immunity, but in reality there is little we can do. I will use this opportunity to press for the restoration of our electicity, as its loss endangers our health. The septic tank for the Embassy's sewage depends entirely on an electically operated pump. While I am protesting and negotiating, Smy in the radio room will have enough time to send a final message to London and Habbaniya, and then destroy our transmitter before we turn it over. Also ask Smy to burn the remaining cipher books and have General Waterhouse present so that he can authenticate their destruction.'

'That means that we will be totally cut off from the outside world, doesn't it?' asked Holman as more of a statement than a question.

'Not quite', said Cornwallis. 'I will hide my Philips radio so that we can get some idea what is happening, and we do have a hidden reserve radio transmitter.'

At the American Legation Paul Knabenshue took stock. He had given shelter to 170 refugees – fifteen Americans, 140 Britons and fifteen people of other nationalities.

Col Page, a retired Indian Army officer, was drilling some of the men, armed with a motley collection of hunting-rifles, shotguns and pistols, while Betty Sulman, the young King's British governess, was organizing food and shelter. It came as a great shock to Betty to encounter lying, cheating and stealing which people who were not normally dishonest or greedy did to increase their rations.

Knabenshue had also lost his radios and telephones to the Iraqis, and was isolated like the British across the river.

Habbaniya

As dusk began to filter in from the east, five Wellingtons of 70 Squadron returned for a second attack on the plateau. Although the Iraqi Air Force intercepted the Wellingtons with two Northrops and two Gladiators and attacked for twenty minutes, there was no damage.

However, ground fire did succeed in hitting one of the Wellingtons, which had force-landed at Habbaniya.

During the early evening the first issue of a daily sheet giving news of the progress of the war, with a note or two about events at Habbaniya, began to roll off the camp printing-press.

With the fall of darkness, combat flying was halted for the day.

Smart called for a briefing at 20.00 hours in his first-floor conference room in the Air Headquarters block.

The number attending this meeting was much smaller than the day before. Smart now presided over the Army officers, Roberts and Everett from the King's Own and Brawn from the Levies, Page from the Armoured Car Company and Savile, Hawtrey and Dudgeon from the Air Striking Force.

The results of just one day's sustained combat were not good.

The Air Striking Force had flown 193 recorded sorties, although there were probably more which went unrecorded in the heat of the engagement. Of the sixty-four aircraft, over one-third, twenty-two, had been shot down, strafed by the Iraqi Air Force, blown up by the Iraqi guns or damaged beyond repair. Many of the remaining aircraft were unfit for service under normal RAF standards, but fitters and riggers working with light from hooded torches behind the hangars and on the polo field were trying desperately to coax them back into the air for tomorrow's battle.

More seriously, ten, more than a quarter of the thirty-nine pilots were dead, missing or hospitalized, and most of the rest were wearing bandages and plasters.

The British casualties were thirteen dead and twenty-nine wounded, including four Levies and nine civilians.

Despite the continuous bombing and strafing campaign, the Iraqis were still firmly ensconced on the plateau, looking down on the camp with the undiminished capacity to shell Habbaniya into submission or to mount an unstoppable ground attack. Iraqi morale was higher than Smart had been expecting, and, more pointedly, showed no signs of weakening.

Smart looked visible shaken by the news, and began to blame Wavell in Cairo, Auchinleck in New Delhi and Bill Fraser in Basra for failing to come to his aid, and the politicians in general for getting Habbaniya into this mess in the first place. 'What else could I have done?' he said. 'We have attacked and it's not working. My station is being destroyed around me and my people are dying and no one is helping us.'

Smart called an end to the meeting, to the relief of the participants embarrassed by his outburst. 'Well,' he concluded as the participants were filing out of the door, 'tomorrow is another day and I will be talking to you about some better ideas after I have spent some time thinking about them.' No one commented on Smart's behaviour as they went their separate ways.

After the disastrous briefing, Dudgeon, Savile and Hawtrey met at the operations room at the back of Hangar Six to discuss tactics for the next day.

'In the face of our experience today and particularly our losses, I think that we should divide our resources differently', Dudgeon said. 'By switching the remaining Audaxes and the Gladiator flight to the polo field, where they are well screened from the Iraqi gunners, they can bomb-up, take-off and land back quicker and safer. Cutting back on my command to just the Oxfords and the Gordons means that I will be able to get them all behind the hangars out of direct sight of the gunners. The corrugated iron of the roofs and walls will also explode most of the incoming shells. This will give my crews their best measure of protection.'

Hawtrey confirmed his agreement, adding, 'It would simplify our tasks as we would each only have to crew two different types of aircraft.'

'We have a problem with the women and children still in the camp, as well as the wounded at the hospital. All require evacuation. Obviously we cannot get them through the Iraqi lines, so the only way out is by air. What about the Oxfords, Dudgeon?', asked Savile.

'The Oxfords can only carry a few at a time and have no passenger comforts', replied Dudgeon. 'However, 31 Squadron at Shaiba has some nice shiny new DC-2s which they commandeered from Indian National Airways and fitted out for troop transport. We could get them to shuttle the women, children and wounded out to Shaiba.'

'The DC-2s are big targets for the Iraqis and we could lose not only the planes but also the women and children', replied Savile.

'As long as we know when they are coming we could have the Audaxes dive-bomb and strafe the Iraqis to keep their heads down', said Hawtrey.

'I'll get in touch with Richard Burberry, the CO of 31 Squadron, and get them to arrive a few minutes after five, just as we start our attack on the plateau, which should keep the Iraqis tied up', agreed Savile.

Savile confirmed the operational plan for the second day and to a 04.00 hours briefing for the crews, with a take-off time scheduled for 05.00 hours the next morning.

After the meeting Hawtrey and Dudgeon toured the polo field and behind the hangars to assess the number of aircraft that would be available for combat the next day, and spoke individually to the fitters, riggers and armourers who were working in virtual darkness, to keep up their morale.

Smart signalled Tedder in Cairo, urgently requesting reinforcements due to the damage suffered by so many of Habbaniya's aircraft and pilots in the first day of combat.

Dudgeon got back to his room shortly before midnight, to be greeted by his long-suffering dachshund, Frankie, who had been frightened out of his wits by the non-stop shelling and bombing. Just as Frankie curled up in Dudgeon's arms, the Iraqis, free from instant retribution by the Air Striking Force, began a sustained bombardment which went on from midnight through to 03.00, pumping over two hundred shells into the camp.

Dudgeon and a shivering and whimpering Frankie crawled underneath the bed just before a near-miss blew in the windows, scattering jagged shards of broken glass, part of the window frame and bits of curtain all over the room and bed. After a few minutes, desperate for sleep, Dudgeon, complete with Frankie, brushed the debris off the bed and climbed in, with Frankie burrowing down under the sheets to curl up at his feet, apparently safe in the belief that his master would protect him.

Cairo

Smart's initial handling of the attack, his dispatch of somewhat hysterical messages, including his failure to press home ground attacks in concert with the bombing and strafing, suggested to Tedder that Smart's judgement might be affected. He began to consider replacing him.

Habbaniya, 3 May 1941

Crew briefing took place at 04.00, and Habbaniya's little air force took off at 05.00, joined by a single serviceable Wellington from Shaiba. The plan was to continue the relentless programme of bombing and machine-gunning the Iraqi positions on the plateau overlooking the camp. As the bombing began the Iraqis resumed their intense shelling of the camp.

When the first of 31 Squadron's DC-2s appeared overhead, still sporting their Indian National Airways livery, John Hawtrey's Audaxes began an intense dive-bombing and strafing attack, which enabled the DC-2 to slip unscathed into Habbaniya. Throughout the airlift only a few DC-2s were damaged, none seriously, and no women or children were wounded or injured.

Paul Holder flew down to Shaiba on the first Douglas flight out of Habbaniya to organize the purchase of meat, vegetables and other foodstuffs to fill the aircraft on their flights up to Habbaniya to restock the camp's food stores.

On the second day there were some tactical changes. Three Wellingtons operating out of Shaiba, together with some dive-bombing Audaxes and Gordons from Habbaniya, took the fight to the enemy. Several Iraqi fighters intercepted the RAF aircraft over Raschid air base, and gunners aboard a Wellington shot down one Nisr and damaged a second. Photographic evidence from Dudgeon's Oxford later showed that the surprise attack on Raschid air base, a little to the south of Baghdad, where the Wellingtons had unloaded 7,100 lb of bombs, damaged twenty-nine of the Iraqi Air Force's Savoia Marchetti bombers and Breda fighters on the ground.

Back at Habbaniya, SM79s and Northrops again attacked the camp. Dicky Cleaver made three passes firing 1,200 rounds, and a Savioa Marchetti left the area trailing black smoke, while Flt Lt May attacked a formation of Northrops and damaged one.

On the way back from the Raschid attack, Plt Off Michael Strange, flying an Audax, saw a lone Iraqi Nisr flying north-north-east away from Habbaniya. Following the same course, he came across a Northrop and a Savoia, both force-landed in the desert, signifying that Cleaver and May had made confirmed kills.

The Nisr disappeared, but could only have come from Baquba air base some seventy miles away on the same course. The Air Striking Force decided to pay Baquba a visit later that day.

A group of Audaxes supported by Gladiators found twenty-one parked Iraqi aircraft at Baquba. The dive-bombing Audaxes took ten on the ground and the Gladiators got three on the ground and one in the air.

While the Raschid attack was accomplished without loss, an Audax was shot down over Baquba with a bullet through its Kestrel engine. The pilot managed to glide away and landed safely on packed sand. Iraqi troops quickly arrived on the scene, none too happy at having their airfield soundly beaten up.

They stripped the two RAF aircrew, tied their hands behind their backs, badly beating them with rifle butts and staves as they made them run barefoot to the air base. Luckily the troops did not resort to the common Iraqi custom of slashing off their prisoners' genitals.

It had been decided to avoid bombing civilians in Iraq since no one wanted to inflict suffering on the population, with whom the British had no quarrel. However, Gordons began dropping leaflets which Cornwallis had composed in Arabic a few days before.

These were designed to assure the population that the British would drive out their enemies and that Rashid Ali and the *Golden Square* had betrayed them for German gold. Not all the leaflet-dropping sorties were received without retaliation and many took ground fire from the Iraqis. Several pilots responded by dropping the wrapped parcels so that the tightly packed paper fell on the heads of their assailants.

Baghdad

At 07.30 Rashid Ali made a radio broadcast which was repeated hourly through the day:

> *To the people of Iraq*
> *We were forced to take defensive measures, and the military operations which have begun are continuing with successes to our Army. The noble Iraqi nation is requested to remain quiet, proving its political maturity, and confidence in our national forces. The people are requested never to attack foreigners among us who will be regarded as our guests.*

The early part of the day at the Embassy was marred by several incidents. The reserve wireless set was up and working by 8 a.m., and by 10 a.m. contact was re-established with Habbaniya. By 11 a.m. an official from the Iraqi Ministry of Foreign Affairs turned up at the main gate with some army officers, demanding the surrender of the reserve wireless set. The Embassy gave the set up and reluctantly allowed a further search of the buildings under protest at the implied threat of force. Around noon the Iraqis requested that the British managers of the Imperial Bank of Iran and the Eastern Bank, who were at the Embassy, and the manager of the Ottoman Bank, who was at the American Legation, hand over their keys. If the managers refused, the Iraqi Ministry of the Interior would open the banks by force. The managers eventually agreed under protest in the face of *force majeure*.

Freya stood on the long, low terrace wall at the foot of the Embassy lawn looking out over the river. It was strange to see the Tigris so silent. Except for the police launch riding quietly off the Embassy wall, the river was devoid of traffic. Normally the 400-metre-wide dirty brown river would still be swollen from the winter run-off of snow in the mountains, and would be alive with river traffic almost as varied as the streets of Baghdad.

Gufas, large round barrel-like coracles made of reeds filled with watermelons would josh with *Kalaks* made up of planks and goatskins from Mosul transporting brushwood and grain. The beautiful slender *Maheiles* with pointed, overhanging prows would slid silently past the long, rectangular *Shahturs*, lateen-sailed *booms* or *Dhows* up from the Gulf with their sharp sterns and nose like a swordfish, Arab *buggalows* with intricately carved sterns and the gondola-like *Bellums*. All the while the passenger ferries operated by the Lynch Brothers would criss-cross the Tigris, darting around the big flat-bottomed British-built river steamers from Basra downstream, who presided over the noise and chaos like disapproving parents looking down on unruly children.

However, Baghdad was a town under curfew, and nothing moved on land or river. Iraqi river commerce was dead. The high-sided ships bringing Welsh coal, Kenyan coffee, Egyptian cotton and Indian spices and tea, and carrying out Arabian horses, dates, gums, hides, liquorice, nuts and wheat, had all gone. The only thing in the river that remained the same was the odd dead dog or donkey floating downstream with the current.

Later in the day the Iraqis had demanded that the Embassy hand over the seven cars and two trucks inside the walls. They went away for a while when this was refused, but were back later with a request for the British to lower the Union Jack on the roof of the Embassy as this could incite hatred

While Loftman and some of the permanent residents became angry, Freya was pleased that Cornwallis overruled them and agreed to lower the flag, since the Iraqi request made sense under the circumstances. A little later he had the Union Flag raised on a flag pole in front of the main Embassy building, which could not be seen from outside the walls, thus pacifying Loftman.

Although Rashid Ali's radio broadcast was designed to keep the lid on popular opinion, this was being inflamed by the broadcasts from Radio Zessen and Radio Bari, which Freya could hear blaring out from nearby houses. Most irritating was the radio in a coffee shop a few yards from the southern boundary wall of the Embassy, which seemed to be amplified every time that Yunis al Bahri ranted and raved about the British. Radio Zessen and Radio Bari transmitted programmes five times a day, including readings from the Koran, anti-British news and German and Italian military successes. Since the outbreak of hostilities the radio broadcasts had begun to add historical descriptions of the glories of the Arab past to strengthen Iraqi self-assurance.

Heavy doses of martial music and a focus on nationalism, rather than religion, constantly calling on Arabs to revolt against the British, was heady stuff in a country with a low level of literacy. A demonstration by the *Futuwwah*, disparagingly known to the British as the 'Footwear', outside earlier in the day had also caused concern among those incarcerated in the Embassy.

Freya looked back and saw that in some windows of the houses overlooking the Embassy Iraqi soldiers had mounted machine-guns, and shivered, hoping that things would not spiral so far out of control that the Iraqi armed forces would either participate in, or turn a blind eye to, a massacre at the Embassy.

Freya could not help but think that the leaflets that the RAF had dropped earlier in the day had been of little use. Although written in Arabic they were not widely read by a largely illiterate population, and they probably helped to inflame rather than convert those who could read the content.

Berlin

Ribbentrop wrote to Hitler in an attempt to force support for Iraq:

> *If the available reports are correct regarding the relatively small forces the English have landed in Iraq so far, there would seem to be a great opportunity for establishing a base for warfare against England through an armed Iraq. A constantly expanding insurrection of the Arab world would be of the greatest help in our decisive advance toward Egypt. The figures regarding the British in Iraq show how weak England still is today at the Suez Canal.*
>
> *The Iraqis have requested that Fritz Grobba be sent to Baghdad at once to help their efforts. Grobba had been our Minister in Baghdad until the war started and relations were broken off. He is our best Iraq expert. He should be flown at once to Iraq to direct and further expand our network of agents in the Near East.*
>
> *The whole Arab world shall then be aroused into rebellion against England from our centre in Iraq.*
>
> *I await your agreement on sending immediately a fighter and bomber squadron to aid the Iraqis, as well as air delivery of arms and ammunition.*

Later in the day Hitler responded favourably to Ribbentrop's request, and the *Reichsaussenminister* sought an immediate meeting with Goering to convince him of the strategic value of the Iraqi operation.

Habbaniya

Dudgeon had a problem with Frankie. He could not leave the Dachshund alone to endure the continuous shelling, which was driving the dog mad. With nowhere to leave him, he decided, against all known RAF rules and regulations, to take Frankie with him on operational sorties.

He figured that as no one of any seniority seemed to be risking his neck if he didn't have to, there was no one close enough to cause him trouble.

After a couple of sorties Frankie had got the hang of flying. As soon as Dudgeon picked up his flying helmet Frankie would trot a few feet in front of him trying to divine which aircraft they would take. When they got to an Oxford Frankie would stand near the door at the rear of the plane waiting to be lifted in, as he was not tall enough to jump in. Once in the Oxford he would scamper up front and look out of the bomb aimer's window in the nose. As soon as they were airborne Frankie would come back and curl up on the floor next to Dudgeon's seat and close his eyes, and sit there undisturbed by all the manoeuvring until Dudgeon throttled back his engines for the approach. Then Frankie would run back to the bomb aimer's window to supervise the landing, only leaving his position to run aft when the aircraft stopped, to wait for the door to open.

Flying a Gladiator or Gordon, both with no floor, where Frankie could not lie beside Dudgeon, almost drove Frankie to distraction, but anything was better for him than leaving him behind among the Iraqi shells and bombs which fell continuously on the camp.

Holder's second Audax was hit in the fuel tank, drenching him in petrol. He crash-landed upside-down on the station's golf course and was trapped with his head in the sand of a bunker. Wad Taylor, whose wounds had been patched up, scrambled clear and with considerable effort raised the aircraft's tail, freeing Holder. They ran for their lives and had made some hundred yards when the Audax blew up.

Roberts, standing outside the Air Headquarters block, made his way between the slit-trenches to two old 18-pounder field guns that graced the entrance to the two-storey building. He had asked around and found out that they had been used against the Turks during the 1916–18 Mesopotamia campaign, and had been sitting around for years until brought to Habbaniya in 1937.

Although they were covered in paint in typical armed services fashion of 'if it doesn't move, paint it', with a coat for every year in place, they had not been disabled.

Roberts decided to fly a Royal Artillery artificer up from Shaiba on the next 31 Squadron flight, plus some 3.3-inch shells for the guns, to see if they could be pressed into service.

London

Churchill, increasingly concerned about the situation, and annoyed with Wavell's continuing reluctance to assume a greater burden, had the Chiefs of Staff send a directive to Cairo:

> *A commitment in Iraq is inevitable. We have to establish a base at Basra and control that port to safeguard Persian oil in case of need.*
>
> *The line of communication to Turkey through Iraq has also assumed greater importance owing to German air superiority in the Aegean Sea. Had we sent no forces to Basra the present situation at Habbaniya might still have arisen under Axis direction, and we should also have had to face an opposed landing at Basra later on instead of being able to secure a bridgehead there without opposition.*
>
> *There can be no question of accepting the Turkish offer of mediation. We can make no concessions. The security of Egypt remains paramount. But it is essential to do all in our power to save Habbaniya and to control the pipeline to the Mediterranean.*

Habbaniya

The meeting with Savile was short and perfunctory. The Iraqis were still on the plateau, seemingly impervious to the death and destruction rained down upon them by the Air Striking Force while sending shell after shell into the camp.

The damage in the camp was beginning to mount. A number of barracks had lost their roofs, some houses and all of the hangars had been hit, slight damage was recorded to the officers' mess, the Assyrian church had been seriously damaged and a number of vehicles, including Smart's car, were write-offs.

As night fell and combat flying ceased, the Iraqi artillery began to use the freedom of darkness to step up their fire on the camp, throwing in about a shell a minute.

The only possible way to reduce the barrage was to bomb at night. Dudgeon and Hawtrey decided on a bold new plan. While they could not, for obvious reasons, use a flare-path which would illuminate them for the Iraqi gunners, they could use hand-held shielded torches among the trees along the polo ground to take-off, and use moonlight to land. While this took care of the Audaxes, the Oxfords faced a more difficult problem.

The polo ground was too short for the Oxfords to land, so they were confined to the main airfield. The final approach run to the main airfield was directly over the plateau, which would expose them to the Iraqi gunners. However, if the run was made without moonlight they could use their landing lights for a few seconds to touch down.

With only three Oxford pilots with night-flying experience, the decision taken was to fly three two-hour patrols, with the last pilot landing at daybreak. The Iraqi gun flashes would give away their positions on the plateau, allowing the Oxfords to target the guns. If the Iraqis did not fire, the Oxfords could drop one of their eight 20 lb bombs every fifteen minutes to encourage the Iraqis to keep their heads down.

Dudgeon took the first sortie shortly before midnight and ten minutes after moonset.

He started up the Oxford's twin Cheetah engines and was guided by shielded torches through the gates out onto the main airfield and into pitch darkness.

Lining up on a set compass course, and guided by his bomb aimer, Sgt Arthur Prickett, Dudgeon set the throttles and taxied forward for 4½ minutes, which brought them close to the plateau, and then turned onto a new compass heading and opened the throttles. The Oxford finally lifted off and Dudgeon brought the aircraft up to 1,000 feet.

Once they were airborne, the darkness was not so intense, and Dudgeon was able to pick out the winding Euphrates in the background, and the canopy of stars above gave him just enough ambient light with which to distinguish trees and roads and water from the desert.

For the next two hours Dudgeon criss-crossed the plateau, dropping bombs every now and again to keep the Iraqis from shelling the camp and from enjoying a good night's sleep.

The tricky bit was landing in pitch darkness. Switching off his cabin lights to regain his night vision, Dudgeon steadily banked to bring the Oxford over the lip of the plateau, and lost height down to 250 feet, lining up on a compass heading that should put the airfield dead-ahead. Counting ten seconds, he descended to just above the airfield, and when the altimeter read 50 feet he switched on his landing-lights. Seconds later the road around the airfield and then the ten-foot dyke flashed beneath his wings.

Dudgeon switched off the landing-lights and snapped the throttles shut at the instant the wheels touched the ground, using the light from the instruments as he braked to a standstill.

The emotional stress of the landing hit Dudgeon hard. He began to shake, hyperventilate and sweat profusely. After several minutes of silence, Arthur Prickett asked over the intercom whether he was all right. He shook his head to clear it and then looked over towards the hangars, and saw shielded torches signalling to him to taxi in.

The other two Oxford pilots did not fare so well. The first, a flying officer, managed to get down in one piece, but got out of the aircraft shaking, uttering, 'Don't ask that again, that's enough.' Dudgeon did not ask him again, nor did he think badly of him for it. The second Oxford, piloted by a WO, turned too early, leaving too short a take-off run. The wheels clipped the edge of the ten-foot dyke, and the Oxford somersaulted into the marshes beyond, the wooden aircraft exploding in a ball of fire: another Oxford lost, as well as a vital crew.

On the plus side, the night shelling of Habbaniya had been significantly reduced as a result of the night combat missions flown by the Audaxes and the Oxfords.

Brawn's fighting Levy patrols at night began to range far and wide outside the camp as they searched for Iraqis in outlying posts. So powerful was the impact of these patrols that the Iraqis began to vacate their forward posts at dusk, and never seriously attempted to penetrate Habbaniya at night.

Habbaniya, 4 May 1941

By the third day of the siege the defenders were getting into a pattern of 04.30 take-offs, strafing and bombing the Iraqis on the plateau at first light in conjunction with the Wellingtons of 37 and 70 Squadrons from Shaiba.

Eight Wellingtons again attacked Raschid Airfield, bombing buildings and strafing aircraft and scoring a direct hit on an Iraqi Nisr.

The Wellingtons attracted significant ground fire as well as interception by the Iraqi Air Force. The rear gunners on two Wellingtons put a Northrop and a Breda fighter out of action. However, one Wellington flew low over a 20 mm anti-aircraft gun while being pursued by an Iraqi Gladiator. Both fighter and guns hit the Wellington, forcing it to land, with the crew being taken prisoner.

The loss of irreplaceable pilots was a growing concern, and Dudgeon decided to push his luck with Savile. While Savile had been doing a sterling job in keeping supplies of fuel, ammunition and bombs going in spite of problems with transportation and shell damage, he disappointed the younger pilots. Dudgeon became more and more frustrated as he saw Savile pouring over the photo-mosaic maps plotting targets and assigning them to the pilots. Although Savile was an instructor of the highest quality and graded fully medically fit for any duty, he rarely flew, in common with almost all the senior officers, and he had not taken part in the strikes against the Iraqis.

Dudgeon, young, fatigued with flying around the clock and intolerant, saw a man dodging his responsibility. Finally, after Savile continuously turned down opportunities to take a sortie as he was too busy, he was confronted by Dudgeon. 'Sir, you have not yet seen the top of the plateau. I and your pilots believe that you should. My aircraft is outside, engines running, bombed-up and ready to hit the targets you just gave me. Come with me and we will be back in twenty minutes.'

'Dudgeon,' replied Savile, 'I just cannot leave the operations centre.'

'Sir, with all due respect I think that your presence in the air will encourage the younger pilots and will boost morale among the hard-pressed ground-crews. A personal example will go a long way to supporting their efforts.'

Savile looked very unhappy, but at last gave in and agreed to go.

After Dudgeon had completed several bombing runs, Savile, sitting next to Tony, asked, 'What are those zipping noises?'

'They are machine-gun and rifle bullets passing close by', responded Dudgeon.

At that instant Savile looked out of the cockpit and saw a row of holes being stitched through the plywood wing. He yelled, 'My God! We've been hit! Go back and land at once.'

Dudgeon as captain ignored the demand and completed the remaining bombing runs of his sortie. Savile sat quietly next to Dudgeon with his hands on his knees, staring straight ahead.

This was the only time a senior RAF officer ventured into combat at Habbaniya.

Dudgeon later regretted what he had done to Savile, whose medal ribbons clearly showed that he had contributed his full share during the Great War.

Smart and his family were evacuated on the first 31 Squadron DC-2 early that morning. The reason for Smart's departure has never been satisfactorily explained. The official view is that he suffered severe injuries including concussion, a broken jaw and multiple fractures in a car crash in the blackout on the night of 3 May. Those on the spot believed that it was nervous exhaustion.

Unexpectedly Sqn Ldr Pike of 203 Squadron arrived with four Blenheim fighters from Cairo. No one had told the defenders that they were coming, and no one had briefed the Blenheims that the plateau was thick with Iraqi anti-aircraft guns.

Coming in to land at Habbaniya with a normal approach over the plateau, 203 Squadron got a rough reception from the Iraqi gunners. Luckily some Audax pilots saw the approach of the Blenheims and did their best to keep the gunners' heads down by dive-bombing ahead of the incoming Blenheims. The arriving pilots were staggered to see airmen waving them in behind the hangars, and hesitated, but bursting Iraqi shells got them to make their minds up. Three of the Blenheims were subsequently found to have bullet holes, while one of the pilots swore that he had flown through the dust of an exploding 250 lb bomb on his approach run.

London

With no response from Wavell, Churchill sent another, more strongly worded, personal directive to Cairo:

> *Our information is that Rashid Ali and his partisans are in desperate straits. However this may be, you are to fight hard against them. The mobile column being prepared in Palestine should advance as you propose, or earlier if possible, and actively engage the enemy, whether at Rutba or Habbaniya. Having joined the Habbaniya forces, you should exploit the situation to the utmost, not hesitating to try to break into Baghdad, even with quite small forces, and running the same kind of risks the Germans are accustomed to run and profit by.*
>
> *There can be no question of negotiation with Rashid Ali. Such negotiations would only lead to delays, during which time the German Air Force will arrive.*
>
> *You do not need to bother much about the long future in Iraq. Your immediate task is to get a friendly government set up in Baghdad, and to beat down Rashid Ali with the utmost vigour.*

Baghdad

Paul Knabenshue at the American Legation was incensed by the Iraqi warning he had received that morning. The Iraqis had threatened to bomb the British refugees in the American Legation in retaliation for an alleged British threat to bomb public buildings in Baghdad if Iraqi forces did not evacuate the Habbaniya area.

Knabenshue agreed to surrender the British refugees only if an Iraqi cabinet minister would sign a statement guaranteeing adequate and safe internment facilities. Since no official would comply, Knabenshue offered the American Legation as an internment camp and accepted responsibility.

The Iraqis reluctantly accepted Knabenshue's offer.

Habbaniya

Lt Kit Wilson of the 3rd Field Regiment, Royal Artillery, beamed happily at the two 18-pounder field guns sitting outside the Air Headquarters block.

He had flown up from Shaiba late on the 3rd with a set of tools, an engineer and an artificer, sitting on three crates of 3.3-inch shells amid a jumble of boxes of tinned foodstuffs and bags of vegetables and meat from Paul Holder's first 'shopping' expedition.

It had taken several hours for the working party to strip off the accumulated paint and get the breech, rifling and firing mechanism cleaned.

Wilson walked over to Ouvry Roberts. 'Well, sir, I think you have got yourself two heavy guns', pointing at the two now gleaming howitzers. 'Would you like me to give a demonstration?' he asked.

Wilson got help from several airmen to turn the guns to point at the plateau. His engineer, together with the artificer, loaded both howitzers with their heavy 23 lb shells while he adjusted the sights for an airburst at the edge of the escarpment.

He walked back to Ouvry Roberts. 'Would you like to join me, sir?' he said, offering the lanyard of one of the guns to the Colonel, who happily accepted the offer.

'On my count of three, pull the lanyard. One, two, three . . . '

Both guns thundered simultaneously, which brought airmen and soldiers running out of the barracks and blocks nearby to see what was happening. They, together with those manning the slit-trenches and the working party, stopped to watch with awe as one shell hit the lip of the plateau and the other exploded about fifty feet further along and twenty feet above the escarpment.

As a loud cheer went up from the Habbaniya defenders, Wilson said to Roberts, 'I think it just needs an adjustment or two.'

Baghdad

Across the river from Knabenshue's 'White House on the Tigris', life in the British Embassy had its trials and tribulations.

Freya had spent part of the previous evening trying to suppress false rumours that Rutba Wells had been taken, and had finally ended the evening with a welcome hand of bridge.

In the morning, up on the Embassy roof Freya could just see the Wellingtons bombing Raschid air base to the south, and hear the dull crump as the bombs exploded and the sharp crackle of returning anti-aircraft fire.

The police in the motor launches retaliated by shooting their rifles every time that they glided past the Embassy, and Freya spent a lot of her time soothing the nineteen female refugees – Iraqi Armenians and Jews, Greeks, an Indian family and a Yugoslav.

Later Freya, together with some Embassy staff and Ernest Main of the *Baghdad Times*, helped to compose, print and distribute a daily news bulletin compiled from the BBC broadcasts.

A drama occurred when a superintendent of the Iraqi police arrived at the main gate. However, this was a false alarm, as he was only there to provide a friendly escort for the Embassy lorry to buy food. Unfortunately all the shops had been closed by their owners, terrified of being bombed by the British. This precipitated strict rationing in the Embassy.

Freya managed to get on friendly terms with many of the police guarding the Embassy, and found them happy to help in any way provided that they were given a little *bakhseesh*.

Late in the day the Iraqi Ministry of Foreign Affairs asked for a list of the names of all people in the Embassy of whatever nationality, accompanied by a certificate giving an assurance that no one would leave the Embassy before the Ministry had been advised. Since no one at the Embassy had any desire to do so, and this contravened diplomatic protocols, the Embassy refused to respond.

Habbaniya

At the end of the day the number of recorded sorties by Habbaniya's Air Striking Force had fallen to fifty-three, added to which were the night sorties flown by the Audaxes in the moonlight and the Oxfords in pitch darkness.

However, the Iraqis were still on the plateau and raining shell, machine-gun and sniper fire down on the camp.

Habbaniya, 5 May 1941

Overnight the ground-crews had been able to repair the bullet holes in the three 203 Squadron Blenheims, and one took off shortly after dawn before the departure of the Air Striking Force to maintain a standing combat patrol over Habbaniya.

The Iraqi Air Force later sent up two of their Pegasus-engined Nisrs to strafe and bomb Habbaniya.

They saw the Blenheim and fled, although one was not fast enough. The Blenheim overhauled the Nisr flying flat-out, low down over the Euphrates, and shot it down into the river with a single burst of its four .303 machine-guns.

As the Blenheim sedately waggled its wings and returned to its combat patrol, a tremendous cheer came from the camp, which must have been heard by the Iraqis on the plateau. From then on the frequency and strength of the Iraqi Air Force raids on Habbaniya declined dramatically.

Two of the Blenheims hit Raschid air base and the civil airport at Baghdad. At Baghdad, a Gladiator and three Nisrs were strafed, while at Raschid a Savoia, a Breda and a Nisr were attacked, with the Nisr being left in flames.

The fourth Blenheim, piloted by Sgt Hemsted, flew a photo-reconnaissance mission to Kirkuk, Baghdad, Solomon Doh and Mosul. At the latter he strafed two Nisrs, but was hit in the tail seven times by anti-aircraft fire.

Cairo

Wavell to Chiefs of Staff:

> *Your message takes little account of realities. You must face facts. I feel it my duty to warn you in the strongest possible terms that I consider that the prolongation of fighting in Iraq will seriously endanger the defence of Palestine and Egypt.*
>
> *The political repercussions will be incalculable and may result in what I have spent the last two years trying to avoid, namely, serious internal troubles in our bases. We should seek to accept a negotiated settlement via Turkish good offices.*

Later that day the operational command for northern Iraq passed from Auchinleck in New Delhi to Wavell in Cairo.

Baghdad

Day after day the temperature soared, reaching 115°F on 5 May. The heat in Baghdad was moist and tropical and oppressive, and added to the air of depression. Men at the Embassy stripped to their shorts, and the women did what they could to stay cool.

To combat depression, life in the beleagured Embassy was taken in hand. The defence of the premises grew daily more complicated as more and more barbed wire was wound around trees and hidden in flower-beds, and more and more sandbags were filled and barricades built – only to be resited the next day. The largest organization in the Embassy was the guard, which, with few exceptions, embraced all the able-bodied European men. Divided into four main and one subsidiary squads, these volunteers watched the perimeter by day and patrolled it by night.

As George Waterhouse was liable to conduct an inspection at any time, all the watchers, wisely, were at their posts and awake – all except an elderly Lancastrian who was provided with a chair for his short post-lunch duty of keeping an eye on the main gate. One afternoon Waterhouse, on a tour of the defences, found him asleep, and severely reprimanded the man. The following day his chair was seen to be facing the Embassy drive, with his back to the gate. The defaulter's superior demanded an explanation, and was told, 'I can see the old bastard better comin' from 'ere!'

There was also a group of roof spotters who did duty from dawn to dusk in the increasingly hot weather to follow the progress of the war in the air. Their reward came from seeing the RAF shoot down Iraqi planes and drop bombs on Raschid air base, the Washash camp and the airport.

Except for his bedroom and a small dining room, Cornwallis had given over the Embassy to his 'guests'.

Catering had been divided into five sections according to dietary habits – European, carnivorous Indian, vegetarian Indian, Arab and Orthodox Jew. The European canteen, catering for about 150, nick-named the 'Corner House', was run by the Matron of Faisal College and one of the nurses from the Royal Hospital, under the supervision of the Director-General of Iraqi State Railways.

Many of the women and the older men sat around in the shade of trees in the garden, and even the police in their motor-boats on the Tigris opposite the Embassy lay stretched out asleep on the thwarts in a square of shade which fell on the water.

The lack of police vigilance made it easier for people to enter and leave the Embassy, and a man was seen hawking a bundle of fish on a pole as he walked in and around the premises.

One of the biggest problems for the Iraqi refugees in the Embassy was an absence of their own bread. Freya, using her Arabic and some *baksheesh,* was able to arrange for supplies of *tannura,* which was gratefully received by the Arabs, Persians and Kurds.

The six horses stabled in the Embassy were getting rather bored by the lack of exercise, and the Kurdish grooms walked them around the grounds and Freya fed them dates.

She found that the leaflets dropped by the RAF were causing more trouble than they were worth. Empty threats and the promise to bomb government buildings had been counter-productive, and Freya advised Ken to telegraph Habbaniya to stop the leaflet drops.

Habbaniya

By the evening of the fourth day Savile, Hawtrey and Dudgeon took stock.

Although the Air Striking Force aided by the Wellingtons out of Shaiba had flown some eighty recorded sorties, only four of the original twenty-seven Oxfords were now 'flyable', and the remaining Audaxes and Gordons were literally held together with fabric patches pasted over the bullet holes. Even more problematical was the fact that in addition to the wounded, evacuated and dead pilots, an additional four, from Dudgeon's original nineteen, had to be relieved of flying duties due to nervous exhaustion.

During the night a fighting patrol of the King's Own and the Levies had tried to drive off the Iraqi troops which had invested Sin el Dhibban. The village lay below the northern end of the escarpment some four miles to the south of Habbaniya and was a vital ferry point across the Euphrates, providing a route to reinforce the Iraqis on the plateau. For the first time they failed to shift 200 Iraqis entrenched in well-defended positions.

Washington DC

'Wild Bill' Donovan had spent the morning with the President, Franklin D. Roosevelt, in the Oval Office finalizing proposals for a new government agency which would combine intelligence gathering with clandestine warfare.

On several trips to Britain as FDR's personal emissary, he had been impressed by SOE and the Commando units, and by Churchill's doctrine of taking the war to the enemy by 'setting Europe alight'.

Although both FRD and Donovan had little doubt that America would be fighting the Germans and the Japanese, sooner rather than later, they had to overcome not only strong domestic political pressures to remain neutral but also the Army, the Navy and the State Department, who would fight to the death to retain their control over intelligence.

FDR had proposed that Donovan be named first as Coordinator of Information in June, followed a year later by the formation of the Office of Strategic Services.

This, believed FDR, would give the military time to adjust to a new agency and Donovan the space to begin recruitment. FDR had also decided to promote Donovan from his current rank of lieutenant-colonel to major-general, to give him more political clout, recognizing that Washington DC was a city where the trappings of power and position were everything.

As Donovan shut the Oval Office door behind him, Marguerite 'Missy' Le Hand, FDR's personal secretary and close confidante, asked Donovan if he could spare a few minutes to talk to the Secretary of State. As Donovan nodded his agreement, Missy called through to Cordell Hull's secretary to advise her that Donovan was on his way over.

It took Donovan a good eight minutes to cross from the White House to the Old State Building, climb the ornate staircase to the second floor, and walk down the long corridor to the Secretary of State's office in the south wing.

Donovan did not have too much time for politicians, especially the brand in Washington, who seemed to be doing their best to line their own pockets or those of their sponsors. But Cordell Hull was different. Genuinely born in a log cabin in Tennessee, Hull, a tall lean man, was earnest and sincere in a way that comes to someone thoroughly convinced of the righteousness of his political and economic policies for peace and justice, as well as the moral and commercial supremacy of the United States.

Hull's secretary was waiting for Donovan and showed him into Hull's office, where Hull, already on his feet, gestured to a dark-green leather-buttoned chesterfield and matching easy chairs that seemed lost in a corner of the large office.

Hull was a no-nonsense politician, and the ornate stencilled wallpaper and the decorative furniture had been panelled over or removed, leaving only the massive fireplace, with its carved mantel and Doric columns as a reminder of Room 208's former richness. For Donovan the nicest feature of the room was the three windows opening onto the south portico, which gave a magnificent view of the Potomac.

'Thank you for coming over to see me, Bill. I heard that you were with the President, and hoped that we could talk for a few minutes.'

'Of course, Cordell, anything for a fellow lawyer, how can I help?'

'The situation in Iraq does not look good for the British. The Iraqis have besieged a British air base, the Regent has fled the country and our Legation is surrounded, and the Iraqis have taken away our radio. All our information now comes from our Ambassador in Cairo, who is briefed by British Headquarters. Adding to the problem is news from our highly placed source in the Vichy government that the Germans want to use Syria as a staging-post to supply the Iraqis with arms and equipment and possibly troops.

'In my eyes the Near East offers the greatest danger of the war, the possible juncture of German and Japanese forces, effectively cutting the world in two. Not only do we have to protect our own economic interests in the area, but the British cannot be seen to lose. It is not the oil that is at stake – we supply 90% of Britain's gasoline – but a British loss of face that would have a catastrophic effect on their position in Egypt, as well as Palestine fanning the flames for revolution. With revolts breaking out all over the Middle East the British would have little option but to disengage, leaving the Germans with North Africa, the Middle East and the Suez Canal.

'However, that is only my opinion. As Secretary of State I have to deal with a set of competing interests which has led to muddled thinking in US policy over Iraq, as well as the whole of the Middle East. Congress will not stomach war, so FDR has gone as far as he can go by virtually declaring economic warfare.

'Added to FDR's problems are the isolationist lobby led by the America First Committee supported by Lindbergh, a bunch of Ivy League intellectuals, a number of influential senators and congressmen and some of the Hollywood set. All of which are financed by a motley collection of industrialists and newspaper magnates.

'FDR is committed to keeping Britain afloat because sooner or later he will have to face the Nazis. FDR puts the defence of the Middle East in fourth place behind that of Britain, Singapore and the Ocean trade routes. FDR is not interested in helping the British to preserve British Imperialism nor their political or commercial pre-eminence in the Middle East after the war. He sees this as an opportunity for the United States.

'This is to do with the interests of US oil companies who want to be able to muscle in on the British monopolies in Iraq and Iran, but also the possibility that there are substantial quantities of oil in Saudi Arabia. It is also to do with the policy we adopted at the end of the Great War, which commits us to the creation of a Jewish national home in Palestine. Those are the interests that I have to contend with.

'Bill, you have been to Baghdad, how do you read the situation?'

'I share your concerns. I was there for a few days this January during my Mediterranean fact-finding trip. In my view the British had done little to quench the flames of dissent. Their then Ambassador spoke only to pro-British Iraqis, people with position and power to maintain, so he had no real idea of what was going on. On the other hand our Ambassador, Knabenshue, was a lot more switched on and had already made strong representations to the Iraqi government to cooperate with the British. Knabenshue fixed up meetings for me with a number of leading anti-British and neutral politicians for me to outline America's firm support and all possible aid short of war to the British.

'I also met with Haj Amin, the Mufti of Jerusalem. He very reluctantly came to see me at the Legation. I expected him to arrive with his retinue, but I think that he concealed his visit as he came alone. He is a malevolent influence and is behind the current problems in Iraq. I explained to the Mufti, in no uncertain terms, that America, though we have not yet declared war, is behind Britain and would resent the activities of people working against her. I told him to look ahead and understand the consequences of actions which, being against the interests of Britain, were against the interests of America. I asked him to explain our position to members of the *Golden Square*.'

'What was his response?'

'He agreed, but I am sure that he did not relay my message to them, as he continued his intrigues. The result has been this revolt.'

'What do you think will happen?'

'It is difficult to judge, as it could go either way. The British are heavily extended and have very little, if anything, left to give. It largely depends on whether the Germans get to Baghdad in strength before the British. If that happens it's the beginning of the end for the British in the Middle East, and it may well signal the end of British resistance to Germany.'

'Is there anything that we could do?'

'We are already doing everything we can short of war', replied Donovan.

Habbaniya, 6 May 1941

The sharp decline in airworthy aircraft and the loss of pilots and aircrew now meant that what was left of the Air Striking Force's resources were at a premium, and they had to husband their ever-diminishing planes and crews.

Savile, Hawtrey and Dugdeon had waited until dawn to send up an

Audax on a photo-reconnaissance run over the plateau and up the Baghdad road as far as Falluja.

The Audax pilot's news was good. By dawn the plateau was beginning to empty of Iraqi troops, who were withdrawing in the direction of Falluja.

Roberts immediately dispatched his armoured cars and infantry patrols in pursuit, clashing with the Iraqis on the Falluja road and in the village of Sin el Dhibban.

The lack of supplies, the continual air attacks and the use of the camp's 18-pounder 'artillery', which suggested that the camp was being reinforced by air, they later found out all contributed to shaky Iraqi morale.

Eight Iraqi Crossley armoured cars out of a column of fourteen were able to withdraw safely to Falluja, but the other six were destroyed as a counter-attack was being prepared to recapture lost Iraqi positions.

The 4th Iraqi Infantry Brigade which had initially been holding the plateau had been withdrawn after two days, being replaced by the 11th Iraqi Infantry Brigade and the 7th Field Artillery Brigade. These were now withdrawing due to the psychological pressure of continuous bombing and strafing and high casualties.

As the Iraqis from the plateau streamed onto the road to Falluja, an Iraqi column was leaving Falluja bound for the plateau to follow Colonel Fahmi Said's orders to recapture the lost Iraqi positions at whatever cost.

A patrolling Audax saw the column of four Crossley armoured cars, the 2nd Infantry Battalion of the 1st Infantry Brigade transported in civilian cars and the 5th Desert Artillery Regiment coming from Falluja meet up with the 11th Infantry Brigade and the 7th Field Artillery Brigade and their equipment, staff cars and trucks retreating from the plateau. This caused a huge nose-to-tail jam of men, vehicles, equipment and horses.

The Audax pilot wasted no time in landing and relaying the situation to the operations room in Hangar Six. The Air Striking Force would never get another opportunity like this, and Savile got every Audax, Gladiator, Gordon and Oxford that could be possibly coaxed into getting off the ground into the air to bomb and machine-gun the Iraqis on the ground. Forty aircraft from Habbaniya went into a pattern of bombing and firing on everything on the Falluja road, racing back to the airfield and the polo ground, rearming with their engines running and taking off again and heading back to the Falluja road to repeat the process.

The Air Striking Force took full advantage to cause mayhem by shooting and bombing everything along the only available road. They first attacked vehicles at the front and rear of the column to wreck their vehicles to trap those in the centre. With marsh and flooded ground on either side of the road, the vehicles had nowhere to go and were destroyed where they had stopped.

In a devastating two-hour attack on the road the Air Striking Force made 139 sorties When the last aircraft left, the pilot reported that the road was a strip of flame hundreds of yards long with ammunition limbers exploding and civilian and Army staff cars and troop transport trucks burning by the dozen. The charred and battered remnants of the two convoys littered the Falluja road for several weeks afterwards.

The Iraqis had lost about seventy vehicles and over five hundred troops killed or wounded in this single engagement, while the Air Striking Force had lost one Audax shot down.

Six Wellingtons of 37 Squadron from Shaiba attacked Raschid air base and Baghdad airport, setting fire to a hangar and inflicting damage on parked aircraft. They then dropped thousands of leaflets over Baghdad and bombed the Washash barracks in the western part of the city. However, the transport Valentias had a bad day. One crashed at Pumping Station K-3, while three more had to land in the open desert for a variety of reasons.

Sin el Dhibban

Unfortunately the Iraqi troops dug in at Sin el Dhibban, on the high ground beyond and in trenches by the New Lake Road did not follow the example of their compatriots and withdraw, but stubbornly held the village, forcing Habbaniya's ground troops into a major offensive.

Roberts's plan was for B Company of the King's Own under Capt David Clayton to attack the village at the eastern end of the plateau from the flank, while D Company under Maj Nigel Gribbon moved around to the west and made a frontal attack.

B Company met stiff resistance from intense Iraqi automatic weapons fire, and started to take heavy casualties. Lt Thompson and Private Owen pressed home the attack, firing bren-guns from the hip and lobbing hand grenades. Thompson came upon an Iraqi heavy machine-gun post, and called on them to surrender. As they raised their arms Thompson lowered his bren-gun and an Iraqi shot him dead. Owen and the last of the platoon finished off the rest of the post. B Company started to extricate themselves, with a wounded Pat Weir giving covering fire from his bren-gun.

D Company had better luck following behind the RAF armoured

cars, and mounted three successive attacks supported by the Levies, the RAF armoured cars and the two 18-pounder field guns to drive the Iraqis out of the village. At one point the Levies had to intervene. Capt Cottingham, RAB100 Stephan Nessan and Sgt Lazar Adam, all from the Levies, loaded up a Commer truck with a Vickers heavy machine-gun and a 3-inch mortar, and were able to get into a position by the sewage farm to enfilade the Iraqi positions. Together with support from a Levie company under RAB100 Khamsi Putros Odisho, their withering fire broke up the dangerous possibility of an Iraqi counter-attack.

D company began to take large numbers of prisoners, which required guards, reducing the strength of the already depleted company. At that moment a Valentia landed at Habbaniya with the band of the King's Own, who were rapidly trucked over to the village and pressed into service to reinforce D Company in mopping-up Sin el Dhibban. A young lance-corporal with a Webley who was seen chasing a terrified Iraqi stopped only to shout to the nearest officer, 'Do we take prisoners, Sir?'

The dust and heat haze, together with the fluid lines and the lack of radio communications, made air-to-ground and artillery cooperation extremely difficult, and much of the action was in hand-to-hand combat.

At the end of the day when the action had finished and the British were in possession of Sin el Dhibban and the plateau, they had lost seven killed and fifteen wounded in action. Together with the estimated five hundred killed on the Falluja road, the Iraqis had lost anything up to one thousand men killed in the battle for Habbaniya.

Basra

Convoy BP1 with the 21st Indian Infantry Brigade, comprising the Frontier Force Rifles and two battalions of the Gurkha Rifles, with two troops of the 13th Lancers equipped with armoured cars and a detachment of Engineers landed at Basra from Bombay. This gave enough strength for the 10th Indian Division to take over more of Basra, including the main telegraph office and the wireless station, albeit at the loss of a few Gurkhas to snipers.

Although Iraqi civil servants, dock workers and the crews of the dredgers keeping the port free from silt still refused to work, the situation in Basra was now stable enough to begin to re-establish communications inside Iraq.

Berlin

The drive from Templehof airfield to the *Reichsluftfahrtministerium* building took only twenty-five minutes, but *Oberst* Werner Junck was late. His flight from Calais, where he was stationed with *Jagdflieger-fuhrer 3* at Wissant, had been delayed by almost an hour due to a violent spring storm over the Ruhr.

It was well known that General Hans Jeschonnek, the *Luftwaffe's* Chief of Staff, detested tardiness. Junck's sense of foreboding increased as he entered the sober façade of the ministry building – another monument on the Wilhelmstrasse to Ernst Sagebiel's National Socialist intimidation style of architecture.

Jeschonnek, a hardworking and intelligent officer, was not best pleased with the mission to Iraq when he was stretched for men and machines with both the up-coming attack on Crete and *Barbarossa*. Nor was he ecstatic with his visitor's tardiness, which he put down to disrespect. None of this was the fault of Junck. But to show his displeasure he had Junck stand in front of his desk for a few moments before looking up.

Jeschonnek was a complex man, and although highly professional he was out of place in the higher echelons of the *Luftwaffe*. He was complex and often abrasive, brusque and sarcastic to his subordinates, while his youth and immaturity made life difficult for him with more experienced leaders.

'Sit down, Junck, this is not a parade ground', Jeschonnek snapped. 'This is a difficult operation. You are to organize and lead a special force, which we have codenamed *Sonderkommando Junck*, to go to Iraq to help them to fight the British. The *Fuhrer* desires an heroic action', he said, pursing his lips.

'What does that mean precisely, Sir?' questioned Junck.

Jeschonnek, realizing that he had treated Junck poorly, replied, in a less aggressive tone, 'This is an operation which would have significant effect, possibly leading to an Arab uprising, in order to start a *Jihad*, or Holy war, against the British.

I want you, as *Fliegerfuhrer Iraq*, to establish your staff headquarters on Rhodes. Reporting to you will be *Oberst* Rodiger von Manteuffel and his team with headquarters at Aleppo airfield in Syria. He is responsible to you for organizing ground support in Syria, including refuelling, flight planning and the transportation of your equipment. You will also have *Hauptmann* Harry Rother who will be in overall command of the transport element, and *Major* Axel von Blomberg who will be your liaison to their Prime Minister, Rashid Ali.

Our operations staff working with the *Oberkommando der Wehrmacht* (OKW) have found you a *Staffel* each of Messerschmitt Bf110 fighters and Heinkel He111 medium bombers, together with a transport element – some Junkers 52s and a few Junkers 90s. We have added the big Junkers to carry bombs, anti-aircraft guns, lubricants and even petrol, as we cannot guarantee the quality of Iraqi-produced aviation spirit. When we finish I suggest that you go down with Blomberg, who is waiting for you outside, to the operations staff office on the third floor, and they will fill you both in on all the details.

We have started negotiating with the Vichy French to provide refuelling and transit rights for Syria. They have been stalling, but the *Fuhrer* has a meeting with Petain in a few days and he will be put under extreme pressure to cooperate.'

'Is there anything else I should know, sir?' asked Junck.

'Yes, *General* Hellmuth Felmy, who is in Athens, has been earmarked as the head of the German military mission to Iraq. You may have heard of Felmy. He is extremely ambitious. Stay out of his way. Your chain of command is through me. Oh, there will also be a civilian involved. His name is Grobba and he is from the *Auswartiges Amt*. Grobba will be based in Baghdad and is the political link with Rashid Ali. He also has the reputation of being a prima donna, so you will need to step carefully on the ground. You should also know that Felmy is Grobba's brother-in-law. Good luck!'

With that he dismissed the *Oberst*.

Junck was left with the distinct feeling that he was stepping into a snake pit.

London

Chiefs of Staff to General Wavell

> *Your telegram of yesterday has been considered by Defence Committee. Settlement by negotiation cannot be entertained except on the basis of a climb-down by the Iraqis, on Iraq. Realities of the situation are that Rashid Ali has all along been hand-in-glove with Axis powers, and was merely waiting until they could support him before exposing his hand. Our arrival at Basra forced him to go off at half-cock before the Axis was ready. Thus there is an excellent chance of restoring the situation by bold action, if it is not delayed.*
>
> *Chiefs of Staff have therefore advised Defence Committee that they are prepared to accept responsibility for dispatch of the force*

specified in your telegram at the earliest moment. Defence Committee direct that the AOC Habbaniya should be informed that he will be given assistance, and in the meanwhile it is his duty to defend Habbaniya to the last. Subject to the security of Egypt being maintained, maximum air support possible should be given to operations in Iraq.

Habbaniya

The Iraqi Air Force hit Habbaniya twice that day. While a Gladiator did intercept and damage a Northrop, Iraqi bombs and machine-gun fire destroyed two Oxfords, one Gladiator and an Audax on the ground, as well as killing seven people and wounding eight more.

The second raid was particularly upsetting for Dudgeon. He was away from his Oxford making his sortie report to Savile and getting details of his next target when an Iraqi plane dropped a stick of bombs nearby. When he returned to the Oxford the engines were still running but his bomb aimer, Arthur Prickett, was lying on his side underneath the aircraft where he had been loading the bomb-racks for the next sortie.

He felt no pulse and, rolling Prickett over, saw a small wound just over his heart with only a little blood. It had been Dudgeon's turn to load the bombs while Prickett reported in to Savile, and by rights Dudgeon should be on the ground

With a heavy heart Dudgeon called for an ambulance to take Prickett's body to the hospital, and told one of the ground-crew to inform Savile. He checked the Oxford for other damage and loaded the remaining three bombs, calling out to the nearest pupil-observer, Stuart Smith, that he was Dudgeon's new bomb aimer. Once aboard, he and Smith, together with Frankie, took off for the next raid on the Falluja road.

Later that night Savile, Hawtrey and Dudgeon met at the operations room at the back of Hangar six for their review of the day's actions and plans for the following day together with Roberts, Everett and Brawn.

'Just before nightfall I sent up an Audax to take a shufti over the plateau,' said Savile, 'to see if there were any Iraqis still there. He dropped some bombs and machine-gunned his way around the plateau, but there was no return fire. He took photos from height and from some low-level passes. But as you can see,' Savile said, and pointed at the new photo-mosaic covering the map table, 'there is no sign of the Iraqis whatsoever.'

With the immediate threat ended, they agreed to wait until the following morning and a second photo-reconnaissance flight to decide upon their next moves.

Dudgeon and Hawtrey retired to the bar at the officers' mess to celebrate their victory over the Iraqi ground forces investing Habbaniya, and to recount their operations.

During the five days of combat in their poorly armed and obsolete training aircraft they had managed to drop well over 3,000 bombs, about fifty tons of ordnance, and had fired 116,000 rounds of ammunition. Savile had recorded 647 sorties, but they both knew that there were many more. Many of the Audax pilots were too tired to walk the half-mile from the polo field to report to the operations room after each sortie, and both Dudgeon and Hawtrey had also sent up the occasional aircraft without reference to Savile.

However, the price had been high. From the school alone they had lost thirteen killed and twenty-one too badly wounded to fly, as well as four grounded by nervous exhaustion. Those who joined from other formations in the camp, serving as both pilots and aircrew, were not included as they were never recorded as casualties by Savile.

It terms of sheer losses sustained in relation to the resources employed, the RAF had lost more men in air combat over Habbaniya than in the Battle of Britain.

In between whiskies, Hawtrey said, 'Do you realize that not one senior officer from Air Headquarters or the padres ever came onto my polo pitch, or down to your airfield, to give us an encouraging word or to comfort the wounded?'

It was a sad but true reflection of the support given by senior non-combatants. Many found themselves in an unexpected situation for which they were unprepared and inexperienced, and they just ground to a halt.

Habbaniya, 7 May 1941

For the first time in more than a week a more relaxed Savile, Hawtrey, Dudgeon and Holder met with Roberts, Everett and Brawn at the operations office at 06.00.

The night had been strangely silent with no Iraqi shelling, and they had all benefited from a night's uninterrupted sleep. The only one put out by the changing fortunes of Habbaniya was Frankie, who no longer slept in Dudgeon's bed.

The reconnaissance Audax had reported that there was no large-scale Iraqi presence in the area surrounding the camp, but only a few small, isolated units, while Page's armoured cars had confirmed that the plateau was completely deserted.

Without the threat of constant shelling, the wreckage of the Wellington and an Oxford, as well as the tractor, could now be cleared away from the main airfield, and aircraft could be repaired and serviced in the hangars in the shade out of the searing heat.

The King's Own and the Levies had begun to collect equipment abandoned by the Iraqis on the plateau, at Sin el Dhibban and along the Falluja road. The haul was impressive – field guns, gun tractors, cannon, machine-guns, a light tank and ten armoured cars, trucks and civilian cars and over three hundred rifles and half a million rounds of ammunition.

All of this equipment was far superior to the arms of both the British and Indian Armies, enabling Roberts to rearm the King's Own and the Levies with more and better weapons.

However, the war was far from finished. The decision taken was that the Air Striking Force's main role would now be in finishing off the Iraqi Air Force as a fighting force, while the ground forces would concentrate on mopping-up the few Iraqi units still in the area and pushing the Iraqis back to Falluja.

A lone Iraqi Nisr raided Habbaniya in mid-morning. A fighter Blenheim was scrambled, piloted by Sgt Hemsted. Giving chase, Hemsted intercepted the Nisr, shooting it down. In the early afternoon two Blenheims flew a reconnaissance over Baquba and found a collection of twenty-one Bredas, Nisrs and Northrops on the ground and strafed them. Later in the afternoon they returned with some of the Air Striking Force's Audaxes and Oxfords. The Blenheims set three Iraqi aircraft on fire while the Audaxes and Oxfords destroyed three more and damaged others.

An Iraqi Gladiator attempted an interception but was engaged by Plt Off Watson in an RAF Gladiator. Watson fired a long burst from astern at point-blank range, and the Nisr rolled over onto its back and was last seen diving steeply away, trailing smoke.

Baghdad

In contrast to previous days it was cool and pleasant at the Embassy. However, an air of depression began to take root as the idea that the problems would not be solved soon began to set in among the residents.

In an effort to fight the growing morale problem, Cecil Hope-Gill turned his public affairs section into an Amusement Committee to keep the enforced inmates happy. He collected all available talent, drew up programmes for the afternoon and evening, and lectures were provided on the most unlikely subjects, as well as producing entertaining diversions like Tea-Time Topics, Siesta Spotlights and the like on widely differing topics.

Every evening there was a least one dance, concert, lecture or cinema show, as well as bridge drives, a treasure hunt, crosswords and puzzles. One of the big moments of the day was the Embassy 'Broadcast' at 7.30 p.m., when Dr Harry Sinderson, doyen of the British medical - community in Baghdad, produced a fifteen-minute roundup of news, anecdotes, jokes and the inevitable limerick under the guise of the Embassy Broadcasting Corporation.

Several RAF air raids occurred that day, and an Iraqi Petroleum Company oil tank was hit to the north on the eastern side of the river. A great plume of black smoke billowed out of the oil tank and rolled over the houses. The fire burned through the night, greeting the dawn with a pall of smoke which hung over Baghdad and the river.

An RAF Audax dropped a message bag into the Embassy during the late afternoon but was driven away by machine-gun fire.

Habbaniya

During the night the AOC's office at Habbaniya received a telegram from Churchill:

> *Your vigorous and splendid action has largely restored the situation. We are all watching the fight you are making. All possible aid will be sent. Keep it up.*

Savile had copies made and posted on notice boards throughout the camp.

Berlin

Grobba, accompanied by Dr Hans-Ulrich Granow, Willi Steffan, two radio technicians and Ahmed Jabr, a Palestinian German from the Brandenberger Regiment, left Staaken airfield in Berlin at 16.10 on a *Luftwaffe* Junkers 52/3m *en route* to Baghdad.

It was going to be a long, circuitous trip. They were scheduled for refuelling stops at Foggia on the Adriatic late that night, which would put them into Rhodes in the Dodecanese by late morning the next day. They would fly on to night-stop at Aleppo in Syria that evening before arriving via Mosul in Baghdad on 11 May.

Habbaniya, 8 May 1941

The Air Striking Force swung into action with renewed vigour, and raided the Iraqi air bases at Baquba, Shahraban, Khaniqin and Kirkuk, destroying twelve aircraft on the ground in fifty sorties.

At first the Air Striking Force raided in penny-packets as so few aircraft were in any fit state to fly. With the lack of shelling and working out of the sun in the hangars the mechanics began to get more and more aircraft back into flyable condition. This enabled the Air Striking Force to increase the size and frequency of the raids.

With little or no Iraqi reaction to the raids, the fighter escorts of Gladiators used up their ammunition strafing ground targets. Within a few days Iraqi air attacks on Habbaniya had fallen to two to three aircraft a day, signalling that Iraqi air power was a spent force.

However, the Air Striking Force was still taking casualties.

An Oxford reconnaissance sortie flown by Flt Sgt Harry Brattan, one of Dudgeon's few remaining qualified pilots, resulted in his death. Iraqi forces in brigade strength were known to be in Ramadi some twenty miles west of Habbaniya on the Euphrates, and a sortie was flown to see if anything had changed and whether they were preparing for an attack against Habbaniya

Even though the Iraqis were quiet, there was no point in taking risks, and Dudgeon ordered Brattan to fly at 3,000 feet, out of range of rifle and machine-gun fire. Brattan disobeyed Dudgeon's orders and came in over Ramadi at 1,500 feet. He learned the hard way when a single bullet came up through the plywood floor of the cockpit and through his left side, severing a main artery. He died within a matter of minutes.

AC Kenneth Clifton, being used as an air gunner, a big step up from operating a wind-driven winch in a target-towing Gordon, left his gun and got Brattan out of the seat. Clifton then took over the controls to bring the Oxford back.

The only problem was that Clifton had only held the controls once before, and his efforts in trying to get the Oxford down in one piece, viewed from the ground, were hair raising.

Finally landing, he attempted to taxi the aircraft in, and was saved by one of the flying instructors, Kenneth Osbourne-Young, who got aboard and had to sit in the pilot's seat full of blood in a cockpit awash with it. Although there was a pupil-pilot on board who was fully capable of flying and landing the aircraft, he was outranked by Clifton until he qualified. Clifton almost got court-martialled until sanity prevailed and he was promoted to leading aircraftman and immediately awarded the Distinguished Flying Medal. However, the DFM caused him immense trouble. The medal was only awarded to aircrew, and he was constantly stopped by officers, NCOs and the RAF police demanding to know why he was wearing the medal.

At the end of the day welcome reinforcements in the shape of five Gladiators from the Storage Unit at Ismalia in Egypt flew in with Sqn Ldr Freddie Wightman, Flt Lt Sir Robert MacRobert, Flg Off Gerard Herrtage and Sgts Bill Dunwoodie and Len Smith.

Baghdad

Starting that day, the Iraqi National Defence Council began to repeat the following statement over Radio Baghdad:

We wish to inform the public that in their joy over the victory they are spending their ammunition in vain. We wish peace to prevail in every place, and after the victory over the British, revenge shall be taken on the internal enemy, and we shall hand him over to your hands for destruction.

Citizens in Baghdad began to respond, often vengefully. A woman whose gold button inadvertently appeared through her black *abba* was detained for signalling the British, as was a French violin teacher accused of carrying a radio in his violin case. Patients in the Meir Eliyahu hospital were accused of signalling the British, and a mob entered the hospital, attacking staff and patients.

Despite a total blackout, crime was down. Schools were closed, businesses paralysed as banks were ordered not to make payments and collections were taken up for the Army and the wounded.

Many hostile and over-enthusiastic members of the paramilitary *Futuwwah* policed Baghdad and used the opportunity to exact personal revenge, and to break into private houses and beat and terrorize people.

News of the Iraqi retreat from Habbaniya reached the Embassy through the BBC broadcasts picked up by their clandestine radio, and Dr Sinderson read out the news to the refugees sitting under the palm trees on the lawn.

Food was still coming in to the Embassy, and Freya went to talk to the police at the main gate to see if she could get any local news. The Iraqis claimed to have shot down forty-five RAF aircraft for the loss of one of their own, and though friendly they refused to give any further news. Freya hoped that London was making political capital out of the fact that the Germans, who had promised aid within two days of hostilities, had still to deliver on their promise.

Later in the day an RAF Gladiator swooped down low over the

Embassy and dropped a letter, confirming that all except thirty-two women and children had been safely evacuated from Habbaniya to Basra. However, an attempt later by an Audax to pick up a message from the Embassy using a hook and cable was abandoned due to intense ground fire.

Jeddah

King Abdul-Aziz Ibn Saud, a tall thin man with a great hook of a nose and drooping eyelids that belied his sharp intellect, sat on a raised chair as Naji al Suwaidi, Rashid Ali's Finance Minister, was ushered into his office in the Summer Palace at Jeddah.

Ibn Saud had little time for town Arabs who donned *keffiyehs* when they came to see him, and had even less time for so-called Arab nationalists, a small band of intellectuals who fought to secure their own power for their own ends rather that that of all Arabs. Although the Hashemites were no friends of the Sauds, deposing a king was a serious business. It set a bad precedent and could not be encouraged in case it spread throughout the Middle East.

'Your Majesty,' began al Suwaidi, 'I have come at the behest of Rashid Ali to seek your support to repel British aggression under the terms of the Treaty, specifically Article 4, signed between our countries in April 1931. Rashid Ali requests your help to mediate with Great Britain to call off the fighting and to send your forces to threaten Transjordan to prevent the Arab Legion being used against the Iraqi Army. Rashid Ali also is proposing a conference be held in Baghdad to make a pact between Iraq, Iran, Turkey, Russia, Germany and Italy and to consider the present situation and the future of the Arab world. He would appreciate your sending a representative to participate in the conference.'

'I have heard the request from Rashid Ali for support from Saudi Arabia', Ibn Saud began. 'As I told you during your visit in April, you should have reached a decisive agreement with Britain, avoided sedition and have no dealings with governments or individuals who seek personal advantage to the detriment of Iraqi interests', he said, taking a swipe at the Mufti, whom he viewed as a vicious zealot, and the Germans and Italians whom he mistrusted. 'Your Prime Minister chose to ignore my advice. Rashid Ali has made a big mistake in fighting Great Britain at such a critical time. If one puts one's hand in a nest of scorpions one will be stung. Any differences of opinion between Iraq and Great Britain should have been solved by peaceful means. You seem to forget that Iraq owes both its nationhood and its independence to Great Britain and, as such, is heavily indebted.

'I am a staunch friend of Great Britain and would have gone to her aid if I had sufficient arms. With the exception of Palestine, Great Britain has done nothing against Arab interests, and the present war is one of life or death for her. Our duty, if not to help Great Britain, is to be neutral. To the people of Iraq I say if you wish us to mediate between you and Great Britain we are willing to do what we can, but do not imagine for a moment that we shall take any steps which could cause a breach between us and the British. Our firm and fixed belief remains that interests of all Arabs lies in friendly cooperation with the British.

'Thank you for your visit. My warmest greetings to Rashid Ali.'

As al Suwaidi turned to leave, Ibn Saud said as an aside to his chamberlain, 'See that he gets one of our new Buick cars and make sure that he leaves quickly.'

Berlin

Ribbentrop waved a paper at Woermann when the latter entered the *Reichsaussenminister*'s office in the *Auswartiges Amt*.

'Abetz, our Ambassador in Paris, has been able to get the following concessions out of Darlan. The stock of French arms under Italian control in Syria can be transported to Iraq, they will help us forward all shipments destined for Iraq, give us permission for our planes to land and take on fuel, make an airfield available specially for Iraq operations and until this is available allow us to use all airfields in Syria.'

'What is the price we have to pay', asked Woermann, always cautious of concessions.

'Surprisingly little', responded Ribbentrop. 'We allow them to rearm six destroyers and seven torpedo-boats, relax travel regulations between Vichy and the rest of France and reduce their payments covering our occupation costs. It's really a few *Reichsmarks* compared to the gains that we could make with Iraq in our hands. I am sending Rahn to supervise the implementation of the details.'

'Do you want me to do anything?'

'No. I have sent my personal aircraft to Paris to pick up Rahn and take him to Syria.'

As Woermann left Ribbentrop's office he wondered what was driving the Foreign Minister. Was it to get back at the British? They had ridiculed his clumsy efforts at diplomacy when he was the Ambassador in London in the mid-1930s. His attempts at mixing with the aristocracy and the élite were rebuffed as they saw nothing but a social climbing 'Champagne salesman', which had made him bitter towards the British.

Or was it his constant need to impress Hitler? Ribbentrop's shameless flattery and sycophancy and his way of always telling Hitler what he wanted to hear were the stuff of legend in the *Auswartiges Amt*. It was probably a combination of both, mused Woermann.

Cairo

Wavell officially assumed operational control of South-Eastern Iraq from Auchinleck, the C-in-C India. Wavell informed the new commander of the 10th Indian Division, General Edward Quinlan, that his task was to secure the Basra–Shaiba area and organize a base to receive further reinforcements.

This contrasted with Auchinleck's policy, which was more aggressive, being designed to move the Army north as quickly as possible to set up a friendly government.

Wavell's strategy was to first ensure the cooperation of local tribes before moving north from Basra, while a force from Palestine, Habforce, would advance on Baghdad from the east.

In 1941 British Intelligence in the Middle East was locked into a turf war marked by failures to communicate and coordinate. At the heart of this was a fight for influence between the War Office and the Foreign Office. The Military wanted to centralize information from the many secret and semi-secret groups operating out of Cairo and to ensure that action was taken. In contrast, the Foreign Office wanted exclusive control over all actions with foreign powers, including those at war with Britain.

Rising above the bitterness and petty squabbles were two military operations that had proved their worth. Security Intelligence Middle East (SIME), formed by Lt Col Raymund Maunsell in Cairo in 1939, was primarily involved in counter-espionage. SIME had captured virtually every Axis agent in the Middle East, and had turned many of them. Modelled after MI5, SIME behaved more like MI6, one of the cover names for the Foreign Office's Secret Intelligence Service . . . and did it better. Maunsell ran SIME on loose and informal lines, with little attention to military proprieties. First names were encouraged, and his senior staff called him R.J.

The other operation was Brig Dudley Clarke's 'A' Force, whose mission was deception and disinformation. 'A' Force was the real reason behind the defeat of 250,000 well-armed and supplied Italians in Cyrenaica and East Africa by Wavell's poorly equipped army of 55,000. A small neat man with sparkling eyes, his laconic, self-depracating manner, cigarette holder and love of the good life masked Clarke's brilliantly clever and imaginative mind and his photographic memory. Maunsell and Clarke had formed an alliance to share information and give assistance in the interests of 'getting the job done'.

The headquarters of British Forces Egypt, where SIME was based, was too close to the intrigue, so Maunsell met Clarke weekly in 'A' Force's headquarters in a four-storey building at 6 Shari Qasr el Nil, a few blocks from Groppi's, the famous Cairo coffee house.

The one thing that Maunsell had not expected was the fact that Clarke's headquarters was on the floor below a fashionable brothel, which Clarke had gallantly permitted to continue. Maunsell was always embarrassed when he entered the building and was greeted cordially by the brothel's ladies, but Clarke reckoned that it was perfect cover, shielding his staff and agents from prying eyes as the constant flow of people in and out of the building was easily explicable.

Today's meeting was a little different. Both had been appalled by the lack of Foreign Office interest in neutralizing the Mufti and in countering Axis and nationalist subversion in Iraq. Clarke was fully aware of the Mufti's objective. He had found an Arabic translation of an IRA booklet on fighting the British when they raided the Mufti's office in Jerusalem, following his flight to Beirut. The Foreign Office's intelligence arm, MI6, and its various cover organizations, like the Allied Services Liaison Unit (ASLU) and the Intelligence Security Liaison Department (ISLD), had done little, if anything, and the result was Rashid Ali's revolt.

Both men had guessed that Wavell had access to high-grade German intelligence, although neither had any idea that the source was ULTRA intercepts or that the Italian diplomatic cipher had been broken, enabling the British to read messages to and from Gabrielli. MI6 kept its information away from all in the Middle East save for Wavell. Wavell had told Maunsell and Clarke that he was expecting German intervention in Iraq and wanted an operation mounted to counter this.

They had invited Maj David Collins from Special Projects Operating Centre (SPOC), the sabotage section of SOE (Special Operations Executive), to discuss how they could intervene to block the Germans supporting the Iraqis.

Collins, a former oil company executive based in the Middle East and a straight-talking Londoner with a reputation for making 'things happen', said nothing for a few minutes before speaking. 'If the Germans come to the aid of Iraq their vulnerability will be their supply lines. They hold no territory adjacent to Iraq, and their nearest Axis base is Rhodes, which is six to seven hours' flying time to northern Iraq. No plane can carry a heavy load for that distance non-stop, which means that they have to refuel in either Turkey or Syria. This will require that they persuade or coerce the Turks or the Vichy French to help them. From what I gather, the Turks show little interest in getting involved either with the Germans or with us, so that leaves the Vichy French. The Vichy do not like us, and with the right pressure they will relent and allow the Germans use of their airfields, roads and railways.'

'What can we do about it?' asked Clarke.

'I do not have enough resources to sabotage every airfield in Syria, but I could take out the railway line between Aleppo and Mosul at a viaduct a few miles before Tel Kotchek, just inside Syria. If they need to ship anything heavy it will have to go by rail, and this is the only railway line.'

'Apart from sabotaging the railway line, what else could be done?' probed Maunsell.

'The one thing that the Germans cannot do is fly in enough aviation spirit to support their aircraft. Petrol is heavy, messy and dangerous to ship by air, and it would use up space that is necessary to support their aircraft, like ammunition, bombs and spare parts.'

'Yes, but Iraq is an oil producer and is awash with the stuff', rejoined Clarke.

'That may be so, but it exports crude oil and has only a small refinery in Baghdad for domestic supplies. If we could sabotage the 90-octane supplies held at the Iraqi Oil Company's storage tanks for their Air Force, we force the Germans to either fly it in or to refine Iraqi oil on the spot.'

'Why?'

'Local Iraqi oil is low-grade 80-octane, and the Germans need a minimum of 87-octane. It would be essential to improve the grade as this has an important effect on aero engine efficiency, particularly in terms of speed, manoeuvrability and climb, as well as engine life.'

'David, can you sabotage these storage tanks?' asked Clarke.

'Yes, but I will need help. Unlike Tel Kotchek, I cannot fly in, blow them up and fly out. We will have to infiltrate people into the middle of an enemy city of almost half a million, which means I will need people who can pass for Iraqis – look, talk and dress.'

Maunsell thought for a moment. 'I think I know where we can get some help. Do you have any problems in working with the Jews, David?'

'None at all, sir, I will work with anyone who is willing to fight our enemies.'

'Good. I will have to pass this by Wavell, but I expect that you will be on a flight to Lydda in the next few days.'

'What about SOE and Thornhill?' questioned Collins.

There was a general feeling among senior officers at GHQ that SOE Cairo was out of control. Although SOE had been operating in Cairo for almost a year at great expense, it had scored few successes. Slack security, inexperience, the cavalier attitude of its operatives, who swaggered around Cairo like 'Good-time Charlies' who could be found at all the up-market restaurants, bars and parties had created suspicion and hostility.

Col Thornhill, one of the leading lights of SOE, was an amiable but very indiscreet man with an insatiable need to know what was going on. Unfortunately he was often to be found propping up the Long Bar at Shepheard's – the centre of the Cairo rumour mill. This was problematic for SIME, who believed, but could never prove, that the bar-man, 'Joe the Swiss', was a German agent.

'David, SOE will receive a change-of-duties order later this afternoon assigning you to Jumbo Wilson's staff ostensibly as an engineer working on the defences in Crete. As from now you will operate out of sight here in Dudley's offices. That should take care of SOE and keep Thornhill away', replied Maunsell.

Transjordanian-Iraqi border

Wavell ordered a mechanized squadron of the Transjordan Frontier Force (TJFF), an Imperial unit with local troops and senior British officers, to link up with Habforce – the column being mobilized in Palestine

King Abdullah of Transjordan, incensed by the treatment of his brother, Abdul Ilah, by Rashid Ali, committed part of his own private army, the Desert Mechanized Regiment of the Arab Legion and its commander, Maj John Glubb, who would act as the political officer, to Habforce.

As the combined Arab force advanced on Rutba Wells from H-3, a number of Arab officers and NCOs of the TJFF made it clear that they would not cross the border into Iraq and fight their Arab brothers. They argued that they had no quarrel with Iraq, but with the British, who made others fight for them.

They were surprised, when they approached the Arab Legion to join them, to be disarmed and led back to the border, where they were dismissed.

The conspirators had not realized the big difference between the two units. The TJFF were mostly Palestinians and Syrians who were promoted on their length of service. In contrast the Arab Legion was picked from the leading families of Transjordan, largely Bedouin, with personal allegiance to Abdullah and where promotion was patriarchal.

After leaving the TJFF stranded over the border, Glubb's force of 350 troopers in Chevrolet and Ford trucks and a few odd-looking armoured cars made by a German company in Haifa, turned around and headed back towards Rutba Wells.

Habbaniya, 9 May 1941

An 05.30 take-off from Habbaniya put two 203 Squadron Blenheims over the Iraqi air base at Mosul two hours later. One of the Blenheims, flown by Flt Lt Gordon-Hall, climbed away after dropping its bomb-load and made for Habbaniya, while Sqn Ldr Pike's aircraft strafed the airfield, destroying four aircraft.

On the way back to Habbaniya, Pike saw Gordon-Hall's crashed aircraft on the ground some thirty miles south of Mosul. Radio Baghdad announced later in the day that the pilot and copilot had been captured, but the gunner had died in the crash

At the same time as the Mosul raid, two ancient Vincents of 244 Squadron carried out a dive-bombing attack on Iraqi Army barracks at Amara in the south, while Wellingtons of 37 Squadron at Shaiba attacked Iraqi airfields at Kirkuk and Mosul.

A Blenheim of 203 Squadron on a reconnaissance mission over Raschid air base saw a Savoia, three Breda 65s and a Nisr on the ground, which he strafed, claiming to have destroyed the SM79.

The Air Striking Force was in action throughout the day, making fifty-three sorties against Iraqi ground forces in the Falluja area.

Baghdad

During the morning the Mufti broadcast over Radio Baghdad, as well as those of Radio Bari and Radio Zessen, a highly inflammatory *fatwa* announcing a *jihad* against Britain, urging every Muslim to join in the struggle against the greatest foe of Islam.

> *In the name of Merciful and Almighty God*
> *I invite all my Muslim brothers throughout the whole world to join in the Holy War for God, for the defence of Islam and her lands against her enemy. Faithful, obey and respond to my call.*
> *O Muslims!*

Proud Iraq has placed herself in the vanguard of this Holy Struggle, and has thrown herself against the strongest enemy of Islam, certain that God will grant her victory.

The English have tried to seize this Arab-Muslim land, but she has risen, full of dignity and pride to defend her safety, to fight for her honour and to safeguard her integrity. Iraq fights the tyranny which has always had as its aim the destruction of Islam in every land. It is the duty of all Muslims to aid Iraq in her struggle and to seek every means to fight the enemy, the traditional traitor in every age and every situation.

Whoever knows the history of the East has everywhere seen the hand of the English working to destroy the Ottoman Empire and to divide the Arab countries. British politics toward the Arab people is masked under a veil of hypocrisy. The minute she sees her chance, England squeezes the prostrate country in her imperialistic grasp, adding futile justifications. She creates discord and division within a country and while feeding it in secret openly she assumes the role of advisor and trusted friend.

The time when England could deceive the peoples of the East is passed. The Arab Nation and the Muslim people have awakened to fight British domination. The English have overthrown the Ottoman Empire, have destroyed Muslim rule in India, inciting one community against another; they stifled the Egyptian awakening, the dream of Mohammed Ali, colonizing Egypt for half a century. They took advantage of the weakening of the Ottoman Empire to stretch out their hands and use every sort of trick to take possession of many Arab countries as happened to Aden, the nine districts, the Hadramut, Oman, Muscat and the Emirates of the Persian Gulf and Transjordania.

The vivid proof of the imperialistic designs of the British is to be found in Muslim Palestine which, although promised by England to Sheriff Hussein, has had to submit to the outrageous infiltration of Jews, shameful politics designed to divide Arab-Muslim countries of Asia from those of Africa. In Palestine the English have committed unheard-of barbarisms; among others, they have profaned the el-Aqsa Mosque and have declared the most unyielding war against Islam, both in deed and in word. The Prime Minister at that time told Parliament that the world would never see peace as long as the Koran existed. What hatred against Islam is stronger than that which publicly declares the Sacred Koran an enemy of human kind? Should such sacrilege go unpunished?

After the dissolution of the Muslim Empire in India and the Ottoman Caliphate, England, adhering to the policy of Gladstone, pursued her work of destruction to Islam, depriving many Islamic states both in the East and in the West of their freedom and independence. The number of Muslims who today live under the rule of England and invoke liberation from their terrible yoke exceeds 220,000,000.

Therefore I invite you, O Brothers, to join in the War for God to preserve Islam. your independence and your lands from English aggression. I invite you to bring all your weight to bear in helping Iraq that she may throw off the shame that torments her.

O Heroic Iraq, God is with Thee, the Arab Nation and the Muslim World are solidly with Thee in Thy Holy Struggle!

Habbaniya

Roberts had a meeting with Everett and Brawn during the early afternoon to finalize the next phase of their ground strategy.

'The further we push the Iraqis back,' Roberts began, 'the safer we will be. We now hold ground as far west as Ramadi, twenty miles away, and to the north of the river a wide arc is free of Iraqi troops. Soon we will have to go forward to Baghdad to release the British and other Westerners in the British Embassy and the American Legation and get a pro-British government in place.

'The choke point is here at Falluja,' he indicated on the map spread across the trestle table, 'which is the only bridge crossing between here and Baghdad. If we hold the bridge we deny the Iraqis the ability to cross the Euphrates and we make it easier to advance on Baghdad. If the Iraqis hold the bridge they are positioned to retake Habbaniya with a counter-offensive. The RAF is already systematically bombing and machine-gunning Iraqi reinforcements, making it difficult for them to build up a strong counter-force. We are now better armed and even have our own artillery', he said, to laughter from Everett and Brawn.

'We need to get the ferry back into operation at Sin el Dhibban. This will help us to put a flying column across the Euphrates which can take Falluja from the rear. Until we are ready to attack Falluja we can start small night reconnaissance patrols across the river to check on both Iraqi strength at Saqlawiya and Falluja and suitable routes for our flying column.'

'What do you think the chances are of capturing Falluja?' asked Everett.

'I don't think that the Iraqis have a hope in Hades against us, and Falluja is a piece of cake', responded an upbeat Roberts.

Baghdad

Freya had kept herself busy at the Embassy by trying to gain news on the evolving situation with the police guards as well as helping out with tasks like a lecture on the lawn the previous evening on Aden in Wartime.

The police had been buoyed by the Mufti's call for a Holy War, and Freya could not understand why the British, seeing the effect other people managed to obtain through propaganda, persisted in thinking it quite useless for themselves.

A long conference had been held that day full of a spirit of vengeance, with plans not only to humiliate Rashid Ali's government but for the one that would replace it to be filled with pro-British politicians. Freya voiced the opinion that they should only deal with the five top people and the Mufti and any found to be working with the Germans, and then work at discrediting the Germans with the Army. Any other approach would be counter-productive, she argued, as the majority of Army officers, like the rank and file, were honest dupes of a small number of ambitious staff officers.

Rutba Wells

The fort at Rutba Wells was two hundred empty miles from anywhere. The fort, with its high windowed walls and four round towers, sat at the convergence of tracks from Amman, Damascus and Baghdad. There were no roads in 1941 except those made by the tracks of previous vehicles, which were quickly blotted out by the sand blown by the wind over the hard, red earth and the beds of flint.

The old fort had been turned into an overnight rest-house in 1927 to accommodate passengers at the Imperial Airways refuelling stop on the route to and from Haifa, Baghdad, the Gulf and India. When Imperial Airways switched to flying-boats, the mud-walled fort, with its bedrooms, lounge and restaurant, became a rest-stop for desert travellers and for the Nairn Brothers' cross-desert bus service from Damascus to Baghdad.

The fort had been seized at the beginning of May by the Iraqi Desert Police. They had been joined by Fawzi al Qawujki, the Syrian guerrilla leader. al Qawujki, a large, red-haired, scar-faced man who had been made a colonel in the Iraqi Army, responsible for irregular forces, brought forty trucks full of irregulars armed with machine-guns to support the Desert Police.

Following the attack on the British road survey party on 1 May, the Europeans working at the H-3 pumping station on the Kirkuk–Haifa pipeline had fled.

With its water source and airfield, the fort could be used as a base by German airborne forces to seize the oil pipeline. The Mechanized Regiment of the Arab Legion arriving from H-4 attempted to secure Rutba Wells. However, the Iraqis put up stiff resistance, and, armed only with Lewis and Hotchkiss machine-guns dating back to the Great War, and without artillery or mortars, the Legion retired to wait for the RAF.

The Iraqis triumphantly announced Glubb's death on Radio Baghdad that evening, which led to the premature publishing of his obituary in *The Times* in London the next day.

Four Blenheims from 84 Squadron operating out of Aqir in Palestine flew in to support the Legion. Each made two passes over Rutba Wells, attracting severe ground fire that damaged all four aircraft, forcing Flg Off Goudge to make a crash-landing near H-3.

Chapter Four

Shortening the Odds

Rhodes, 9 May 1941

Two weeks earlier, Dr Rudolf Rahn had been on holiday in the Obersdorff on a short break from his post at the German Embassy in Paris. He had been summoned urgently back to Paris and told by the Ambassador, Otto Abetz, that he had been selected to go immediately to Syria to help to save the Iraqi revolt.

Rahn, a young man going places, was not surprised to have been selected for the mission. He had had trouble-shooting assignments in Iran, Turkey and South America, as well as stints in the legal, oriental and press departments at the *Auswartiges Amt* under his belt. While he liked the ambience of war-time Paris, where he could enjoy the culture and, as a German, still get a gourmet meal, he needed a new challenge – particularly one that would advance his career.

Abetz had hinted privately that some of the Arabists at the Wilhelmstrasse had encouraged an Iraqi coup d'état, followed by a revolt, without thinking of the consequences. Iraq's military action had failed to stop the British, and the revolt was now in serious trouble

The *Luftwaffe* was *en route* with two *Staffeln*, and Rahn's job would be to ensure that the Vichy French in Syria complied with Admiral Darlan's directive to provide refuelling facilities and release weapons and ammunition stored by the Italian Control Commission, and transfer these to Iraq.

He had arrived just before noon at Rhodes' Gaddura airfield in Ribbentrop's personal Heinkel 111 transport to refuel on his way to Aleppo. He noticed a number of two- and three-engined *Luftwaffe* aircraft among a collection of *Regia Aeronautica*'s Savoia bombers and FIAT biplane fighters crowding the grass along the single paved runway.

All the *Luftwaffe* aircraft seemed to be in various stages of refuelling, and there were Italian ground-crews, supervised by the aircrews, busy painting out the *Balkenkreuz* and the *Swastika* national markings, and

113

overpainting them with what seemed to be, at a distance, green triangles outlined in red.

As they left the plane, an Italian staff car drew up alongside the Heinkel, and a young *tenente* stepped out and greeted them. 'Would you please join me,' he said, pointing at the Lancia, 'and I will take you to our mess, where you can wait in comfort.'

'*Tenente*, what are you painting on the aircraft?' asked Rahn.

'We have been requested to repaint the aircraft with Royal Iraqi Air Force markings', he replied.

Rahn and his translator, Eital Malhausen, an Austrian born in Smyrna of a French mother, were driven across to Gaddura's administration block by the helpful *tenente*, who ushered them into the small mess hall.

The room was empty with the exception of one table by the window, where six men were seated. One detached himself and walked over to Rahn and Malhausen. 'You must be Rahn', he said, ignoring Malhausen. 'My name is Grobba. We should talk', and he guided Rahn by his elbow to a table by the far wall, leaving Malhausen to join the others.

They both ordered coffee from a mess waiter, and sat quietly sizing each-other up while they waited.

Rahn knew that Grobba was the ranking Iraqi specialist at the *Auswartiges Amt*. Although he had the reputation of being obstinate and high handed, he had been placed in charge of supervising the revolt on the spot by Ribbentrop.

Conversely Grobba was well aware that Abetz was part of Ribbentrop's inner circle, a personal Foreign Office nicknamed *Dienstelle Ribbentrop*, which met in a private office across the Wilhemstrasse from the 'official' *Auswartiges Amt*. Rahn was supported by Abetz and Ribbentrop, who at Abetz's suggestion, had given Rahn plenipotentiary powers, as well as use of his personal VIP Heinkel transport.

Both realized that they had more to gain by cooperating than competing: if the Iraqis got the weapons and equipment both men would benefit. However, what the Iraqis did with those arms was out of both men's control.

'I am travelling under the name Gehreke,' began Grobba rather self-importantly, 'to confuse British spies.'

'Is that why you have repainted the aircraft in Iraqi colours?' responded Rahn.

'Oh, no, that is political. We do not want to be identified as German until our success is virtually guaranteed.'

They had just finished agreeing on how Rahn would notify Grobba of where and when the arms were to be delivered, and Rahn's acceptance of one of Grobba's radio technicians, Hontsch, when the *tenente* returned to announce that their planes had been refuelled.

Forty minutes later Grobba and Rahn, together with a third Heinkel, left Gaddura for the 400-mile flight to Aleppo, where they landed later that evening.

Aleppo

At Aleppo Grobba received bad news. The Iraqi Consul-General met the aircraft and advised him that the British had broken the siege of Habbaniya and seemed to be set to march on Baghdad.

Grobba decided to fly on that night to Mosul, to be in Baghdad early the next morning.

Rutba Wells, 10 May 1941

Just after noon, two Blenheims of 203 Squadron operating out of H-4's airfield, flown by Sqn Ldr Gethin and Flg Off Watson, attacked the fort at Rutba Wells, making several strafing and bombing attacks. Two columns of vehicles were seen to be engaged in a fight, but Gethin and Watson refrained from attacking as it was uncertain which of the columns was British.

Both aircraft took heavy rifle and machine-gun fire, and Gethin flew off in the direction of the column, but the Blenheim lost height and crash-landed. Watson landed alongside, and together with Gethin tried to get the other members of the aircrew out of the crashed and burning aircraft. The intense heat and the exploding ammunition and fire from some Iraqi armoured cars drove them back. They were lucky to get off the ground with the surviving Blenheim, but Gethin died of his injuries a few hours after they landed back at H-4.

One of the columns of vehicles that Gethin and Watson had seen fighting al Qawujki's machine-gun-armed trucks was a forward detachment of No. 2 Armoured Car Company RAF. On Thursday, three days before, Sqn Ldr Casano's Rolls Royce armoured cars – similar in type and vintage to those at Habbaniya – were guarding an RAF airfield one thousand miles away at Sidi Barrani in the Western Desert. Casano made an epic journey in record time to get to Iraq, arriving at Rutba Wells on Saturday.

During the night the Iraqis, shaken by the bombing and the appearance of the British armoured cars, evacuated the fort and retired to the east.

Baghdad

There was relief at the Embassy that the RAF made no low-level passes that day. The Iraqi machine-guns were now quite visible around the Embassy, and there was concern that the Iraqis would shoot down an RAF plane.

The BBC reported that the Iraqi Army was dispersed and their Air Force destroyed. But there was no confirmation that the Iraqis were in trouble. Things had settled down, and life in the Embassy was one of ease and boredom.

Freya had managed to get cigarettes for the servants, which helped to ease the problem of supplying them with a special diet. Pat Domvile told Freya that he wanted to become a servant so that she would look after him. Freya had now collected a 'family' of forty-five, including Embassy and personal servants, grooms and gardeners to look after.

Freya was invited to dine with Ken and enjoyed the opportunity to wear her evening gown and sit at a well-set table. But the conversation was stilted – not because of the situation, but because the guests were chosen in order of merit, which had nothing to do with the art of conversation. 'Keeping up appearances' in the face of adversity was maybe good for morale, mused Freya, but it was hard going.

Habbaniya, 11 May 1941

At 05.10 the Air Striking Force's Audaxes and Oxfords, escorted by two Blenhiems of 203 Squadron and the Gladiators of A Squadron from Habbaniya, attacked Raschid air base. The Audaxes, Oxfords and Blenheims bombed, while the Gladiators strafed. Several more attacks were made on Raschid that day, and formed the pattern of Habbaniya air strikes over the next three days.

Baghdad

As the three-engined Junkers taxied to the terminal at Baghdad's civil airport, Grobba could smell the city through the partly opened sliding window. For good reason the city of 1001 nights was referred to by its foreign residents as the city of 1001 smells. He remembered every city by its distinctive odour, and the smell of Baghdad, which would require an entire perfume industry to mask, brought memories of the eight years that he had spent there flooding back.

A big, fair, rugged-faced man, Grobba had arrived in Baghdad in 1932 to set up the German Legation. Gregarious by nature, and a Mason and a democrat by conviction, he and his wife had worked diligently to create a wide circle of important local dignitaries and to fit into the expatriate community, becoming friendly with many British families. Unlike most Germans, he maintained close friendships with foreign and Iraqi Jews long after Hitler's time. Although he left Masonry after Hitler's accession to power, he still gave the Masonic grip when he met a fellow Mason. His success was also a factor of his staying power and his command of Arabic. While non-Arabic-speaking British Ambassadors came and left year after year, Grobba remained solidly in place from 1932.

Grobba's forte was intrigue, and in manipulating relationships and fixing deals, leaving politics and propaganda to Dr Julius Jordan, a German archaeologist and a rabid Nazi, who worked for the Iraqi National Museum.

Grobba's career was in the ascent until he was declared *person non grata* in September 1939, when Iraq, under Nuri al Said's government, broke off diplomatic relations following the British declaration of war against Germany.

Twenty months at the Wilmhelmstrasse among the Junker aristocrats, the Nazis and the bureaucrats had taken its toll, and he was happy to be back in the field with an opportunity to kick-start his stalled career.

He was highly ambitious, and was determined that nothing would stand in the way of his achieving a promotion to the top ranks of the *Auswartiges Amt*. A victory in Iraq, he believed, would catapult him to his rightful place over the heads of the old-school network, the political appointees and the time servers.

He had survived the last two years in Baghdad walking on a very thin tightrope between Iraqi demands for arms, money and recognition and Germany's reluctance to get involved. It was a tribute to his ability to influence people that the Iraqis had requested his presence in Baghdad as the German liaison.

His assignment now was more difficult. Rashid Ali and the *Golden Square* needed to be motivated to continue to resist the British for the next few weeks until Germany could rearm the Iraqis and the *Luftwaffe* could destroy the RAF.

Jerusalem

Wavell and Jumbo Wilson flew into Lydda Airport early in the morning in a 267 Squadron Lodestar and took the waiting Humber staff car to their appointment with George Clark at Force Headquarters in the King David Hotel in Jerusalem.

Although the King David was a massive building of some seven storeys with two hundred rooms, which towered above its surroundings, it fitted in. Municipal regulations in 1918 decreed that the front of every building be at least partially made of local 'Jerusalem' limestone with its gold or ochre hue. This meant that even the largest, highest and even ugliest of buildings seemed to blend with the city, giving a semblance of conformity.

In 1939 the British had taken over the entire southern wing of the hotel, housing their communications gear in the basement and building a side entrance which linked the hotel with the Army camp at its side.

The barbed wire and the armed guards at the airport, in the escorts that had accompanied Wavell and Wilson, and at the entrance to the hotel were not there as a precaution against the Axis. They served as a reminder of the fragile peace in Palestine between the Arabs and the Jews, and the fact that the British were caught in the cross-fire between the warring sides.

Maj Gen George Clark, together with AVM John D'Albiac, who was to replace Smart at Habbaniya, were waiting for Wavell and Wilson in the large top-floor conference room which overlooked the old city and gave a magnificent view of Jerusalem and the Dome of the Rock.

Wavell, a man of few words, quickly got to the point, after the introductions had been made and the coffee served. 'Although the encirclement of Habbaniya has been broken, we still need to send a force to pre-empt Rashid Ali joining with the Germans to oust us from Iraq. As you all know,' he explained, 'we have elements of the 10th Indian Division here,' he pointed at the map, 'south at Basra. They have encountered great problems in moving north to Baghdad due to the seasonal floods. The Iraqis have added to the problem by cutting the roads and destroying rail and telegraph communications, making movement out of Basra impossible. Our only option for timely intervention is from Palestine. Time is of the essence, gentlemen. George, what is happening?'

'We have put together a relief column, Habforce, consisting of 6,000 men and almost 1,000 vehicles', Clark responded. 'Obviously this quantity of men and equipment will take time to get to Habbaniya, so we have divided up the force into two components. Joe Kingstone, the Commander of the 4th Cavalry Brigade, has formed a small advance striking-force, Kingcol, with 2,000 men, together with the Arab Legion, who are at Rutba Wells. They will make a dash for Habbaniya. The bulk of Habforce will follow on Joe's tail.'

'When will you move?' interjected Wilson.

'Joe moved out from his camp at Nathanya at first light this morning.

The rest of Habforce is moving into position and will rendezvous at the Beit Lied crossroads late today.'

Wavell smiled at Clark. 'You have done a first-class job! When do you think that you will be able to relieve the siege of the Embassy in Baghdad?'

'Baghdad!' exploded Clark, 'No one said anything about Baghdad!'

'We need to get to Baghdad and the Embassy and get rid of Rashid Ali', said Wilson, raising his voice. 'Your job is to do that. Do I make myself clear?'

Visibly shaken by Wilson's outburst, Clark responded, 'Of course I will follow orders, but you all need to be aware of the risks that we face. First, it's a long way: it's four hundred and seventy miles to Habbaniya and a further fifty-five miles on to Baghdad. Most of it is across unmapped desert and we will be facing temperatures of over 100 degrees. Water and heat exhaustion will be our greatest problems. The Met Office predicts the highest temperatures in the desert for the last twenty-five years. Second it is hostile territory the whole way. John here', he indicated D'Albiac, 'cannot guarantee me fighter cover over Habforce. Our column will be thirty to fifty miles long, which is a difficult target for any aircraft to miss. There are at least two untouched Iraqi divisions and remnants of a third, plus an armoured brigade, and we have no armour.'

Wilson, now furious, began to get out of his chair. Wavell leaned across, placing his hand on Wilson's arm, and said, 'Jumbo, we need to hear from George.'

Determined to make his point, Clark went on, 'And we have men and equipment problems. The Household Cavalry, the Life Guards and the Blues, only made the move from horses to vehicles last month. They have never fought as a mechanized unit, they have had little training and many of the other ranks cannot drive. The Royal Artillery battery was unable to calibrate its 25-pounders before moving off, and the RAF Armoured Car unit with its museum-pieces, got on station only yesterday. To make ourselves mobile we have had to hire scores of resentful Jewish and Arab drivers and their trucks and buses from Jerusalem and Haifa, as well as borrowing twenty trucks and drivers from the Palestine Police and commandeering some taxis from Haifa. We have little or no modern equipment, and even our machine-guns date back to the First World War.'

Before anyone could speak, Clark held up his hand. 'That being said, we are all as keen as mustard, and morale is very high throughout Habforce.'

'Well, George, you seem to have things well under control. Keep us briefed', Wavell said, rising from his chair, so signalling that the meeting was over. 'Jumbo and I have to get back to Cairo, as that Rommel fellow is giving us a bit of trouble at Tobruk', he said, making his way to the door. As he turned the handle he paused and looked back at Clark. 'It is long odds, but I think that you will make it,'

Nathanya

At first light Kingcol had begun to move out from Brigade Headquarters of the 4th Cavalry at Nathanya, by the Mediterranean.

The previous days had been a blur of frantic activity as the various units assigned to Kingcol hunted for spare parts, traded equipment and loaded up on ordnance. No one had been briefed on the mission, but cleaning two-gallon petrol cans, marking them 'water' and filling them, as well as numerous canvas bags reminiscent of the traditional seven-pint goatskin *chargules*, with water suggested an imminent desert crossing.

The previous evening Brigadier John Joseph 'Joe' Kingstone, who had been acting as commander of the 1st Cavalry Division at Haifa, resumed control of the 4th Cavalry Brigade. He held a brief meeting in the wooden hut which served as the Brigade mess. to outline to his senior officers the formation of Kingcol and its mission to relieve Habbaniya. Peter Grant-Lawson, the Brigade Major, impressed on the officers that this was a fighting column crossing a desert that no conquering army had ever crossed, and Kingcol needed to be self-supporting in water, fuel, oil and ammunition. They were to take the minimum of personal equipment in their vehicles, as every nook and cranny would be needed for Kingcol's supplies.

To ensure that every one got the message, Grant-Lawson concluded with a sobering comment: 'Gentlemen, we will be travelling with twelve days of rations, five days of water and five days of fuel for the column, There are 2,000 of us in two hundred vehicles, so that is a lot of food, water and fuel to carry. This means that we will not be able to take anything along with us under any circumstances that we cannot fight with, eat, drink or drive. That means, Bobo,' to the Duke of Roxburghe, 'you can't bring your dinner jacket,' to peals of laughter, 'but it also means that you and your men can't take along the exotic pets you have collected in our stay here. You have to get rid of them tonight. Our most precious commodity is water. Officers are personally responsible for water discipline. It's one gallon per man per day and one gallon per vehicle per day. There are no exceptions. You will allow drinking only at scheduled halts.'

Kingcol in its ageing Morris 15 cwt trucks borrowed from the Scots Greys at Rehovot, together with a motley collection of RASC 3-ton trucks, commandeered taxis, buses and even some decrepit flat-bed trucks with solid tyres and little or no spare parts, driven by a bunch of rebellious civilians, together with a sprinkling of new Chevrolet staff cars, streamed out of Nathanya at dawn.

As the leading elements of Kingcol pulled out of the camp gates, Sgt Major Hugh Seekings of the Royal Military Police turned to Staff Sgt Jack Holmes, the Field Security Officer. 'Kingstone's got more nobles with him than Henry V. There's the Duke of Roxburghe, a lord, an earl, a marquesss, two viscounts, a couple of baronets and at least half a dozen knights. Oh, yes, there are also two Members of Parliament.'

'He will need all the help he can get. Where he's going the odds are far greater than they ever were at Agincourt', replied Holmes.

The road skirted the lower, northern slopes of Mount Carmel and then plunged down to the wide clay-covered plain of Esdraelon, until it crossed the eastern part of the plain to reach Beisan, where the Jordan Valley met the Plain of Jezreel. At Beisan Kingcol halted for the first of the 'twenty minutes every two hours' halts designed to minimize heat exhaustion and dehydration. The men got out of their vehicles for their first water stop, some taking advantage of the time to stretch their legs, others to buy some oranges, while a few looked out across the Jordan valley to the desert hills of Transjordan shimmering in the heat haze.

After the halt Kingcol crossed the narrow-gauge railway line of the old Hejaz Railway and turned north down the Jordan Valley, which contained the heat like a furnace. It passed over the three bridges over the swift-flowing Jordan, passing a sign which indicated that it was at sea level, and, reaching Josr Majami, began the ascent up the long, winding and steep gorge, then on the dusty road through rugged, wild and inhospitable country to Irbid. Beyond Irbid Kingcol reached a stretch of tarmac road which took it out onto the high desert plateau of Transjordan to the column's night stop at Mafraq.

An hour or so later Kingcol was joined by Maj Keith May, who brought A and D companies of the 1st Essex in requisitioned Haifa buses and two bren-gun carriers – christened *Chelmsford* and *Colchester* – carried on RASC lifting transport.

The column was dispersed over a large area, and dug in as a precautionary measure. Mafraq, a desolate place consisting of nothing but a few old huts, was just twenty-five miles south of Deraa in Vichy-controlled Syria. Deraa had a rail junction and an airfield which could be used by either the Vichy or the Germans as a base from which to attack Kingcol.

But Kingcol's luck held. At that point the *Luftwaffe* had not yet arrived in strength in Syria, and the Vichy French were not interested in attacking the British. Kingstone was also pleased with Kingcol's performance – they had covered 140 miles in the first day.

Beirut

Shortly before nine in the morning, Rahn and Malhausen arrived in their Heinkel from Aleppo at Beirut airport, where they were met by Jacques Guerard, Admiral Darlan's (the Vichy military leader) special representative, who was to take them to General Henri Dentz, the Vichy High Commissioner for Syria.

After the introductions Guerard took Rahn aside. 'Dentz argues about everything with everyone. His problem at the moment is the loyalty of his troops to Vichy, as the Free French in Palestine have been making overtures across the border. He is also angry at the Italian Control Commission, who have secured a large number of his weapons and who generally strut around as if they own Syria. My job is to smooth the way for you to accomplish your mission. It would help us both if you were very diplomatic with Dentz. He does not like to be reminded of the surrender, added to which he is an Alsatian. He is only pro-German in the sense that he believes that the British let down the French.'

Rahn smiled and nodded in agreement.

The Vichy administrative and military headquarters for Syria was based at the Grand Serail. The striking 430-room, three-storey building with its red roof, yellowish walls and windows encased in white limestone was built by the Ottomans in the French Romantic style in the 1820s. It was imposing, not only because of its size, but by its location, crowning the Serail hill, which gave it a sweeping view across the city to the sea, being framed against the Lebanon Mountains which rose in the background.

Guerard ushered them through the entrance and up the wide marble staircase, to Dentz's second-floor office suite located above the portico.

The meeting started off badly, with Dentz in turn being aggressive, resentful and sarcastic. However, Rahn, a skilful and accomplished diplomat, managed to get Dentz on side by impressing and charming him with his good humour and modesty.

'Whatever the recent differences between our countries, General, the supply of weapons to Iraq, for which we will pay in both gold and French francs, is a great opportunity for a new chapter in Franco-German relations, and offers the prospect of seeing the British defeated in its colony', Rahn began. 'The victory in Iraq will also clear away the plan to invade Syria by the British and Free French from Palestine It will also give us the chance to work together to throw the British out of the Middle East and North Africa for good.'

Proffering the papers he had taken out of his case, Guerard added, 'This has been thoroughly discussed with and agreed by Admiral Darlan, who has given me these written instructions to enable you to comply urgently with this request.'

'Is this a request or an order?' responded Dentz.

'The Admiral prefers to see this as a request. However, he has asked me to impress upon you the importance of the successful accomplishment of our mission to Vichy and to the Admiral in particular', answered Guerard.

'What will you do about General di Giorgis, who is responsible for the arms which are stored under his supervision by the Italian Control Commission? I have no authority over the Italians', Dentz said.

'This has already been agreed, and di Giorgis has been informed', replied Rahn.

'What weapons do you want from the arms stored under the Control Commission's supervision?' asked Dentz

'For the first shipment,' responded Rahn, 'I require the following items: 15,500 rifles and 200 machine-guns with 6 million cartridges and 900 filled belts of ammunition, four 7.5 cm field guns and 10,000 shells with all the necessary equipment and spare parts'

'I am not sure if we have that much ordnance on hand', began Dentz.

'I have the latest inventory here from the Control Commission, and this is just a fraction of what they have', Rahn said, smiling at Dentz.

Dentz sidestepped Rahn's response and asked, 'How do you plan to get these weapons to Iraq?'

'These are too heavy to send by air, so we will use the railway from Aleppo to ship the arms to Mosul', said Rahn.

'North of Aleppo the railway passes through Turkish territory parallel to the border up to the town of Kamishli, where it re-enters Syrian territory. I am sure that the Turks will not give you permission to ship the arms to Iraq through Turkey', opined Dentz.

'If you say that they are urgently needed to strengthen French forces along your northern border with Iraq, I am sure that the Turks will agree', Rahns said, again smiling at Dentz. 'The Turks do not need to know the final destination. The railway passes from Kamishli to Tel Kochek, where it intersects with the Syrian-Iraqi border and from there runs directly to Mosul and Baghdad.'

'The Franco-Turkish Convention allows the Turks five days' advance notice for military shipments on the railway, and I see no way around this', said Dentz

'I am sure that you will find a way, General', Rahn responded.

Guerard turned to Rahn, 'Would you kindly give us a few moments, M. Rahn?'

After Rahn had left the room, Guerard looked at Dentz for a few moments before speaking. 'Please do not keep trying to make this more difficult than it is. Yesterday Marshal Petain meet with Hitler and Ribbentrop at Berchtesgaden. A part of their discussion concerned Syria and Iraq. Although I do not have all the details, the Marshal agreed to four main points. Firstly to turn over three-quarters of the war materials stored in Syria. Secondly, to allow the landing of German and Italian aircraft, to provide them with fuel and make available to the *Luftwaffe* a special base at Aleppo. Thirdly, permitting the use of roads, ports and railways for transporting arms to Iraq, and fourthly to train in Syria Iraqi soldiers equipped with French weapons. I have here General Huntzinger's written authorization. Your Air Commander will receive today a telegram from General Bergeret confirming that he also must give every assistance to the Germans and Italians. You should think very carefully. Admiral Darlan asked me to convey to you that you personally bear the full responsibility for the suffering which non-compliance would certainly lead the Germans to inflict on France.'

They rejoined Rahn, and a now mischievous Dentz said, 'As this is a clandestine operation what name do you want to be known by?'

'Renoir', responded Rahn, to which Dentz replied sarcastically, as he wrote out his orders, 'Renouard it will be.'

'You are an unusual German, Renouard. The Iraqi coup d'état has been badly handled and the fighting even more so, and I fear that these weapon shipments will fall into the hands of the British. Nevertheless I wish you good luck.'

Rahn reluctantly declined Dentz's invitation to dinner that evening at his official residence at *Les Pins*, near the racecourse, as he needed to get back to Aleppo to advise Grobba of his progress over a secure radio link.

Dentz later spoke directly with Fedzi Pasha, the Turkish Military Commissioner, who, having no grounds for suspicion, immediately granted the request for trains with military stores destined for the protection of the northern Syrian border to pass through Turkish territory.

Baghdad

The Embassy was like an oven, 111°F in the shade, with the hot *Khamsin* wind from the north made humid by the floodwaters.

Freya could not face a siesta in the garden with heaps of sleeping people, or in her dormitory with the seventeen women, or on her balcony, but was able to sleep on a borrowed mattress on the floor in a friend's office. It was surprising to Freya how small things like sleeping and waking, a cool breeze from the river, and the scent of flowers could give such pleasure.

Church was down to just thirty people that morning, which together with a poor service suggested that people wanted something more profound.

The police were less amiable, and the servants confirmed to Freya that this was a response to the Mufti's *fatwa*; they said that the police promised to massacre the Iraqi servants who stayed in the Embassy.

Later that evening, as Ken walked around the garden with Freya, he asked, 'Who do you think that we should have to deal with Anglo-Arab relations after this fiasco, Freya?'

'Ken, it would be disastrous to have the wrong man. This may well be our last chance, and our very last chance, to set good relations with Iraq on their feet once more. There is bound to be resentment, but it should not be beyond us to switch this against the Germans', Freya replied.

Aleppo, 12 May 1941

Rahn was aboard the first train which left Aleppo central station at 10.00 a.m. with 300 tons of French weapons and ammunition destined for Tel Kochek on the Syrian-Iraqi border. At noon a second train followed, carrying 160 tons of weapons and ammunition. Each train was accompanied by half a company of the 16th Tunisian Tirailleurs, to give a semblance of reality to Dentz's request to Fedzi Pasha.

Baghdad

At nine thirty in the morning, Grobba was ushered into Rashid Ali's office in the Serai Building, and found that the Mufti had already arrived and was deep in conversation with the Prime Minister.

'Dr Grobba, welcome again to my office. It seems ages since you were last here', Rashid Ali said as he stood up to greet Grobba.

'I hope that my stay this time in Iraq will be longer', the German answered as they shook hands.

The Mufti also rose from his seat and took Grobba's hand between his own two hands and said, 'It is nice to see our old friends once more.'

'It is good to be back among my friends', replied Grobba.

'Gentlemen', he began, 'I am pleased that we could meet privately before the others join us. We have a number of delicate issues to discuss. I have brought financial assistance as we had agreed', he said, walking to the open door, where his private secretary, Ahmed Jabr, and his radio operator, Emde, were waiting with two wooden boxes which he had them bring into Rashid Ali's office. He had them open the boxes on Rashid Ali's desk and then retire, closing the door behind them.

He reached into one of the boxes, handing Rashid Ali a 250 g gold bar, and then turned to Haj Amin and reached into the second box, bringing out a small stack of $50 bills. 'The boxes', he said, 'contain £10,000 in gold and $15, 000 in notes. 'This', Grobba said, pointing at the money, 'is the first instalment, and more is to follow when Dr Granow arrives from Berlin next week.

'We propose to extend to you a credit agreement of £1 million, and in addition the Italian government will assign 10 million lira to Iraq. Within the next few days advance elements of *Sonderkommando Junck* with *Luftwaffe* bombers and fighters will be arriving, followed by aircraft from Italy's *Regia Aeronautica*. We have also arranged to have weapons and ammunition shipped to you through Syria. The first consignment will arrive by train in Mosul in a day or two.

'However, you must realize that in exchange for this considerable assistance we require something from Iraq. I have a document here which lays out the agreement between Iraq and Germany in respect of our support during these difficult times. Let me explain what these conditions are. Firstly that Iraq transfers to Germany the concessions for the Iraqi oilfields with royalties to be paid in German commodities. Secondly that Germany has control of all Iraqi airfields for the duration of the war, and finally that Iraq recognizes the original concession granted to Germany by the Ottomans for the Baghdad–Istanbul railway.'

The growing bonhomie which had filled Rashid Ali and Haj Amin as they had listened to Grobba explain Germany's largesse gave way to silence as they took in the implications of Germany's quid pro quo.

The only noise for several minutes in the room was the two slowly revolving fans in the high-ceilinged room, as they tried in vain to create a cooling breeze from the humid air which seemed to just hang there.

Finally Haj Amin spoke. 'From my perspective I think that this is something that we must accept to achieve a greater good. However, you must realize that anything which affects our hard-won independence or places us in thrall to another country would be totally unacceptable to all Iraqis. Until we have had time to digest your document. this should remain between us. The *Golden Square* will see this as merely replacing the British with the Germans. While we know that not to be the case, it would serve all our interests if this were not to be discussed during our forthcoming meeting. Rashid Ali and I need to develop an approach that will not antagonize the Colonels.'

Rashid Ali, Haj Amin and Grobba moved to the adjacent conference room just before 10.00 to await the arrival of the four Colonels and the Defence Minister, Naji Shawkat.

Shawkat, together with Rashid Ali and Haj Amin, had formed the party welcoming Grobba the day before at Baghdad's civil airport. However, this was the first time that Grobba had seen al Sabbagh, Fahmi Said, Mahmud Salman and Kamil Shabib since he had been deported in September 1939.

All four Colonels looked tired and drawn, highlighting the self-imposed stresses and strains of a war which they had unleashed. Fahmi Said in particular seemed very agitated, and spent most of the meeting trying unsuccessfully to sit still.

Rashid Ali opened the meeting, welcoming Grobba profusely, outlined the course of events since the coup of 2 April, and then he suggested that each of the Colonels bring him up to date with the current battlefield situation.

Grobba had lived sufficiently long in the Middle East, and knew each of the participants well enough, to be able to pick out reality from banter and fact from enthusiastic exaggeration. While the Colonels each tried to put forward a positive position, the reality was quite different. The British from Habbaniya were still contained by the Iraqis holding the bridge at Falluja, and the floods and broken rail links in the south stopped the British from moving up to Baghdad. However, it was only a matter of time before a relief column from Palestine arrived, which would dramatically change the situation. The Royal Iraqi Air Force was no longer in any position to support the Iraqi Army, and everything depended on the Iraqis holding out for a few weeks. Grobba began to have serious doubts whether the Iraqis could hold things together long enough for the *Luftwaffe* and the arms from Syria to make a material difference to the outcome of the revolt.

When his turn came, he outlined both the financial and military commitments that the Germans and Italians were making, and the necessity that the Iraqis hold firm for a week to ten days until the *Luftwaffe* and the arms from Syria could be brought to bear.

'My feeling is that the *Luftwaffe* should send General Felmy as military adviser to Iraq', proposed Grobba, sensing that the Iraqis badly needed both some seasoned military advice as well as a stiffening of their resolve.

'That is precisely what the British wanted to do in connexion with the Anglo-Iraqi Treaty of 1930, which is why we are sitting here today', an annoyed al Sabbagh responded, sensitive about his own position as the *de facto* commander of all Iraqi forces.

'Felmy would only have the *Luftwaffe* under his command', Grobba countered quickly to defuse the hostility. 'Felmy is one of our ablest and youngest generals, and would be an ideal person to act as a liaison between the Iraqi and German forces.'

'Gentlemen,' Haj Amin interrupted, 'I think that this is an excellent suggestion. We get a first-class military adviser who is not involved in the day-to-day operation of the Iraqi Army so that we have all the benefits and none of the drawbacks that we experienced under the British.'

'What do we need to do to get your General Felmy here?' asked the Mufti.

'Rashid Ali should make a formal request, as postings at this level are strictly approved by the *Fuhrer*', Grobba said, pleased that they were making practical progress.

The meeting lasted another hour as Grobba outlined the fuel and accommodation needs of the German forces which were *en route* to Mosul.

The constant heat, the anxiety of not knowing what was going to happen, and the wear and tear of having to listen to Radio Baghdad blaring out depressing news for six hours up to ten o'clock in the evening, accompanied by the rantings of Yunis al Bahri on Radio Zessen, began to tell. The BBC News was no better, reporting that things were 'all quiet in Iraq', with complete forgetfulness of the Embassy's precarious situation. People became increasingly short tempered, and arguments seemed to erupt over the slightest thing.

Freya was shocked to see a rifle and three boxes of cartridges outside the Secretariat, and both of the large doors leading into the Embassy building shut and locked, with their handles tied with rope. It seemed to reinforce their desperate situation.

Freya's overriding goal today was to try to get face-powder out of the Iraqis.

Within the Embassy a number of things beside defence and food required organization. The doctors set up a surgery and dispensary capable of dealing with anything from a headache to a major operation – although there was fortunately no need for the latter. The doctors also presided over the 'decontamination squad' which paraded every morning to wash out the bathrooms and 'Flit' all the rooms, while the 'water controller' had to cope with the fact that the Embassy drainage system was only designed to cater for fifteen people.

Mosul

During the day, advance elements of *Sonderkommando Junck* began landing at Mosul.

Hauptmann Harry Rother's Junkers 90 had left Gaddura at 22.00 the night before and had overflown Syria during the night as the *Luftwaffe* had still to receive landing permission. Rother was well aware of the need to support the incoming aircraft, and had ensured that they began by first delivering the anti-aircraft defence and the ground-crews.

Rother's aircraft carried the *Flakzug*'s three *Flak* 38 mountings which made up the battery, together with their twelve-man crew and ammunition, while the accompanying Junkers 90 had brought in the thirty-man *Zug* of aircraft, engine, instrument and wireless mechanics and fitters, and their equipment for the Messerschmitt fighters.

Rother was appalled to see that the Royal Iraqi Air Force, despite being at war, had made no preparations for air defence. This shortcoming was highlighted by the wrecks of several of their aircraft which had been destroyed in RAF air raids.

Before leaving on his return trip to Gaddura, Rother had had the single-barrelled 20 mm *Flak* 38s mounted to give defensive fire across the airfield, while the ground-crews dug slit-trenches and constructed fire-control points. He had improvised around the lack of revetments, and had the ground-crews mark out random stands for the incoming aircraft, which would help to make destroying more than one aircraft at a time from the air more difficult.

During the morning all twelve Messerschmitt 110Cs of the 4th *Staffel* of *Zerstorergeschwader* 76 (4/ZG 76), the '*Haifischgruppen*', under *Oberleutnant* Max Hobein, together with three Heinkel 111H6s of the 4th *Staffel* of *Kampfgeschwader* 4 '*General Wever*' (4/KG 4) led by *Hauptman* Schwanhauser, landed, having flown through Aleppo. The Bf 110s were weighted down. On the inside they carried a third 'crew member', one of the ground-crew, cramped up inside the long cockpit 'greenhouse', and on the outside they sported two 900-litre external fuel tanks to extend their range.

The pressure to get *Sonderkommando Junck* in place as quickly as possible to bolster their flagging ally meant that units had been commandeered from all over Europe. For example, 4/ZG 76 had been transferred virtually overnight from its base in Belgrade.

The transport element was composed of twenty Junkers 52/3ms and a few large four-engined Junkers 90s. All of the transports had been snatched away from the build-up at Athens Tatoi airfield in readiness for Student's airborne invasion of Crete. The transport aircraft began an immediate shuttle between Aleppo and Mosul, bringing in spare parts, ammunition and bombs.

Three of the Junkers 52s stayed at Mosul. One was completely equipped as a powerful mobile radio station to keep Junck in contact with Aleppo, Athens and Jeschonnek in Berlin. Of the other two, one was fitted out as a chemical laboratory to analyse and determine the additives necessary to bring Iraqi aviation spirit up to German standards, while the other was designed to mix the additives with the fuel.

The logistics of assembling the force at such short notice, together with delays by some of the Vichy French in Syria, either due to their reluctance to help their recent conquerors or as a result of German condescension to the defeated French, meant that Junck's forces were flying in to Mosul piecemeal.

The final three Heinkel 111s of 4/KG 4 flew into Mosul on 13 May, while two Bf 110Cs of *Zerstorergeschwader 26* (*ZG 26*) under *Lieutnant* Woerner arrived on 14 May.

Wadi Tarifa

With an early start, Kingcol moved into the Great Black Lava Belt on its way to H-4. For mile after mile the column passed through a wilderness of black basalt rocks polished smooth by time and the sun's heat, and so densely packed off-road that it was almost impossible to step between them. They passed A25, a wide patch of sand which had been cleared of the black rocks to provide a landing-ground, to a point where the road bent towards the north-east and the Iraqi border.

Emerging from the Lava Belt, Kingcol made good time on the tarmac road to H-4 near the Iraqi frontier, although making 122 miles in eight hours was an exhausting journey. H-4, like all the pumping stations, was a section of some ten acres of desert fenced-in by a high perimeter wire to keep out the *kleptiwallahs*. Inside were the large pumping units, used to boost the flow of oil along the pipeline, as well as sleeping and administrative quarters for the crew.

Kingstone decided against a bivouac inside the H-4 compound in view of the excellent target the pumping station presented to the *Luftwaffe*, and stopped seven miles beyond at Wadi Tarifa to camp for the night. The next day, Kingcol would cross the frontier into Iraq and face the Iraqi Army on its run down to Habbaniya and the beleaguered Embassy in Baghdad.

Tel Kotchek, 13 May 1941

The two trains carrying the Vichy French arms and ammunition arrived at the Syrian-Iraqi border at 04.00 that morning.

To Rahn's chagrin, Grobba was not there to meet him. Even worse, the Iraqis had failed to send a locomotive to take over from the Syrian engine. Finally Dentz's right-hand man, *Commandant* Teze, ordered the station-master to form the two trains into one and have them drawn to Mosul by a Syrian train. The station-master, confused, called Aleppo for confirmation, and was ordered to do as he was told. The train arrived just after noon that day in Mosul.

Grobba, back from his meeting in Baghdad, met Rahn at the station. They arranged for the Iraqi officer commanding the Mosul garrison, Colonel Qasim Maqsud, to sign a three-year agreement with Rahn to pay for the arms with shipments of Iraqi grain, rice, sugar and oil to Syria. The train was scheduled to return to Syria the next day filled with grain. This was Rahn's gesture to Dentz to help him to overcome the serious shortage of bread which had created riots across Syria

Mosul

The first *Luftwaffe* interception took place when a Messerschitt Bf 110 of 4/ZG 76 attacked a Blenheim of 203 Squadron on a reconnaissance flight over Mosul. Although the Blenheim was attacked four times, it suffered no damage. On a bombing mission on the Mosul–Tel Awainot railway later that day, Flt Lt Plinston of 84 Squadron saw a Bf 110 in the air over Mosul, confirming that the *Luftwaffe* had arrived in some force.

Habbaniya

A section of the Madras Sappers and Miners, flown in from Shaiba, and guarded by a company of Levies, built a flying ferry across the Euphrates at Sin el Dhibban

Here the river was over 750 feet wide, and very fast and swollen by the winter rains in the Turkish mountains. It required 1,500 feet of wire hawser to secure the raft. A platoon of the 2nd Levy Company took up positions on the northern shore to guard the bridgehead against an Iraqi attack.

Baghdad

The previous day Freya had noticed an aircraft with strange markings flying over the city making for the civil airport. No one recognized the aircraft, although someone had suggested it might be the Persian weekly mail flight.

The BBC News depressed the Embassy. Soviet recognition of Iraq was a blow, as was the return of von Papen to Ankara. The third day of hearing that Rutba Wells was in British hands seemed to irritate everyone. Freya firmly expected to remain at the Embassy for a week to ten days, although it seemed to her to be wishful thinking.

Freya kept herself busy making out a list of cosmetics and soaps for the ladies and giving it to Vyvyan Holt, the Oriental Secretary, who negotiated with the Iraqi Ministry of Foreign Affairs for all their food and supplies.

Cornwallis had the Embassy spread Union Flags flat on the roof to warn the RAF away from mistakenly bombing their refuge.

A later institution in the Embassy was the keep-fit class held on the temporary 'bowling green', the bowls being small cannon balls for which General Waterhouse could find no other use. The keep-fit, or 'Physical Jerks' class, was held at 06.30 every morning. While the attendance was very good, their gymnastics were put in the shade by an elderly Indian, who, at the same time, used to stand on his head, without using his hands to keep him there, for a full five minutes.

Rome

Mussolini entered the war gambling that the early German victories would continue, enabling Italy to profit handsomely and cheaply. Within a year *Il Duce* was chaffing at his relegation to a junior partner while Hitler dictated events. To redress the balance he made the fateful decision to invade Greece. His easy victory turned into a catastrophe as the small Greek Army drove the Italians back into Albania. Hitler was forced to bail out Italy by diverting troops and aircraft, which delayed the launch of *Barbarossa*.

Nevertheless, Mussolini still harboured grandiose aims of making

Italy a world power, and saw the opportunity of creating an Italian *Imperium* in Africa and the Middle East centred on oil-rich Iraq. With Rommel in Africa recapturing the whole of Cyrenaica, which Graziani had lost to a very much smaller British force, Mussolini's power of independent decision making and of acting separately from Hitler was fast eroding. Iraq was Mussolini's last throw of the dice. Mussolini was a firm believer in his own infallibility, and was buoyed by subordinates who pandered to his ego by telling him what he wanted to hear. Galeazzo Ciano, who had married *Il Duce*'s daughter Edda, owed his position as Foreign Minister to Mussolini. Ciano, a young, inexperienced dilettante, who nursed ambitions of succeeding Mussolini, went along with *Il Duce*'s delusions of conquest, giving personal opinion which suited the mood rather than the professional advice of his experienced diplomats.

Publically Ciano seemed to be a poor copy, slavishly imitating Mussolini's pugnacious gestures and scowling facial poses. In private Ciano was a charming, educated and intelligent man undecieved by Mussolini's pretensions of reviving the Roman empire.

Mussolini sat back in his chair in his large and ostentatious office in the Palazzo Venezia, and turned to Ribbentrop. 'Well, that covers all but one item on our agenda. What is your thinking on Iraq, Minister?' he enquired.

'Excellency,' he replied, 'the Count', gesturing to Ciano, the Italian Foreign Minister, who sat opposite, 'and I have discussed in broad terms the need to help Iraq. If a sizeable shipment of arms could reach Iraq, airborne troops could then be brought into the area. With the material on hand they could advance against the British and, in certain circumstances, attack Egypt from the East', voicing an opinion quite independently from that of Hitler. 'Iraq has to be helped. As you suggest, arms shipments and airborne forces could open up a new front against the British and start a revolt, not only of Arabs but of a great number of Muslims. Already the Mufti has summoned the Arabs of the world to a holy war against Britain.'

'The possession of Iraq and its oil wells might well have a more profound effect upon the British world position than a landing in the British Isles themselves', responded Mussolini. 'It would be necessary to get possession of Crete and Cyprus, the anterooms, if you like, to Syria. If we could get French permission to land troops and planes in Syria, our help to Iraq could be substantial. We have already prepared five planes which could proceed to Baghdad via Rhodes. They can transport 400 machine-guns as well as twenty anti-tank guns. We also have a squadron of fighters ready for action. Should the passage of arms through Turkey prove impossible, we would have to march against Britain through Syria. The great advantage here is that an attack on Egypt from Syria would require crossing a desert of only 100 km compared with the 500 km stretch of desert if we attack Egypt from the west.'

'How long, Excellency, do you think that Iraq would be able to hold out against the British?' asked Ribbentrop.

'The Prime Minister has assured us that he can hold his own against the British provided that he receives war material. If he receives no aid the British would overwhelm the Iraqis in three to four weeks', *Il Duce* replied. 'But will Darlan let us send men and material across Syria?'

'That has all been taken care of, Excellency. German weapons, ammunition and aircraft are arriving in Mosul as we speak.'

Mussolini, not wanting to be left out of any spoils that could be gained, turned to Ciano and said to his son-in-law, 'Please arrange for our aircraft and our weapons to be sent to Iraq immediately.'

When Ribbentrop had left, Mussolini sat with his Foreign Minister and reviewed their meeting. 'Galeazzo, we have to make sure that we have Italian soldiers and airmen in Iraq when it is freed from the British. If not, we shall give the Germans complete access to the Middle East, the oil and the Persian Gulf, and we shall become minor partners in the Axis. I do not want to have to beg for access to the oil. Make sure that you talk to Darlan immediately to secure transit and refuelling rights for the *Regia Aeronautica*.'

Ciano agreed and asked, '*Duce*, what do you make of von Ribbentrop?'

Mussolini replied, dismissively, 'He belongs to the category of Germans who are a disaster for their country. He talks about making war right and left without naming an enemy or defining an objective.'

'The King hosted Ribbentrop at the Quirinale Palace, and could not wait until he was gone. The King regards him as a cross between a head butler and a pimp', Ciano added mischievously.

Ankara

'My dear Minister,' Franz von Papen, the German Ambassador, said, turning as Naji Shawkat, Rashid Ali's Defence Minister, entered his office, 'it is so nice to see you again.'

Von Papen had just returned from a difficult week in Berlin with Ribbentrop at a high-level *Auswartiges Amt* briefing on *Barbarossa*. The very last thing he wanted was a session of hand-holding with the Iraqi.

'I am leaving for Baghdad this afternoon, and I needed to see you before I leave. I have had several meetings with Sukru Saracoglu, the Foreign Minister, concerning Turkey's mediation on our behalf with the British.'

'I hope, Minister, that your government has not decided to capitulate', a concerned Von Papen replied.

'No, no. We see this merely as a truce, a ploy, to give us time to organize political, economic and military aid so that we can renew our fight. We are only pursuing mediation for a postponement of hostilities. We are not changing our political orientation.'

'As I have said before, Minister, I and my government feel that the Iraqi revolt was premature. You must keep pressure on the British for another two weeks until we can send to you the aid that you have been promised. You must hold the airfields and the railways, as they are the keys to German aid. According to a message that I received earlier today, two train loads of weapons and ammunition which we have arranged for you have crossed the Syrian border this morning on their way to Mosul.'

'That is most pleasing, Ambassador.'

'What do you think are the chances for a successful mediation?' questioned Von Papen.

'I am afraid that they are slim. My government will not cede any ground on the number of British troops in Iraq, and Saracoglu does not see the British accepting our position.'

H-3

Kingstone, in his staff car, a low-slung Plymouth taxi from Haifa, painted a vivid green, accompanied by an escort of two trucks full of motorized troops from the Household Cavalry and Lt Somerset de Chair, his intelligence officer, set off across the Iraqi border. They arrived at the next pumping station, H-3, ten miles over the Iraqi border, just after six o'clock in the evening.

Waiting for Kingstone at H-3 was Sqn Ldr Michael Casano, the commander of No. 2 RAF Armoured Car Company, with six of his Fordson vehicles. A tall, dashing and colourful character with a big black moustache, red-spotted scarf and hat set at a rakish angle, he was waiting for Joe at the lead armoured car. As Joe walked up he was met with a raffish salute from Casano and a growl from Casano's black and white mongrel, Butch, who had been wisely sitting in the shade.

'What happened at Rutba? Kingstone asked Casano.

'The Arab Legion got there first and was involved in a fire-fight with the Iraqi Desert Police who were holding the Fort. The Legion had to make a strategic withdrawal when Fawzi al Qawujki turned up, reinforcing Rutba with a motorized column. The RAF attacked with Blenheims, but they lost two aircraft to Iraqi ground fire. At that point we arrived and evened up the score. After an hour or so of intense fighting, Fawzi and the Desert Police withdrew to the east. '

'Fawzi's a nasty piece of work. He is a competent guerrilla leader and gave us a lot of trouble in Palestine in the 1936–39 revolt. Did you leave any troops to guard Rutba?' probed Kingstone.

'Glubb Pasha, the commander of the Arab Legion, is there with about three hundred and fifty legionnaires. I left two cars in case Fawzi tried to retake Rutba', replied Casano.

'How long will it take to get to Rutba?' Kingstone asked.

'About three hours', replied Casano. 'We have five miles of tarmac highway, then it's another forty-five miles across the desert using astral navigation.'

'Let's go to Rutba and meet up with this Glubb Pasha', said Kingstone, turning back towards his staff car.

Rutba Wells

They made good time across the desert in the cool of the night, and rolled into Rutba Wells at nine in the evening.

Joe left the escort and Casano's cars on the outskirts. He drove on through the small town with de Chair past the single-storey mud brick dwellings until they reached the eastern end, dominated by the large fort silhouetted against the starry night.

Dismounting among a jumble of Chevrolet and Ford trucks, with Lewis guns on plinths, they walked through the massive open wooden gates of the fort. Inside they were greeted by a mass of khaki-robed Bedouins with red-and-white check *keffiyehs* and red sashes, wearing bandoliers full of ammunition, long silver-handled daggers and .38 revolvers in their belts, and Lee-Enfield rifles slung over their shoulders. The legionnaires quickly became affectionately known as 'Glubb's Girls' by cavalry and infantrymen alike.

As Kingstone and de Chair moved through the throng, they met a short man in a khaki-drill uniform and a yellow *keffiyeh* with double ropes of a black silk *aqal*.

The man beckoned to them and led them through the courtyard, which still displayed tangled and charred wreckage from the fire-fight, down a corridor into a large hall. Judging by the refectory-style tables and a blackboard on one of the walls, with 'Roast Beef & Yorkshire pudding and custard tart' written in faded white chalk, this was the restaurant.

He sat down at one of the tables, putting his riding-boots up on the table. The hall was illuminated by several candles thrust into empty beer bottles. The flickering light showed the man to have a dent in the side of his jaw and a sandy moustache.

'Please sit down', said the man. 'My name is John Glubb and I command the Arab Legion.'

Kingstone, a tall, red-faced man, stood towering above Glubb. He did not know what to make of Glubb, with the many ribbons on his chest and the crossed swords and stars of an unknown design on his shoulder tabs.

Establishing that the wells were working, Kingstone went outside with de Chair. 'He thinks he is the King of Saudi Arabia. I am going to get him out of the way. The trouble is, I don't know if he is senior to me or not.'

de Chair replied, unhelpfully, 'With all those insignia I thought he looked like a lieutenant-general.'

'You go ahead', said Kingstone. 'I am going to have a word with Glubb.'

As Glubb reached the main gateway, Kingstone stepped back to talk to him. They looked like two lions sizing each other up to find out who would win the fight to lead the pride.

'Are you senior to me?' Kingstone asked Glubb.

'That does not arise, because I am a civilian', answered Glubb.

'Yes, but aren't you seconded from the Army', he persisted, determined to get to the bottom of this.

'No. I resigned my commission in 1925 and I am now a colonial civil servant', replied Glubb.

Both looked a little nonplussed as they parted company. Kingstone drove back to the escort camped on the outskirts, where he bedded down for the night under the desert sky, lit by a large, bright moon.

The last thing he remembered was the conversation of two troopers on guard, as they patrolled noisily around the camp. 'I have absolutely no idea why they brought us to this sodding place, do you?' said the first.

'Well I wouldn't give you tuppence for Transjordan, and as for this place I wouldn't give you a bloody penny for it', replied the second.

Rutba Wells, 14 May 1941

Starting just after 04.00, the rest of Kingcol began to trickle into Rutba

Wells, with the final vehicles straggling in at around 08.00. All the vehicles were dispersed with the armoured cars on point, backed up by the 25-pounder battery with their barrels pointing outwards.

The Brigade was to move out at first light on the 15th, and the day was spent filling up with water and fuel, repairing vehicles and equipment, and checking ammunition and weapons.

In the early afternoon Kingstone held a meeting around the Brigade Office truck. As there were too many people and it was too hot to sit inside the truck, the awnings had been opened up and chairs brought outside to accommodate the participants in the shade, out of the 122°F heat.

Kingstone, regarded as one of the best fighting brigadiers in the British Army, was an inclusive officer, and in addition to his staff of Grant-Lawson and de Chair, and the outsiders Casano and Glubb, who were now included in Kingcol, another twelve officers gathered at the Brigade Office truck for the briefing.

It was a tight squeeze under the awning. There were Lt Col Andrew Ferguson, who commanded the Life Guards and the Royal Horse Guards, Maj Keith 'Steve' May who had brought A and D Companies of 1st Battalion Essex Regiment and the two bren-gun carriers, Maj Jack 'Daddy' Wright with 237 Battery 60th Field Regiment Royal Artillery and his useful punch of 25-pounder field guns, Lt Barraclough with No. 1 Anti-Tank Troop, Royal Artillery, with 2-pounder guns to take care of enemy armour, Lt 'Fish' Ackroyd of the Light Aid Detachment to repair vehicles, Maj 'Doc' Arundel of 166 Field Ambulance to patch up the wounded, Capt Dick Shuster of the Middlesex Yeomanry's Signals Troop, Maj Newmarsh of the RASC, commanding 552 Transport Company providing heavy trucks, and Lt 'Cheeky Chappie' Oldhan with a troop of Royal Engineers from the 2nd (Cheshire) Field Squadron. Together with the non-combatants Capt Corpe, Lt John Hampton the transport officer and Maj Victor Toler-Aylward the camp commander, this represented all the combat and support elements in Kingcol.

'Tomorrow at first light we are making a dash for RAF Habbaniya, which is fifty-five miles west of Baghdad. Habbaniya has been under siege, which was lifted by the RAF a few days ago', Kingstone began. 'However, there are substantial Iraqi forces in the area which still pose a threat and have to be neutralized. We will join up with Habforce, which is following closely in our wake, and move on Baghdad to relieve our Embassy, which is under siege. We will first go east for 220 miles to Kilo 25 here,' he indicated on the map, 'which is about fourteen miles west of Ramadi. We will bivouac there overnight and then turn south. The RAF has established that there is an Iraqi Brigade well dug in at Ramadi. We are going to leave that for Habforce to finish off while we strike south to Wadi Abu Faruk. We will then turn east around the south of Lake Habbaniya, cross the Mujara bridge, here, and enter Habbaniya from the south. RAF reconnaissance shows that the land between Ramadi and the north shore of Lake Habbaniya has been deliberately flooded. The Iraqis have destroyed a long culvert west of Ramadi on the road to Habbaniya, which adds to the problem. This will necessitate Kingcol striking south. rather than east, and puts perhaps half a day on our journey.

'Now to formations. Glubb Pasha of the Arab Legion is splitting his force into three. He is leaving fifty men each to occupy H-3 and Rutba, and the remaining 250 Legionnaires in their trucks will scout ahead and form a rearguard for the column. Casano's armoured cars will be strategically placed in pairs throughout the column. The trucked infantry, the Cavalry and the Essexes will be in the vanguard, followed by the guns, with the RASC heavy trucks and the support units bringing up the rear. Kingcol will move at fifteen miles an hour with twenty vehicles to the mile.

'There are some important things that you all need to note. Fish's Light Aid Detachment will be at the end of the column. If your vehicle breaks down stay where you are and Fish's chaps will fix it. We are not going to stop or wait for anyone. We made the mistake of hiring the trucks and buses from Haifa and Jerusalem by the day, and a number of the owners are having frequent breakdowns, as this increases their charges. John,' to the Transport Manager, 'we need to stop this. Tell them that if they break down we will offload what we can and will leave them and their vehicle behind. That should put a stop to their game.

'Gentlemen, this is the desert. It is very inhospitable and waterless. It's sand and stone all the way. There is a main track but there are no reference points and no maps, so we will be using compasses to guide us. Do not get lost. We are not going to stop and go looking for you. It is now 15.00 and the temperature under our awning is 124°F. Outside there is no shade. You are all responsible to see that you and your men wear topees or sun hats as well as shirts. I do not want to hear that anyone in Kingcol has heat stroke or has been burned by the sun. Finally the RAF has notified us that German aircraft are passing through Syria and some are already in Mosul in the north of Iraq. Our column is a big and tempting target spread out across the desert. A number of the trucks have anti-aircraft mountings, and you should attach your Lewis guns. We need to be vigilant and be able to hit back if we are attacked. I know that you all have lots to do, so I suggest that you get cracking. Corporal of Horse Barnes will be setting up mess tables here tonight, and dinner will be at 19.00 sharp.'

Although forbidden, two pets had been smuggled aboard Kingcol – Trooper Dan's rabbit and the unofficial mascot, a small monkey. The intense heat that day was too much for the rabbit. Well out of sight of Kingstone and Grant-Lawson, 'A' Squadron buried the rabbit with full military honours. The monkey, however, survived, but was not best pleased with the heat. Put down onto the sand, he would run quickly, hopping from one foot to the other, to the nearest patch of shade. Kingstone had wisely prevented Grant-Lawson from telling Casano to get rid of Butch, deciding to let 'sleeping dogs lie'. Butch and Casano were inseparable. Casano displayed that rare trait of respect, and engendered an *esprit de corps* that officers earn only by leading by example. 'Cass's Men', as they liked to be called, and their armoured cars, museum pieces maybe, were critical to Kingcol.

Baghdad

The record heat wave brought an announcement at the Embassy that all people should wear topees to guard against heat stroke.

Freya could feel and see that the enforced incarceration was beginning to tell, and many people, particularly those who worked outside the Embassy, were becoming impatient. Freya thought it sad that all the traits that people thought of as Nazi were surfacing each time that there was a problem and people gave vent to their anger. Luckily the Embassy seemed to have kept its 'Nazis' under control, but there was a limit to how long a spirit of amiability could be maintained.

At least the women were very pleased with the face-powder that Freya had organized.

Bet Yar

Lt Adrian Mumford sat nervously with his back against the wall, with a Smith & Wesson .38 Police Special resting on his knee under the table.

'For God's sake put that bloody gun away! This is not the Wild West', said Maj David Collins.

'Yes, but you are not armed. We are meeting against my better judgement with the Irgun, a gang of terrorists. This could be a trap.'

Collins was fed up with Mumford's petulant whining, which he had had to endure from the moment the man picked him up at Lydda airport's small terminal an hour and twenty minutes ago. 'Stop thinking of your own safety and what it would do to your career if the Irgun killed me. No one is going to do anything, although you could drop the gun and injure someone. So put that bloody gun away and look as if this meeting is important to you. If you can't do this, go and sit in the car.'

Collins regretted that he had to involve MI6, but Wavell, a stickler for form, had insisted that Maunsell go through channels. However, he had not bargained for this popinjay from the ASLU, the MI6 cover organization, in Jerusalem. It was all he could do to keep his hands off Mumford's throat.

Collins had flown in on Misr's DH 86 flight that morning from Cairo to be collected by Mumford and driven the sixteen miles to the village of Bet Yar on the coast just south of Tel Aviv. Maunsell had arranged a meeting with David Raziel, the head of the Irgun Zvai Leumi, through Ralph Harari, whose family was part of Cairo's *haute Juiverie*. Harari had contacted Arey Posek, the Irgun's liaison with British Intelligence, to arrange a meeting for Collins. The rendezvous had been fixed for 12.30 at the Neptune restaurant, where they were to sit inside and wait for Raziel.

Collins was not worried what Raziel, a Lithuanian-born Jew and a naturalized Palestinian, would do. Although Raziel had had some brushes with the Palestine Police, he was not anti-British, and wanted only to create a state for the Jews – by force if necessary. At the beginning of the war Raziel had argued successfully, on the principle of 'my enemy's enemy is my friend', for a suspension of all offensive action against the British in Palestine that could assist the greater enemy of the Jews – the Nazis.

Not all members of the Irgun agreed. Avraham Stern had ceded from the Irgun to found his own organization, Lehi, better known as the Stern Gang. Stern's extremism, especially the robberies of wealthy Jews, had already earned the emnity not only of the British but of many Jews.

A few minutes before the appointed time, Posek, together with a youthful, handsome man in a white, open-necked shirt and dark trousers entered the room.

'I am David Raziel', the young man said, shaking hands with both men and sitting down with his back to the door. 'There is no need for weapons', he went on. 'No one followed you from the airport and my men have secured the area. To save time, as I know that the Major will need to be back at Lydda to catch the return Misr flight at 4.30 p.m., I have ordered sea bass, which I think that you will like.'

Mumford was taken aback by Raziel's effrontery, his presumptions and his knowledge. The lieutenant was a career Foreign Office man who considered, like many of the Arabists in the FO, that the Jews were troublemakers who were upsetting the apple-cart, not only in Palestine, but throughout the Middle East. A meeting with Raziel was out of order. It looked as if the British were coming cap in hand to the terrorists. He had already voiced his concerns to Collins, who had said that he would go alone. He was also deeply concerned about the lack of an escort and Collins's veto of prior surveillance. All this just confirmed his misgivings.

After the meal Raziel sat back, opened a pack of Capstans and lit up a cigarette.

'So, Major, what can I do to help you?'

'Mr Raziel, we have a problem in Iraq, and I think that it may be to our mutual benefit to cooperate. The *Luftwaffe* has already flown into Mosul to reinforce Rashid Ali's revolt. Intelligence indicates that they have problems in getting adequate supplies of high-octane aviation fuel. The Iraqis have stocks of 90-octane fuel in storage tanks at the Iraqi Oil Company's facility in Baghdad. If we could sabotage these tanks it would stop the Germans from gaining a hold in Iraq. I don't need to tell you what that would mean for the Jews throughout the Middle East. We need a small team of saboteurs who can pass as Iraqis to cross our lines at Falluja, enter Baghdad and blow up these storage tanks.'

Raziel sat back, slowly sipping his black coffee to give him time to think. 'If you can fly us into Habbaniya, give us explosives and defensive weapons, we can take out these storage tanks for you. We have some Iraqi Jews who can pass as Arabs, and many of us have experience with explosives. There is, however, one thing that we want:' Raziel waited a few seconds to get everyone's attention before adding, 'a free hand with the Mufti.'

Mumford spluttered and was about to open his mouth when he saw the hostile glance from Collins signalling him to shut up.

'Obviously my government cannot and will not give you any encouragement to take the law into your own hands. However,' he added with a wry smile, 'in the confusion following your destruction of the storage tanks you might well find yourself in Zahawi Street. What happens then is, of course, none of our concern.'

'Give me two days to assemble my team and we can be at your military airfield at Tel Nor at 07.00 for a flight to Habbaniya on 17 May', responded Raziel.

All four men got up to leave the restaurant. Outside they shook hands and Collins walked across to the driver's side on Mumford's Morris 10 and asked for the key.

As Collins and Mumford's car disappeared into the distance, Posek, who had been quiet throughout the meeting, turned to Raziel. 'David. Doing a deal with the British is one thing, but going on the mission yourself is foolish. We need you here.'

'Arey, I have no choice. Stern has made me vulnerable. I have to be seen as a man of action, not merely a committee member going to endless meetings like those in the Haganah. I also have to be seen to be getting something from the British in exchange for our cooperation. By ridding ourselves of the Mufti we not only destroy a rallying-point for all Arabs but we show all Jews that the link with the British is to our advantage. If we demonstrate to the British that we can be trusted, our next move is to have them train and arm a Jewish brigade to fight the Germans, This will give us a cadre of trained, disciplined and experienced troops to form the nucleus of a Jewish Army.'

A very different conversation was taking place in the car driven by Collins.

'I just cannot believe that you will be using Jews on a sensitive mission and have given them the green light to commit murder. This is unconscionable. The British do not do this sort of thing. Where will it stop. The FO is not going to like this one little bit', whined Mumford.

With that Collins wrenched the steering wheel to the right and slammed on the brakes, stopping the car in its tracks. As Mumford picked himself off the dashboard Collins grabbed the younger man's shirt-front. 'Right, you little shit. Let's get things straight. Your behaviour in the restaurant almost ruined this mission. The Colonial Office buggered about in the 20s and 30s and even made Haj Amin Mufti. They compounded the error by not stopping him when he led the Arab revolt in the mid-1930s. Then the Foreign Office allowed the Mufti to set up shop in Baghdad and poison the Iraqis. The Foreign Office did nothing about the Mufti and his gang. We would not be in this position now if your masters in Whitehall had been doing their job. The issue is that the Foreign Office still does not want to do anything in case it upsets the Arabs. We have a problem where time is of the essence. I don't care what he is or where he comes from, but Raziel can help us to solve this problem. What they do in their spare time is none of our business. Frankly if they take out the Mufti it will save us all a lot of bother.

'Forget what you have heard about SOE. What little time I spend in Cairo does not involve propping up the bar at the Continental, eating roast pigeon at the Roof Garden, dancing the night away at the Kit Kat or playing tennis at the Gezira Club. My job is to take the fight to the enemy, and I take on the unpleasant but necessary jobs to help to win this war. This involves using and killing people. The Chiefs of the

Imperial General Staff outrank the Foreign Office in a war zone and I outrank you. If you try to thwart me I will have your guts for garters. I will make it my personal business to have you transferred to the Regular Army and push a desk in the remotest posting there is in the Empire.'

With that, he let go of Mumford's shirt-front, switched the engine on, put the car into gear and let the clutch out, and swung the car back onto the road for Lydda. 'Let's see if we can get a cup of coffee at the airport before you see me off', added Collins casually, knowing that he had got his point across to a very confused and dazed Mumford.

H-4

To find out where the *Luftwaffe* was refuelling its aircraft *en route* to Mosul, 203 Squadron flew two reconnaisance sorties. The first sortie showed a Junkers 90 taking off from Palmyra, while the second identified three large and four small aircraft being refuelled at Aleppo.

Plt Off Watson, who had flown the sorties, asked Gp Capt Brown if he could go back with a fighter Blenheim and attack the aircraft. Brown referred him to the newly arrived Habforce commander, George Clark. Clark turned on Watson and barked, 'Do you want to declare war on Syria?'

Watson, unfazed by Clark's rank, responded, 'I think that would be a bloody good idea, sir', much to the delight of the General's staff.

Sense prevailed and an attack on Palmyra was ordered and timed for 17.40.

Two 84 Squadron Blenheims and two 250 Squadron Tomahawks, which had flown in for the raid from Aqir in Palestine, and the 203 Squadron fighter Blenheim took off to attack all German aircraft found at Palmyra. The British raid missed three *Luftwaffe* Heinkel 111s which had taken off for Mosul an hour earlier, and they were able to destroy only two German aircraft on the ground.

Baghdad, 15 May 1941

Major Axel von Blomberg was grateful to Jeschonneck for selecting him for *Sonderkommando Junck*. For the first time he hoped to be able to prove his own worth and come out of the shadow that is inevitably cast over your career when your father, in this case a field marshal, is a senior serving officer.

Von Blomberg was flying as a passenger on a Heinkel 111 from Mosul to Baghdad to take on the task of air liaison with Rashid Ali.

His first assignment was to set up a council-of-war meeting between Junck and the Iraqi government on 16 May.

The Heinkel pilot had deliberately flown low hoping to avoid British fighters on its way to Baghdad. The pilot brought the plane down low over the Tigris so that he could make a sweeping starboard turn just after the King Feisal Bridge to line the Heinkel up with the runway to get the aircraft as quickly as possible down into the civil airport in the western suburbs of Baghdad.

As the Heinkel approached the King Feisal Bridge, Hassan al Bassam, a corporal in the 6th Infantry Brigade, saw an unfamiliar aircraft coming head-on to the bridge he was guarding. Unable to see the Iraqi markings newly painted on the side of the Heinkel, al Bassam unslung his Lee-Enfield rifle, released the safety catch and fired three rounds into the belly of the low-flying plane as it passed directly over his position.

Only after the Heinkel had landed did the crew find Von Blomberg slumped forward in his seat, dead. One of al Bassam's rounds had passed vertically through the floor, entering Von Blomberg's throat and travelling on up into his brain. If the Major had not sat forward to see Baghdad through the small side-window, the bullet would have completely missed him.

Rutba Wells

Kingcol column left Rutba Wells at daybreak. As the vehicles moved out onto the desert they began to kick up a yellow dust cloud which created a huge funnel in their wake, stretching back almost thirty miles.

The enormity of crossing the desert to Habbaniya began to strike home to Kingstone on the road to Ramadi. It all depended on de Chair – one small man with a simple compass riding in the back of a pale yellow Chevrolet staff car at the head of the column.

The heat of the desert was staggering: a fierce, parched heat which made you feel as if you were standing on the edge of a huge fire in a high wind, being licked by gusts of flame. Those that would leave Iraq would bear the permanent impression of the country burnt into them – a cicatrix for life. Then there were the almost daily dust storms – a sudden darkness, a rustle and a shadow, a pillar of dust swirling around its base tearing across the desert, which then almost as quickly stopped. Then there were groups of 'Dust Devils' – near-vertical whirlwinds drawn up from the desert in swirling pillars that could reach up several thousand feet and then wander across the skies, and seemed to leap up and spiral around, almost at will.

No stretch of the desert excluded the fly. Iraq in May was plagued with dust, heat and flies, and the greatest scourge of all was the fly. Flies in the tents, in the hastily dug anti-aircraft trenches and in the desert were unbelievable and hard to describe. Flies settled in clouds on everything from equipment and uniforms to food. The troops never seemed to be free of flies; they were their constant companions whether they moved, sat, slept or ate.

Then there was the problem of navigation. de Chair, who was leading the brigade, was faced with a dilemma. Should he follow the camel tracks of the Old Damascus Road marked on all the old maps, or follow the cairns which marked the rough course of the beginning of the proposed Haifa–Baghdad road, which was being surveyed by Brooks & Murdoch, a civil engineering firm in Baghdad? He decided to follow the cairns.

It was a few minutes before 08.00 when de Chair climbed a rise in the ground and looked back at the column, stretching back into the distance like a long, black snake. At that point several explosions, followed by the eruption of clouds of black smoke, came from somewhere to the rear. This was followed by several streams of tracer arcing up towards three aircraft high above the column.

It was not until the stop for water at noon that de Chair heard that Kingcol had been attacked by Heinkels. One of the trucks carrying the Essexes had been hit, and there were several casualties.

The noonday halt was for two hours, to help to limit dehydration in the appalling heat. Following the military manual, the troops began trying to dig slit-trenches in case of another air raid. However, the desert at the halt contained only a thin layer of sand over rock, so most had to do with six-inch-deep trenches – useless against any air raid.

Kingcol was lucky: there were no more air raids that day.

de Chair became concerned about Kingcol's position. Driving back down the column, he found Peter Brooks, a partner in the road surveyors, who had offered to help out with his knowledge of the area.

He motioned for Brooks, who was driving sedately in his blue Packard, to pull his car out of the column and join him. Brooks, a short, quiet, grey-haired man, sauntered over to de Chair's car.

'Are we on the right route?' de Chair asked.

'Yes. You can strike left up ahead until you hit the Old Damascus Road, which is about ten miles away. The alternative is to keep going in this direction along the course of the new Haifa–Baghdad Road. You will meet an area of treacherous sand in about fifteen miles which stretches between the two roads. You should be able to cross the sand trap provided you rush it at speed. Its only sixty to a hundred feet wide, and then you connect with the foundation of the new road', said

Brooks. 'Later you will come across the beginning of a seventy-mile stretch of tarmac road which leads out into the desert west of Ramadi.'

They reached the sand trap an hour later. Despite a few heart-stopping incidents, all the Kingcol vehicles managed to cross the barrier and link up with the metalled road. Picking up speed from its customary fifteen miles an hour, the column made up time along the tarmac, and finally pulled off the road twenty-five miles short of Ramadi at 21.00, with every man and vehicle up at the finish.

After dispersing the vehicles Kingstone held a conference at the Brigade truck at 21.30. 'We strike out tomorrow at 07.00 and turn south fourteen miles before Ramadi, heading towards Abu Farouk. Two companies of the Essexes will lead off under Maj May, followed by Maj Newmarsh's RASC trucks and the rest of the support units. The Household Cavalry will act as our rearguard. At Abu Farouk we turn west, skirting Lake Habbaniya and passing over the bridge at Mujara, before we turn north into the RAF station. Glubb Pasha and the Arab Legion will scout north of the column and will protect our flank.'

After almost 160 tortuous miles in intense heat, the officers and men of Kingcol were tired, dirty and impatient for a meal and a night's rest before their last day in the desert.

Baghdad

A small sensation swept through the Embassy. One of the women, nick-named the Prima Donna, caused a scandal by strolling about in just a camisole and sleeping in the women's dormitory in the nude. One of the senior Embassy wives was forced to confront the woman as a result of the complaints from the other women. Freya was amused that there were no complaints from the men.

Cecil Hope-Gill let it slip to Freya that he was beginning to realize the full import of the phrase 'stark naked'. Freya was furious, and refused to talk to him again. Private relations in the Amusement Committee were not as happy as their public achievements. Hope-Gill usually found himself at loggerheads with the majority. The limerick from one of his colleagues sealed his fate with Freya:

> *Beware of Miss Poison-pen Stark,*
> *Whose bite is far worse than her bark.*
> *She has glutted her fill,*
> *With the blood of Hope-Gill,*
> *And thinks it is only a lark.*

Hope-Gill later remarked that he thought that was the reason that Freya had left him out of her account of the siege.

A rumour in the market-place was that Fritz Grobba was back in Baghdad and German planes were in Mosul. The BBC News later confirmed that the RAF had bombed German planes in Syria and that Germans were indeed in Iraq.

Freya managed to buy two fish from one of the policemen in the launch guarding the Embassy from the river.

Baghdad, 16 May 1941

Despite the unfortunate death of the valuable Von Blomberg, Junck had hastily arranged a meeting with Rashid Ali and a number of key Iraqi officers to set priorities for *Sonderkommando Junck* and to stiffen Iraqi resolve.

Junck flew in to Baghdad's civil airport from Mosul, landing at first light in a Messerschmitt, and was met by *Hauptman* Erik Kohlhaas, the *Abwehr*'s head of station in Iraq. Kohlhaas took Junck to the Maude Hotel for breakfast and to give Junck a briefing.

Junck and Kohlhaas sat under the awning in the restaurant on the first-floor balcony of the Maude. They looked out across a tranquil Tigris and a Baghdad slowly coming to life shimmering in an early-morning heat haze. Junck found it strange, sitting on the balcony, that there was a war going on and men dying less than a hundred kilometres away to the west. Kohlhass, sensing Junck's interest, gave him a quick thumb-nail sketch of Baghdad and Iraq

'To our right, across the river, is the British Embassy,' he said, pointing at a large villa-style building with tall windows and decorative pilasters, 'which is under siege by the Iraqis. The Iraqis have also laid siege to the American Legation, which is a little further down on this side of the river. The Ghazi and the Feisal Bridges were built in the last five years. Before that you could cross the river only by ferry or on a rickety wooden bridge built across boats lashed together. All the government offices, including the Ministry of Defence, where you will have your meeting, are on this side of the Tigris, about a mile upstream. Iraq is a place with a lot of history, the present is a bit of a quandary and the future is clouded.'

'Why do you say that?'

'The politics in Baghdad are as labyrinthine as its streets. Beneath the surface are all sorts of tribal and religious factions attempting to upset the status quo. To me, the only way power is exercised in Iraq is by strong military force. Brutalizing Iraqis appears to be the way that power is maintained. It seems that all that they respect is force. The more brutal, the more respect. This is not just the British and the Turks; before them it has a long history, going back beyond Gengis Khan and even Alexander the Great. Without this the minority élite, the Sunni, would lose their power to tribes and religious factions, and the country would then fall apart. Unity is not one of Iraq's strong points.'

Kohlhaas then provided enough insight on the poor showing of the Iraqi military against a much smaller and weakly armed foe, and on the lack of military skills and morale fibre among the Iraqi officers, to make Junck realize that helping the Iraqis to win would be an up-hill battle. A lack of coordination, poor command skills and little enemy intelligence would be difficult to overcome in the short term.

Kohlhaas, however, was damning in his portrayal of Grobba. 'Grobba is arrogant and he has an insulting personal style. He has deliberately distorted the facts with self-justifying and exaggerated reports to build his importance here in Iraq with the Wilhelmstrasse. He is an obsessive with all things Arab and likes to present himself as the 'German Lawrence'. He is unscrupulously ambitious, and we at the *Abwehr,* both here and on the Tirpitzüfer in Berlin, have found to our cost that we cannot trust him. *Oberst*, I suggest that you are very careful in your dealings with Grobba. He is neither a Nazi nor a Junker, but he is protected by von Ribbentrop, and it would do you no good to confront him.'

Junck entered the second-floor conference room in the Citadel at 10.00 a.m., hoping that Kohlhaas's analysis of the situation and the people was exaggerated due to some personal or professional animosity. He was to find, to his chagrin, that the *Abwehr* head of station's portrayal was all too accurate.

Grobba welcomed him, rather perfunctorily, and introduced him to Rashid Ali, to the Chief of Staff, General Amin Zaki, and his Chief of Operations, Colonel Nur ed Din Mahmud, and the head of what was left of the Royal Iraqi Air Force, Mahmud Salman.

To Junck's surprise, Grobba ran the meeting, building up each of the Iraqis before their presentations and commenting favourably, even when it was clear that the decisions which had been taken and the resulting performance of the Iraqi armed forces were deeply flawed.

Junck realized that the *Luftwaffe* would have to take the initiative, and soon, if the Iraqis were to overcome their fear of British air attacks and regain their self-confidence.

'*Oberst* Junck. You have heard from our Iraqi colleagues in detail. What do plan to do to help them at this critical point', Grobba asked pointedly, as if Junck was his subordinate.

Junck did not rise to the bait, and directly addressed the Iraqis. 'Gentlemen, thank you for your candour. With the British reinforcements isolated in the Basra area I believe that we have two important priorities. Our first order of business is to stop their relief column from Palestine, which is now in Iraq on its way to Habbaniya. Our second priority is to eliminate the British presence by capturing the British base at Habbaniya.

'*Sonderkommando Junck* will provide you with air cover, while the considerable forces at your disposal, which have not yet been committed, the 2nd Division in Kirkuk and the 3rd Division, here in Baghdad, will retake Habbaniya and stop the remnants of the Palestine column. We need to take the initiative, and I have already authorized a substantial raid on Habbaniya which is taking place as we speak. We found and bombed the British relief column in the desert near Ramadi yesterday.

'Gentlemen, to help you I need to know your positions and the situation on a daily basis. In that way we can be sure that the *Luftwaffe* brings you the right support, at the right place and at the right time.'

The Iraqis seemed delighted with Junck's direct approach, and agreed to the programme that they subsequently elaborated with him that morning.

An Iraqi staff car was to take Junck back to the airport, but as Junck walked through the main entrance and down the steps of the Citadel to the waiting car, Grobba caught up with him and pulled him aside.

'What do you think you are trying to do?' he said accusingly to Junck. 'These are very difficult times and we need to handle these people very carefully. Everything must be cleared by me first. You must not make commitments to them or expect them to make commitments to you. I have to coordinate everything. Do you understand, *Oberst*?'

Junck pointedly removed Grobba's hand from his arm. 'Firstly, you asked me what I planned to do for the Iraqis and I told them. Secondly, I am happy to work with you but I do not work for you. I report directly to General Jeshonneck. Thirdly, until General Felmy and the Military Mission arrive I make the decisions on military issues. I will be happy to discuss these in advance of meetings with the Iraqis, but my decision must be final in these matters.'

As Junck turned to go, Grobba yelled after him, 'I warn you, do not try to sabotage my mission here in Iraq. I have the *Fuhrer*'s support!'

However, earlier that day the RAF and the *Luftwaffe* had been in combat with the Germans, drawing first blood. The first to attack was Flg Off Lane-Sansome of 203 Squadron, who arrived over the main airfield at Mosul at first light in a Blenheim.

Lane-Sansome saw a number of Messerschmitt fighters and Heinkel bombers, as well as some single-engined monoplanes on the ground – most probably some of the surviving Iraqi Bredas and Northrops. He dropped a few 20 lb bombs, and as he prepared to drop down to strafe the airfield at low level he found a Bf 110 trying to line up on his tail. Lane-Sansome was lucky and had enough height to pull some violent manoeuvres, managing to give the Messerschmitt the slip before flying the ninety minutes back to Habbaniya.

At 09.35 a *Kette* of Heinkels of 4/KG 4 led by their commander, *Hauptmann* Schwanhauser, raided Habbaniya. Schwanhauser split his force into three, leading one of the Heinkels into a low-level attack on the camp while the remaining aircraft swung to port to bomb aircraft parked on the ground. All three aircraft then made a second pass, bombing the hangars and causing more damage than that of the past Iraqi air raids combined, and killing a number of RAF personnel.

During the attack a lone Gladiator of 94 Squadron, piloted by Flg Off Gerald Herrtage of 94 Squadron, managed to get airborne and closed with the Heinkels as they began their run back to Mosul. Herrtage lined up on the middle Heinkel and began to pump .303 rounds at point-blank range into its port wing, causing white vapour from a ruptured fuel line to stream out behind it. However, the upper and lower gunners in all three Heinkels opened up on the Gladiator, bracketing Herrtage in a withering cross-fire. Herrtage died at the controls of the Gladiator, which then slowly banked away from the Heinkels, tipped over on its starboard wing and then rolled over and drove straight into the ground.

LAC Ernest 'Mel 'Melluish, an armourer from the Armoured Car Company, was on guard at the powerhouse. The three large diesel generators powered the whole camp and, importantly, brought water from the Euphrates, purified it and then pumped it sixty feet up to the 250,000-gallon assembly of storage tanks which dominated the skyline.

At 10.30, when the air raid sirens began to wail, Mel decided to stay out of the slit-trench which ran alongside the diesel storage tanks. As bullets began to fly and holes appeared in the blast-wall of sandbags, Mel's interpretation of guard duty changed, and he quickly jumped into the trench. He saw the Heinkels cross the sky overhead, pursued by a lone Gladiator, and as the gunfire erupted he hugged the ground face down at the bottom of the slit-trench. A slight moaning sound, followed by a tremendous blow in the small of his back, convinced Mel that he had sustained a serious injury. He decided to get out of the trench and look for medical aid. As he stood up, several things dropped off his back, and he reached down into the trench, where he found some empty cartridge cases. Feeling rather sheepish, he put the cartridge cases in his pocket and decided not to tell anyone about the 'incident'.

KG 4's Heinkels were not unscathed. *Oberleutnant* Karl-Heinz Graubner, flying the aircraft attacked by Herrtage, began to lose oil pressure, the temperature rose and his port engine threatened to shake itself off its mountings. After ten minutes the engine died and Graubner's crew began to throw everything out of the aircraft in a vain attempt to maintain height. After several failed attempts to restart the engine, the Heinkel had lost so much height that a crash-landing in the desert was unavoidable. The crew strapped themselves and braced themselves for the crash, while Graubner turned off the fuel cocks. The aircraft was later found wheels-up alongside the Haditha road, pointing towards Mosul. This was the one and only raid flown by *KG 4*'s Heinkels in Iraq.

In retaliation for the raid on Habbaniya, two Blenheims of 203 Squadron, flown by Sqn Ldr Pike and Flg Off Lane-Sansome, hit the airfield at Mosul with a low-level strafing attack at dusk. Both reported to have damaged aircraft on the ground.

Later in the day four more Blenheims arrived at Habbaniya, three from 84 Squadron, and the remaining 203 Squadron aircraft from H-4.

South of Kilo 25

Thursday had been a bad night for Kingcol. After the dust, heat and flies of the day, mosquitoes and sandflies in the night completed the vicious circle. The mosquito nets were not fine enough to exclude the sandflies, which had free rein to bite their hosts unmercifully throughout the night, denying the tired troops any rest.

Friday was an equally bad day for Kingcol. At 07.00 de Chair, joined by Maj Henry Abel-Smith, took up position by a rusty iron plate on a pole which pointed west, with the words 'Ramadi 25 kilos'.

With the Arab Legion scouting ahead, de Chair estimated a compass course of 140, and added three minutes to the bearing to compensate for the magnetic deviation. He passed the bearing to Maj Newmarsh and the RASC drivers, with instructions to follow compass bearing 143 until they came to Abu Farouk, and then to head west to Mujara.

Just over two hours later the column began to flounder, and took to driving along the wadi beds, which were firmer than the ridges. However, the relief was short lived, and less than an hour later the whole column ground to a halt. The heat was now a punishing 122°F and water was becoming scarce. They had not been able to replenish since Rutba Wells, and would have to reach Mujara before they could top up their water supply.

Men were exhausted by the heat. Adding to their discomfort was sweat, which began to soak through their clothing, making it uncomfortable. Everything not covered – metal gun-barrels, plastic steering-wheels, even leather map-cases – became too hot to touch, while those wearing spectacles and sunglasses and goggles had them steam-up.

Moving to the head of the column, Kingstone saw the problem. The big three-ton RASC supply trucks littered the desert. They had broken through the hard crust into the soft sand beneath and floundered up to their axles. A frustrated Newmarsh watched his crews digging out the sand from in front of the wheels, insert metal sand channels under them to give grip and then try to drive themselves out. They would heave themselves out, like a horse getting up, lurching from side to side in a cloud of steam and sand, only to move a few feet forward before getting embedded again.

One of the vital water-trucks had been emptied out onto the sand. Several of the trucks carrying petrol had been unloaded, and the bare, thin sheet-metal of the piles of petrol tins reflected the sun, acting like a gigantic mirror and providing a beacon for any passing enemy aircraft.

By mid-afternoon the temperature was up to 130°F and it became impossible to work, and the crews lay exhausted under their trucks. Kingstone reluctantly admitted defeat, ordering all disabled vehicles to be left where they stood and directing the column to turn around and head back to Kilo 25.

At the Kilo 25 marker Kingstone held a brief conference early that evening when the temperature began to fall and the men were somewhat refreshed. 'I am not going to go over the events of today – we all know what happened. Luckily Maj Newmarsh has had to abandon only two of the RASC trucks, so we are still pretty much intact. The bad news is that we lost one of our precious water cargoes. We have enough supplies of water, on reduced rations, to stay here one more day. After that we have to go on to Habbaniya, or we go back to Rutba. Gentlemen, let's talk about this tomorrow after a good night's sleep.'

As the officers dispersed back to their units, Kingstone turned to Glubb, who had arrived back from shielding the column to the north. 'Tomorrow I need the Legion's help in finding us an alternative route. I know that we can get one or two trucks through, but I have to get all two hundred to Habbaniya.'

Kingcol suffered its first *Turab* as the sun went down, The darkening sky quickly turned ochre, blocking out the remaining sun as the dust storm hit the camp. The wind pushed dust into the eyes, ears and mouths of the troops and into the tiniest cracks and crevices in their clothes, vehicles, weapons and supplies.

Baghdad

Freya was amused by the reaction of the Iraqi police at the gate to the amount of cosmetics that had been sent for. The sergeant said that he could not think why the women needed such things as face-powder when they were all to be murdered in a few days. One of the women later said to Freya that she wondered if they should stop using lipstick, but Freya responded that at least her face was going to be in order if she was going to die.

The Embassy was beginning to look like a camp of immigrants. In the ballroom people were defending their little islands of privacy with pathetic barricades of boxes and suitcases, and two of the offices had been converted into dining areas, instead of the outdoor trestle tables, to get people indoors and out of the ferocious heat. Ominously Dr Sinderson began to vaccinate everyone in the Embassy to guard against typhoid.

Habbaniya, 17 May 1941

Just after 07.00 two 94 Squadron Gladiators looking for 'trade' over Raschid airfield saw two Bf 110s of *ZG26* taking off below them.

Sgts Bill Dunwoodie and Len Smith dived behind the Messerschmitts and lined up for a quarter attack. Dunwoodie got in a few short burts, then moved into an excellent position astern and put a sustained stream of fire into the 110. The first that *Unteroffizier* Werner Fischer knew of the danger was a line of Dunwoodie's .303 bullets stitching their way through his wing from outboard of the starboard engine across the aircraft to the front of the long 'greenhouse' canopy. Before he could bring his rear-mounted machine-gun to bear to return fire, his pilot, *Lieutnant* Kai Woerner, leader of the *ZG26 Rotte*, slumped over, pushing the control column forward. A terrible flash followed, and the 110 became a mass of flame before disintegrating in a mid-air explosion. Almost simultaneously, Smith's target slammed into the desert two hundred feet outside the Raschid airfield perimeter.

Savile, conscious of the need to thwart a build-up of *Luftwaffe* aircraft so near to Habbaniya, ordered a strike on Raschid. At 09.45 six Blenheims of 84 Squadron, escorted by six Gladiators, bombed and strafed the Iraqi Air Force's main base.

To prepare for the arrival of Kingcol the bridge at Mujara had to be secured. During the morning two companies of the King's Own, some Sappers and three armoured cars, accompanied by Roberts and civilian guides, set off for a twenty-five-mile drive across the desert to the south of Lake Habbaniya.

There was no Iraqi opposition and Mujara was deserted, but there was damage to the irrigation plant and to the wooden trestle bridge. These could be repaired, and D Company and two of the armoured cars remained to provide protection for the Sappers. It was extremely hot, 125°F, with no shade, and D Company and the Sappers had a tough time. The company was under strength, and desert sores and boils began to take their toll. The flies at Mujara were the largest and most blood-thirsty that the King's Own had encountered, and they became a byword for the hostile environment.

At noon four Hurricane fighters flew in from Aboukir in Egypt and were handed over to No. 1 Flight of A squadron. Two of the Hurricanes were IIcs. With extra tankage and four 20 mm cannon, they would give the Air Striking Force the range and punch to do some serious damage to the *Luftwaffe* in Mosul 220 miles away. The Gladiators had barely enough fuel to reach Mosul, and had no reserves for a dogfight, which put the Blenheim bombers at risk to the cannon-firing Bf 110s.

Savile decided to hit quickly with his new resources, and immediately arranged a long-range strike at Mosul with a mixed force of Hurricanes and Blenheims.

During the late afternoon two further companies of the Essex Regiment with their CO, Lt Col 'Crasher' Nichols, arrived by air and took over some of the duties of the King's Own, who had been in combat for over two weeks.

Mosul

Flak Oberfeldwebel Oscar Unternahrer sat smoking a pipe under the canvas awning that had been erected to keep the fierce sun off the *Flak 38* anti-aircraft cannon. The afternoon heat had been intense, and all the aircraft dispersed around the airfield had their canopies and their main wheels draped in canvas to keep off the sun. On the nearest Bf 110 of ZG76, still sporting its distinctive shark's-mouth *Haifischmaul* nose insignia, one of the ground-crew, wearing an unwieldy canvas-covered cork *tropenheim*, was adding an Iraqi flag to the line of flags, which ran beneath the cockpit window, of the nations that the *Geschwader* had fought over or been based in – Poland, Denmark, Norway, Belgium, Holland, France, Great Britain and Yugoslavia.

On his other side Unternahrer could see a ground-crew being urged on by an energetic *Erst Wart* struggling to repair a Jumo engine from one of the 4/*KG 4* Heinkel 111s which hung from an 'A'-frame trestle.

He had heard from one of the ground-crew that operating in this intense heat, in the open, with wind-blown sand and a lack of tropicalization, such as special oil and dust filters, was beginning to tax the mechanics, who had limited access to spare parts. Adding to the problem was the fact that the Iraqis had not supplied them with aviation spirit and modern lubricants – just rather poor-quality fuel and heavy-grade oil. This meant that the *Luftwaffe* was dependent on the mobile laboratory and the mixing unit aboard the Ju 52/3ms to refine the Iraqi fuel for use by *Sonderkommando Junck*.

The RAF raid on Mosul caught the Germans completely by surprise. The six Blenheims, preceded by two of the cannon-armed Hurricane IICs, came in fast and low from the west, putting the sun directly in the eyes of the defenders. A lucky burst from a Hurricane's cannon caught the ammunition of a *Flak* 38, which exploded in a fire-ball, sending 20 mm shells in all directions across the airfield and making the defenders dive for cover. The Blenheims came next, and each unloaded four 250 lb bombs on and around aircraft and buildings. By the time the two remaining *Flak* 38 crews had lined up on the attackers and started pumping out shells, the raiders had cleared the airfield and were disappearing to the south.

Junck came out of the slit-trench nearest the administration block, which he had commandeered, to survey the damage. While Unternahrer's gun crew had managed to take out one of the .303-armed Hurricanes which followed in the wake of the Blenheims, this was poor recompense. *Sonderkommando Junck* had just lost two more planes destroyed, and the ground-crews now had to contend with trying to repair four more damaged aircraft.

In just two days of fighting Junck had lost a third of his combat forces on the ground and in the air in Iraq and in Syria, and he now had only four Heinkel 111s and eight Bf 110s and two Ju 52/3ms transports left in his command. That evening he told his pilots that new tactics were to conserve aircraft, aircrew, and fuel by bombing and strafing at frequent but irregular intervals, and to come in fast from a shallow dive, make one pass and then fly away.

Kilo 25

Dawn brought a camp covered in a heavy layer of sand and dust. The troops stayed put all day at Kilo 25, brushing away the dust and digging out the wind-driven sand, which had drifted as high as the tops of the wheels of Kingcol's cars and trucks.

This delay gave the Arab Legion time to send three reconnaissance parties out into the desert, looking for ways around the soft sand to Mujara.

de Chair decided to look for water, and with Glubb and Brook's advice he back-tracked along the tarmac road to the Kilo 40 signpost, and turned south into the desert along a track which descended sharply through a small gorge and opened up to a vast lake of dried asphalt. They found pools of sulphurous water at Abu Jir which would be useful for the radiators of the column's vehicles. After a welcome swim, they headed west until they reached an abandoned oil boring site at Awasil, and then went on to reach the Euphrates at Abu Tibir.

de Chair got back to Kilo 25 to see a lone Heinkel circling the camp and dropping bombs.

Later, as he was arranging for the RASC to send out light trucks to collect the water from Abu Jir in old petrol tins, one of the Legion's reconnaissance parties returned with the news that they had discovered a route through to Habbaniya. Although it required a long detour, the whole column could follow the route in single file.

Kingstone and Glubb had gone on by car from Mujara to Habbaniya, and were flown back in a Blenheim, which landed near Kilo 25 a few minutes before 20.00, just as the light was fading. In that night's conference Kingstone announced that the next day the column would strike out for Mujara and Habbaniya.

Baghdad

From the Embassy they saw the two Messerschmitts fall over Raschid in the early morning, and at noon heard over their clandestine radio from a BBC news broadcast that the Vichy French had by 'accident' allowed some thirty German aircraft to force-land in Syria. The former evoked no cries of joy, and the latter just helped to feed the despondency of the people interned in the Embassy.

Freya refused to share the feeling of gloom, and tried to remain positive. The daily list prepared for the Iraqi *Chef de Protocol* for the Embassy supplies always gave Freya a lift. This time it included ten tins of Brylcream, Kotex and mothballs – hardly the order of pessimists.

Nevertheless, everything in the Embassy was now strictly rationed.

Hammond's Bund, 18 May 1941

It was a tight fit in the four-door Ford Prefect. David Raziel sat up front with Capt Tim Arnold, SOE's man at Habbaniya. Raziel's second-in-command, Yaakov Meridor, sat squashed in the back with the two Iraqis, Yaakov Aharoni and Yaakov Harazi.

They had flown in to Habbaniya from Tel Nor in a Bombay transport before noon the day before. Arnold had arranged their overnight accommodation and meals away from prying eyes in one of the bungalows recently vacated by an Assyrian family who had been evacuated to Basra. He briefed them with a new objective to reflect changing circumstances. The mission was no longer about sabotaging the Iraqi Oil Company's 90-octane fuel tanks in Baghdad It was now about gathering intelligence on Iraqi troop dispositions – numbers, units and weapons – in and around Baghdad. The British were still outnumbered by the Iraqi Army by around twenty to one, and it was vital to know who, where and what they would be facing on their way to Baghdad.

Arnold purposely did not mention Raziel's arrangement with Collins, but ensured that the group was armed with pistols and hand grenades, as well as two limpet mines. Only Mirador knew Raziel's true identity, and that the primary target would be the Mufti.

Early on the 18th they had changed into Iraqi-made clothing which RAF Intelligence had acquired from some of the Iraqi employees on the base. Raziel and Mirador, who were Ashkenazi, dressed in suits and wore fezzes to pass as *Effendis*, while Aharoni and Harazi, who were both Hasidim, with more swarthy complexions, dressed in robes and *keffiyehs* like *fellaheen*.

They left Habbaniya at 13.00, reaching Hammond's Bund just after two. They had driven along the top of the Bund for a mile or so until they found a small rowing-boat. Arnold stopped the Prefect, and after Raziel had pronounced the boat 'river worthy' they had all followed him down the bank to the river.

The frail boat was too small to accommodate all four of Raziel's party and their weapons, so Mirador had rowed Aharoni and Harazi across first. He then turned the small boat around to return to pick up Raziel and the weapons.

Raziel and Arnold, who were standing at the water's edge, simultaneously heard the noise of an aircraft. The engine note changed, taking on a more urgent note as it began to drop lower and head directly towards them.

Hauptman Erich Vogel and his rear gunner, *Unteroffizier* Joachim Elmann, had been looking for British troops and vehicles across the Euphrates opposite Falluja. Vogel had found a small troop concentration which had looked tempting. As they flew lower they had been greeted by bursts of concentrated anti-aircraft fire from guns on plinths, as well as a truck mounting a 20 mm cannon. Vogel and Ellmann had no idea that they were on the receiving end of some Iraqi ordnance which Roberts had pressed into service. The wall of shells and bullets reaching up to the low-flying Bf 110 made Vogel quickly decide that finding easier prey was the most sensible course of action, and they had moved on.

'Erich, we have something at your 9.00 o'clock.' Normally Vogel would not have bothered with a single car and a few people. However, there was no flak, and this was a quick and easy kill. He banked to the east and swung around until he faced west, and then lined up with the Bund and eased the Bf 110 lower so that the nose-mounted package of two 20 mm cannon and four 7. 9 mm machine-guns were lined up with the target.

As Vogel closed on the target, he switched on the reflector gunsight mounted on top of the main instrument coaming. As the target began to fill the sight he saw two figures scrambling up the bank towards the car and into his field of fire. He flicked off the hinged cover and pressed the red gun button. Raziel and Arnold were, perhaps, ten feet below the Prefect, which was parked on top of the Bund. Vogel's fusillade of shells and bullets 'walked' up the bank from the water's edge, slammed into both men and continued up the bank to shred the car. As Mirador reached the shore and ran up the slope towards the two mangled bodies, Vogel had already gained height and turned east looking for more 'trade'

Mirador knelt over Raziel's shattered remains and began to cry over the body of a man whom he had admired and who had held so much promise, who had died so needlessly.

Kilo 25

A patrol led by Lt the Hon. Charles Wood carried out a daybreak reconnaissance towards Ramadi, and was fired upon but suffered no casualties. This was Kincol's first contact with the enemy on the ground.

Kingcol's reveille was at 07.00, and breakfast of tinned bully-beef and biscuits, all that was left of their dwindling food rations followed half an hour later. The column got on the move just before nine, after loading the vehicles and filling the radiators and petrol tanks.

They were now down to less than half a gallon of water per man per day, if you could call it water. Sometimes it was black and at other times purple; sometimes it had to be left for ten minutes until the sediment settled. Some of the water came all the way from Egypt.

First they would go south-west, away from Mujara , to bypass the soft sand before swinging west, pointing towards Mujara . There they would cross the wooden trestle bridge before turning north to drive into the RAF cantonment.

In the lead was Glubb in a Ford 8 cwt of the Arab Legion, which had reconnoiterd the route, followed by a Morris 15 cwt full of troopers of the Blues, with Kingstone's commandeered taxi bringing up the rear of the advance party. The heavy 3-ton Bedford trucks of the RASC moved off directly behind Kingstone, followed by the towed guns, while the fighting-troops brought up the rear. All vehicles were to follow directly in the tracks of the truck in front. If a vehicle broke down for any reason it was to be left where it stood, with those in the rear passing as close to it as possible.

The word had been passed from Kingstone that there would be no stopping, even for the twenty-minute water and rest halts. This was a race to get to Habbaniya. Yesterday's visit by a Heinkel meant that the *Luftwaffe* had Kingcol's rough location, and today's forty-mile-long column of vehicles in single file was a very big and tempting target. All the anti-aircraft plinths were to be manned, and everyone not driving had to keep his eyes peeled for aircraft.

While Kingcol was safe from the sand barrier on the new route, travelling in single file had quickly become uncomfortable. The heavy lead vehicles threw up great clouds of dusty sand, forcing those following to use sand-goggles, sun-glasses and even spectacles to see, and handkerchiefs and scarves over their faces to breathe. Worse still, the heavier RASC trucks and the towed 25-pounder guns had scored deep ruts into the hard, packed soil, which forced the troops following in their lighter trucks and buses to lurch from side to side and porpoise up and down, straining the chassis and destroying the springs.

Leutnant Kurt Eisenach leading a *Schwarm* of ZG76's Messerschmitts looking for Kingcol was frustrated. Eisenach was unaware of the soft sand that Kingcol had encountered, and of the waterlogged ground along the Euphrates. He had assumed, from the Heinkel pilot's debriefing, that Kingcol had moved due south from Ramadi along the Euphrates, as this was the quickest route to Habbaniya.

The *Schwarm* had cruised up and down the west bank of the Euphrates between Ramadi and the top of Lake Habbaniya several times. Fuel was getting low, and Eisenach was wary of getting into dogfights with the RAF's faster Hurricanes, or even the ageing Gladiators, which were much more manoeuvrable than the 110s.

As Eisenarch neared Ramadi on what was to be their final sweep before heading back to Mosul, a shout from the rear gunner in his wingman's aircraft changed the picture. 'A dust cloud at 11.00 o'clock', yelled *Obergreifreiter* Weber.

Eisenach could see a large cloud of dust in the far distance, some way to the west of Ramadi. He looked quickly at his instruments before making a decision. 'We have fuel for just one pass. Circle to the east to put the sun in their eyes, then drop down low and follow me in. Kai, I want you to fly top cover in case we attract any Hurricanes or Gladiators.'

Just after 09.15, as C Squadron of the Household Cavalry left Kilo 25 to form the rearguard of Kingcol, the three 110s of ZG76 came in low, at about fifty feet, out of the sun. They began to strafe the column with their cannon and machine-guns even before they were in range. C Squadron's troopers were caught by surprise, quickly sustaining four casualties and two destroyed Morris trucks.

Ancient Hotchkiss machine-guns, 1915-vintage Lewis guns and even troopers with Lee-Enfield rifles and officers with Webley .45 pistols from all along the column opened up on the *Schwarm*.

In a lone Arab Legion Chevrolet truck parked directly in the path of the attackers, two Legionnaires calmly stood their ground and brought their plinth-mounted Lewis gun unhurriedly to bear on Eisenbach. As the nose with its white upper coaming began to fill the sight, the gunner, Mutr Fuqaan, began to fire controlled bursts in text-book fashion at the oncoming lead aircraft. As Eisenbach, who had been firing contin-uously, lined up on this new threat he ran out of 20 mm shells and fired the last remaining rounds from his 7.9 mm machine-guns. Those few rounds were enough to kill Mutr Fuqaan and seriously wound his loader, Mibrad Mohamad, in the face when he bent down to pick up a new 47-round drum of .303 ammunition for the Lewis gun.

As the rest of the column ground on towards Mujara , Doc Arundel arrived with one of 166 Field Ambulance's vehicles. He dressed the wounds of the injured Legionnaire and Cavalry troopers and, together with the dead *bedou,* put them on stretchers and loaded them into the ambulance. The wall of fire from the ground was so intense that the other two Messerschmitts that had followed Eisenach down and had hit the column near its centre, wounding several men and disabling two trucks and a bus, broke off their attack.

There were no further attacks, and Kingcol rolled into Mujara just after 16.00 and crossed over the wooden bridge, beneath which raced the run-off from Lake Habbaniya, and turned north for the run into the cantonment.

'Well, isn't this a pretty sight. It looks as if the Cavalry toffs have had a hard day in the desert', said Sgt Alfred Humphreys of the King's Own, as Kingcol turned onto the tarmac road which his platoon was guarding.

Lance Corporal 'Stinky' Evans added, 'It's like something out of that film, *Beau Geste*, we saw at the NAAFI in Karachi a few months ago.'

Humphreys walked slowly down from the ridge into the road in front of the column and raised his arm for the lead vehicles to stop. To his right, behind him on the small ridge, a group of the King's Own with Lewis guns on tripods pointing their way, backed up by a pair of RAF armoured cars on his left, guarded the southern route into Habbaniya.

An immaculate Humphreys walked slowly over to the lead vehicle, the dust-covered taxi and its grimy occupants, looked at Kingstone and snapped off a prarade-ground salute. 'Good afternoon, sir. Our dispatch rider will take you about twenty miles up this road to your camp site by the lake. It's tarmac for another eight miles, then gravel desert for twelve miles to where you camp. Then it's another fifteen miles or so on tarmac road into the cantonment.'

'Stinky' Evans, riding the BSA they used for dispatch duty, drove down the slope from the ridge, and with a rather dramatic flourish of his arm to Kingcol rode off down the road.

Humphreys saluted, then walked back up the ridge to get out of the dust while Kingcol began to file past. The men of the King's Own showed mild interest as the long column snaked past their ridge, but there was no waving or shouting. An hour later Kingcol reached its bivouac area on the shores of the lake near to the Airways Rest House, and began to form up in their defensive positions. The rough undulating gravel gave way to soft sand in some areas of the camp, and the RASC was again busy digging out their 3-ton trucks.

After the tribulations of the desert, and particularly the lack of water for washing, everyone found the bathing offered by the lake a great relief.

While the rest of the column seemed to be intent on getting into the water, Kingstone and de Chair met briefly before they each took their staff cars and set out for Habbaniya – Kingstone to talk to Roberts, and de Chair to meet with RAF Intelligence.

'The King's Own certainly did not shown any reverence at our achievement in crossing the desert to get to them. It's almost as if we are spare grooms at a wedding', said a slightly miffed de Chair.

'Somerset, you need to be more charitable. No one came to their aid, and their 1,500 or so men had to beat back over 9,000 Iraqis, which is a tremendous military feat. They have held out for another twelve days without any support. We just look like tourists to these men. So when you are in Habbaniya say little. Remember, our job is to take Baghdad, not to talk about yesterday's battle.'

Habbaniya

Arriving at the Air Headquarters block, Kingstone was shown upstairs to the large conference room. He was surprised to find George Clark, the Habforce commander, and John D'Albiac, Smart's replacement, who had flown in earlier that day, as well as a room full of Army and RAF officers.

'Hello, Joe, good to see you. You are just in time for our final planning meeting for the attack on Falluja in the morning. I'll introduce you around while we organize a beer for you. Sandwiches, I am afraid, are out of the question. Everyone here is on hard rations.'

The introductions made, and a bottle of beer on the table in front of Kingstone, Clark gestured for Roberts to begin.

'Falluja occupies a strategic position. It is on the Euphrates midway between Habbaniya and Baghdad, and home to the only bridge across the river for fifty miles in either direction. Complicating any operation against Falluja is the fact that the Iraqis have flooded the approaches to the town, limiting our approach to a single causeway. They have breached the banks of the Euphrates and they have opened the regulator of the Saqlawiya Canal, flooding the ground to their north. We have no landing craft, specialized equipment or heavy artillery support, nevertheless our job is to secure the bridge before the Iraqis blow it up and isolate us. Securing the bridge intact is vital. Falluja is less than thirty miles from Baghdad, and with the bridge in our hands we can dictate the course of events. The objective of this operation is to cut off, isolate and bombard Falluja into submission.

'Phase One will be a massive air raid on the town by Bill Savile's Air Striking Force. This is timed to start at dawn. We will call up dive-bombing attacks on specific targets as and when necessary.

'Phase Two covers the land operations. Also at daybreak, Reese, with V Column, will be air-landed with C Company of the King's Own, a machine-gun section and two Boys rifles here,' he gestured at the large wall map, 'about two miles north of Falluja. Reese will take up position covering the Falluja–Baghdad road to prevent Iraqi troops from leaving Falluja, as well as stop any forces sent from Baghdad to relieve the town.

'Tonight, A Column, under Anderson, will cross the Sin el Dhibban ferry. His company of Levies with a detachment of Sappers and Miners will capture the Police Post and the Regulator Bridge a mile west of Saqlawiya. Anderson will then move south to the high ground just north of Falluja. Going across the ferry after Anderson will be Strickland with a detachment of the 2/4 Gurka Rifles plus four of Habbaniya's captured 3.7-inch howitzers. This is S Column. Strickland's job is to protect the rear and flanks of A Column. Following on Strickland's heels will be L Column under Hilliard, with an Armoured Car section, a platoon of the King's Own, some Sappers and Miners and a lorry-borne raft. They will strike north and then west, and put a ferry across the Notch Fall Regulator.

'Graham with G Column, consisting of a platoon of Levies, six of Joe Kingstone's 25-pounders and some Sappers and Miners, are to get in front of the bridge and then take it.'

Clark, well pleased with the plan, wanted to control the operation himself, using the argument that he was now the senior land officer. But Roberts had devised the plan, had fought with most of the participants during the Habbaniya crisis and had their loyalty and infected them with his enthusiasm. Clark eventually, and wisely, relented and agreed that Roberts could continue without interference.

After the meeting over another beer, Clark got Kingstone to bring him up to date with Kingcol's dash across the desert. Just before he left, Kingstone asked Clark what he thought of Roberts.

'Although he is forceful and intolerant of inefficiency, everyone who has fought with him – The King's Own, the Levies and the RAF armoured cars – will follow him anywhere. The other thing is that he is unfailingly confident, and those under his command say that they always seem to get a laugh out of him, even under the worst conditions.'

'Not a bad man to have around', mused Kingstone.

However, D'Albiac was extremely unhappy with Roberts's plan, which involved integrated air-land operations. D'Albiac believed, as did many senior RAF officers, that the services were designed to operate independently, and Roberts's plan set a very dangerous precedent. D'Albiac had not been present during the early days of the Habbaniya siege, and was unaware of the tremendous psychological effect of continuous heavy bombing, backed up by aggressive ground action, which enabled a far smaller force to prevail. Combined Operations, which were to become the norm in the Western Desert within eighteen months, was still in its infancy in early 1941. While Roberts had seen the opportunity and witnessed the result, D'Albiac was furious that Army commanders could call on his resources seemingly at will, deflecting them away from what he believed was the RAF's real job –

defeating the *Luftwaffe*. Although D'Albiac did not fight Roberts's plan, he made sure that Tedder in Cairo was aware of his misgivings.

While Kingcol bivouacked at the lake, the Levies, the King's Own and the Gurkhas began to move out of Habbaniya to take up their positions for the attack on Felluja the following day. Leaving at 17.00, it took some two and a half hours to get A, S and L Columns across the Euphrates on the Sin el Dhibban ferry with their mules, armoured cars and captured Iraqi artillery and a few trucks.

At 19.00 G Column under Alistair Graham left Habbaniya to set up positions on a bluff overlooking Canal Turn, while Advanced Brigade and Battalion Headquarters were set up in a well-camouflaged position in direct contact with both companies of the Levies and with Habbaniya. However, this took all night, as the Levies had first to cross the gap blown in Hammond's Bund by the Iraqis, using a combination of rafts and sailing-boats manhandled from the RAF Yacht Club on Lake Habbaniya to the river.

Only half of the Levy column arrived, and Graham had to return and extricate the remaining vehicles, which had been driven into the ditch in the darkness. The river crossing was made in absolute silence. Despite several water-logged boats, the Levies managed to get all their weapons and ammunition across the flooded ground and onto dry land. Only two incidents marred the crossing. One was a Gunner officer and his signaller who upset their boat when trying to lay a cable across the breach in Hammond's Bund, and had to be saved from drowning. The other was the ten mules who lived up to their reputation: having gone halfway across the water they panicked and returned to the shore, despite furious efforts by their handlers to stop them.

Shortly before dawn the whole company was in position at Palm Grove, overlooking Falluja, which lay some two thousand yards to the east.

Chapter Five

The Road to Baghdad

Falluja, 19 May 1941

From first light, the Air Striking Force began to soften up Falluja, some fifteen miles east of Habbaniya, with a fifty-seven-aircraft strike against Iraqi ground forces in the town. This time 4 Service Flying Training School's Audaxes, Gordons and Oxfords were supplemented by the heavier bomb-loads of 84 and 203 Squadrons' Blenheims.

Simultaneously Lt David Reese's C Company of the King's Own was flown in four of the Habbaniya Communications Flight's ancient Valentias, and landed two miles to the north-east of Falluja to cut the Baghdad–Falluja road. The airborne operation went well, with each aircraft remaining on the ground for less than sixty seconds, speaking well for Reese, who had drilled his company assiduously in getting themselves, weapons and equipment out of the Valentias in the minimum possible time.

To prevent the Iraqis summoning reinforcements, the Air Striking Force had been tasked to cut the telephone lines from Falluja. There were two telephone lines. One, with a few wires which led across the cultivated ground, was easily destroyed by an Audax that flew backwards and forwards just above the ground between the telephone poles for about a mile, using its propeller blades to cut the wire. The other telephone line, with a large number of wires, ran across the desert behind Falluja. There were too many wires to use the propeller, and the Audaxes had little success in bombing the poles.

A frustrated pilot officer, Martin Bennett, flew back to Habbaniya. While his Audax was being rearmed and refuelled, he walked over to the workshop at the back of Hangar Two and borrowed a pair of metal shears and an axe. Bennett flew the Audax back to the line of telephone poles which snaked from Falluja towards Baghdad, landed and taxied in between two of the poles. While his gunner gave him covering fire, Bennett calmly stood up on the main plane and cut the telephone wires with the pair of metal shears. To make certain the Iraqis could not repair their landline communications, he then took an axe and unhurriedly cut the telegraph poles on either side of the Audax before returning to the plane to take off and fly back to Habbaniya.

However, Falluja was holding out, and Clark began to worry. By mid-morning he started to pester Roberts to throw more troops into the battle. Roberts steadfastly resisted, as he wanted at all costs to avoid a pitched house-to-house battle with his limited number of troops and the large number of unnecessary casualties that he would take.

Following a lull, Roberts ordered an intensive dive-bombing attack concentrated on the eastern edge of the bridge just before three in the afternoon. After the ten-minute air strike, the same area was subjected to a thirty-five-minute bombardment by Kingcol's 25-pounder guns which had been manhandled across Hammond's Bund the previous night.

Crouched in a filthy ditch fifty feet from the western edge of the bridge, Capt Alistair Graham scanned the eastern edge of the bridge through his binoculars. Fires from the bombing were burning all over the town, and a pall of grey smoke drifted across the face of the buildings opposite, obscuring them and the far end of the bridge.

Graham turned to his Levy lieutenants, RAB100 Baijan Peeku and Khamsi Lazar Oshana: 'If we can't see them, they can't see us. We will use the armoured cars as shields and rush the bridge as they give us covering fire. Pass the word to fix bayonets, and after the count of three follow me. One, Two, Three . . . '

As Graham pounded across the bridge with the Levies at his heels and Iraqi bullets buzzing past his head, the other end of the 177-foot bridge seemed an awfully long way away. When the Levies reached the end of the bridge they were met by a party of Iraqis with a white flag, who surrendered the whole of the Iraqi force in Falluja.

The bridge had been captured without incurring a single casualty, and a large quantity of rifles, machine-guns and ammunition which had been abandoned by the Iraqis was shared out among the Levies and the King's Own. After establishing a bridgehead, the Levies were reinforced by Capt Cottingham, who brought two mortars and a machine-gun section. A little later they were all amused to see Alastair Brawn riding into view on a large white mule which he had used to cross the water.

By 17.00 the town was secure. Although the three northern columns, A, S and L, took no part in the fighting due to numerous delays and difficulties in crossing canals, Roberts's plan had worked well beyond everyone's expectations. The softening-up process, with 134 sorties dropping over ten tons of bombs, had so demoralized the Iraqis that three hundred prisoners, including twenty-seven officers, were captured with a remarkable lack of British casualties.

Col Everett of the King's Own arrived with D Company from Mujara to take command, and the air-landed troops of C Company to the north moved into the town to take up defensive positions, while a Levy platoon under Capt Armstrong returned to Habbaniya with the Iraqi prisoners.

Falluja was badly damaged. There was no water or power and no glass in the windows. Most of the inhabitants had fled, and those who remained were formed into burial-parties and working-parties to help to clean up the town. The intense heat, mosquito infestation and a lack of mosquito nets, coupled with battle rations and continuing offensive actions against pockets of local resistance, made life difficult for the King's Own.

Mosul

Cutting the telephone wires had prevented any news of the battle reaching Baghdad, and it was not until early evening that an Iraqi captain managed to phone the Citadel with the news from Khan Nuqta.

Junck, who had already been forewarned of the Iraqi defeat at Falluja by Kohlhaas, was more than ready for Grobba's call later that evening.

'Junck, where was the *Luftwaffe*? The Iraqis have sustained a major set-back around Falluja and they need immediate support.'

'Get one thing straight, Grobba. At our meeting with the Iraqis I told you that you must keep me informed of the Iraqis' military plans. This you have conspicuously failed to do, and Falluja is the result of your lack of communication. We have no radio messages in our log from you about the Iraqi attack on Falluja, and I am not a mind reader. Let us finish with arguing who is at fault and get down to how we can help them. I will have my fighters and bombers all over Falluja and Habbaniya tomorrow from daybreak. While we take on the British in the air and on the ground, you have the Iraqis mount a counter-attack. We must resecure that bridge at all costs, as it is the only way to and from Habbaniya and Baghdad. Whoever controls that bridge controls the outcome of the revolt. Remember, I am counting on you to convince Rashid Ali and the Colonels that they must give this counter-attack all they have.'

With that, Junck switched off the radio before a stunned Grobba could reply, and got back to the serious business of planning his operations for the following day. Truth be told, Junck was a very worried commander. Not only had he begun to take significant losses from enemy action and suffer from a lack of spare parts, but he had received a signal from Athens, warning of the recall of all his transports.

Operation *Merkur*, Student's airborne invasion of Crete, was to begin the next day, and Student had commandeered all transport aircraft in the region.

Baghdad

News reaching the Embassy indicates that no one really knows what is happening here, mused Freya. The water supply was turned off, and although it was said to be so throughout Baghdad, Freya thought that it might be just a ruse to pressure the Embassy. She made sure that the *cawasses* were fed, although she began to worry that with the war growing closer to Baghdad they might soon run out of food. There was still no answer from the Iraqi government to their protests that the *cawasses* were being threatened with death.

Although Rashid Ali had gone to von Blomberg's funeral, there was still no official admission by the Iraqis of the presence of Germans in Iraq.

Falluja, 20 May 1941

Just after first light, three Gladiators of A Flight encountered a Messerschmitt ground-attacking British troops around Falluja, and drove it off. A little later, two Hurricanes on patrol west of Ramadi chased away four 110s, trying to sneak into Habbaniya from the west. Both engagements resulted in no wins or losses for either side.

Flt Sgt Smith was a lucky man. He was one of four Gladiators flying top cover over an Audax which had force-landed in the desert. The Gladiators were attacked by five 110s of *ZG76*. The Messerschmitts concentrated their fire on Smith's aircraft, and he only just managed to escape after his Gladiator had suffered severe damage. *Leutnant* Martin Drewes mistakenly claimed Smith as his first victory.

The Hurricanes scrambled seven more times that day. Two Hurricanes chased another 110 strafing troops around Falluja and Hammond's Bund. The latter attack almost killed Everett, RAB200 Yacob Khoshaba Aboona and Maj David Rose, who were machine-gunned by the 110, which wounded their driver in the head and riddled their car. Two other Hurricanes found a *Kette* of Heinkels of *KG4*. The Hurricanes all reported damaging their opponents

By the end of the day A and B Companies of the King's Own, who had been in or near Habbaniya, began to drift into Falluja in penny packets by launch, truck, swimming and walking. One of the immediate tasks should have been a thorough house-to-house search for hidden Iraqi soldiers, weapons and potential snipers. However, with the very small number of troops available, this was out of the question. It was not even possible to prevent refugees from returning to Falluja at night – some of whom were undoubtably Iraqi soldiers – a good many of whom were dressed as women wearing *abbas*.

Communications were tenuous. Everett had one radio, an ancient heliograph and a mirror.

Habbaniya

While the Hurricanes were away, the *Luftwaffe* played. Six 110s strafed Habbaniya, destroying a Blenheim of 84 Squadron, a DC-2 and two Valentias of 31 Squadron, and damaging two more Blenheims. They left several fires belching columns of black smoke and several dead and wounded in their wake

In the late afternoon six Blenheims with four Gladiators attacked Raschid air base, with two Hurricanes flying top cover, in a bid to destroy all the airfield's large hangars to deny the Germans their use.

Baghdad

The largest meeting room in the Citadel was on the ground floor. It was windowless and in the centre of the building to provide a cool, safe working environment. However, the notable chill in the air had nothing to do with the location of the room.

Ostensibly General Amin Zaki, the Chief of Staff of the Iraqi Army, presided over the meeting. However, Grobba's earlier stormy meeting with the General had set the tone of the conference. Grobba was incensed that the 3rd Infantry Brigade defending Falluja had failed to blow the bridge as planned. Privately he had told Zaki that if there was not an immediate Iraqi counter-attack the *Luftwaffe* would withdraw.

al Sabbagh, as C-in-C of Western Command, introduced Colonel Nur al Din Mahmud, Director of Military Operations at the Ministry of Defence, who was to present the plan.

'The best plan is a tried and tested plan. The British Military Mission devised a number of operational training plans for the Iraqi Army, which included a counter-attack. The last time we practised this plan was just over a year ago, and Colonel Yahin Hasan', he indicated an officer sitting to his right, 'commanded the exercise with the 6th Infantry Brigade. We have a tested plan, the officer commanding and the troops who have practised the exercise. Our best course of action is to use them as the blueprint for our counter-attack using the directing staff solutions.'

Observing the nods of assent from around the table, Mahmud passed the presentation over to Hasan, who at 35 was young to hold the rank of colonel.

Hasan described in detail the plan and his intention to support the attack with two light tanks and two mechanized machine-gun companies which would help to cover the attack, capture and demolish the bridge, and block the escape route of the British troops.

'When do you plan to attack?' asked Grobba.

'I plan to get into place tonight and begin the attack in the early hours of tomorrow morning.'

'So quickly and at night?' countered Zaki, more to show that he was still in charge of the meeting than concern for the operation.

'Yes. I want to catch the British off guard and give them little time to fortify Falluja. By daybreak we should be in possession of the town. This will limit the effectiveness of their bombers.'

With the blessing of the participants, Hasan left the meeting to prepare for the operation.

Habbaniya

An hour later, Clark held a meeting at D'Albiac's conference room at the Air Headquarters block to hammer out the plan for the advance on Baghdad.

In addition to Clark, the Army was represented by Kingstone, Ferguson and de Chair from Kingcol, Everett of the King's Own, Nichols of the Essexes, Strickland of the Gurkhas and Glubb Pasha.

With the arrival of Habforce, Roberts had relinquished command of Habbaniya ground forces. He had flown back to Shaiba late that afternoon to rejoin the 10th Indian Division as Chief of Staff to Maj Gen Bill Slim, who had replaced William Fraser.

The RAF contingent included D'Albiac, Savile, Hawtrey, Casey and Dudgeon, the Blenheim squadron commanders, Wightman of 94 Squadron and Pike of 203 Squadron, the two armoured-car commanders, Casano and Page and Brawn and Graham of the Levies.

The room was crowded. Clark sat on the conference table with his legs dangling, Kingstone and de Chair sat on the floor behind D'Albiac with their backs to the wall, while the rest of the participants sat at tables, on chairs and on the floor.

After some two hours of debate and discussion around Dudgeon's new photo-mosaic map, which covered the whole Falluja–Baghdad sector, Clark, supported by D'Albiac, summarized the strategy to take Baghdad. 'We are going to play a gigantic game of bluff. It worked at

Habbaniya and it worked at Falluja, and there is every reason to believe that we can pull it off again. However, everything depends on our maintaining our momentum, giving the Iraqis no time to recover and regroup. There are two things in our favour. The Iraqis clearly have no intelligence on our strength. We have to continue to convince them that we are the vanguard of many. The Iraqi Air Force has ceased to exist for all intents and purposes, and the *Luftwaffe* seems to be attacking sporadically. We can rely on the RAF to provide us with ground-attack support, which has proved to be a very effective weapon in softening-up the Iraqis, as well as protecting us from attack by the Germans. We are all agreed that we need two days to finish our preparations for the ground assault.

'We will split our force into two columns to form a pincer movement. On 25 May one column will leave Habbaniya and head north from Falluja and advance to the north to Khadimain to cut the road and rail link between Mosul and Baghdad. This is designed to stop the Iraqis from moving their 2nd Division down from Mosul and Kirkuk to reinforce their 1st, 5th, and what's left of their 3rd Divisions around Baghdad.

'The northern column under Andrew Ferguson will comprise A and B Squadrons of the Household Cavalry under Eion Merry and Eric Gooch, three armoured cars, one troop of 237 Battery's 25-pounder guns, a detachment of the Field Troop of Royal Engineers and one of the 166th's ambulances.

'The southern column leaving on the 26th will take the shorter, more direct, Falluja–Baghdad route under the command of Joe Kingstone. Joe will have C squadron of the Household Cavalry under Rupert Hardy, Steve May with A and D Companies of the Essexes, 237 Battery's 25-pounders less one troop, the anti-tank troop with their 2-pounder guns, three armoured cars and one of the 166th's ambulances. There will be around 700 men in each column.

'Supplementing Andrew's and Joe's troops will be Glubb's Legionnaires, who will run guerrilla operations in the Jezirah – the area between the Euphrates and the Tigris from Falluja to Mosul. The Legion will hamper the passage of reinforcements and ammunition, deny road access and generally create alarm and despondency. They will be tasked with riding around the countryside ahead and on the flanks of both columns, distributing *baksheesh* to the local headmen and sheikhs and advising them to keep out of the way of the mighty British force on its way from Habbaniya to Baghdad. This is designed to stop the tribes from harassing our columns, as well as getting the word through to Baghdad that the Iraqi Army faces impossible odds.

'I am afraid that the food situation is still critical, so you will be carrying seven days of hard rations and water for five days. Each column will be carrying enough petrol for 460 miles.'

'Anything to add, John?' Clark asked D'Albiac.

'Yes, George. The RAF will be flying fighter cover over both columns to keep the Germans and any stray Iraqis off your backs. The Air Striking Force will be kept ready bombed-up at Habbaniya to give you air support. Casey and his man with Ferguson will be able to call up support over their radios. Dudgeon will continue to fly reconnaissance missions so that you are kept in the picture.'

After they wound up the meeting, Clark sat across the desk from D'Albiac in Smart's old office, nursing a whisky. 'What are the odds of pulling this off, George?'

'To be truthful it's touch and go. The bulk of Habforce is tied up around Ramadi, engaged in fighting a very aggressive Iraqi brigade. We have some 1,450 lightly armed troops facing at least 30,000 heavily armed Iraqis supported by armour and artillery. The Iraqis have some good, fresh troops, some professional commanders, and their formations are largely intact. We have to pray that the Iraqis do not stand and fight or take the initiative and attack.'

'What happens if we cannot take Baghdad?'

'Then we have to wait until Slim's 10th Indian Division arrives from the south and the rest of Habforce from the west. Then it depends upon the Iraqis. We certainly do not want to have to take Baghdad house by house and street by street.'

'And the Embassy?'

'They will just have to take their chance', he shrugged.

'It's been a long journey from Jerusalem to Baghdad', remarked D'Albiac.

'It's only the last fifty-five miles that really count', replied Clark.

Baghdad

Shortly before midnight Hasan took the decision to postpone the counter-attack until the night of 21/22 May. He had encountered serious delays in getting fuel for his tanks and vehicles from Baghdad, and in fixing the ground navigation lights to guide his troops into position for the attack. Everything depended on a successful counter-attack, and Hasan decided to err on the side of caution.

Habbaniya, 21 May 1941

Out by the lake, Kingcol refitted, rearmed, refuelled and reprovisioned ready for its first combat. The advance Brigade headquarters was withdrawn from Falluja to Habbaniya, leaving a small force of Levies and King's Own to patrol the town.

Kingstone had the Household Cavalry supplement the Madras Miners and Sappers and the Royal Engineers shovelling earth and sand to plug the gap in Hammond's Bund in preparation for the movement of the two columns across the river.

In early afternoon D'Albiac held a strategy meeting with the Air Striking Force and the rest of his operational commanders. 'We have to eliminate the *Luftwaffe* as a threat. For the last seven days we have been conducting raids on Vichy airfields at Damascus, Mezzo, Palmyra and Kayak to choke off their supply route. While we have caught a number of their aircraft on the ground, we have also destroyed Vichy aircraft. We are not far off an invasion of Syria, but that is not our concern. Habbaniya's Order of Battle has changed substantially. A Squadron now consists of thirteen Gladiators and five Hurricanes. Together with B, C and D Squadrons of the Air Striking Wing, with its serviceable Audaxes, Gordons and Oxfords, and 84 and 203 squadrons, each with seven Blenheims, we now have a lot of firepower. The Germans are still striking at Habbaniya and destroying aircraft and killing people, and they continue to strafe our ground troops, and this has to stop. Without radar we have been forced to mount standing patrols, which are wearing out our pilots and aircraft. As the *Luftwaffe* is still getting through, the only thing we can do is to hit them hard where it hurts most – at their airfields. I have ordered a dusk strike at Raschid, and tomorrow morning I want reconnaissance over Mosul and their other airfields so that we can plan our strikes.'

At dusk the Air Striking Force with fourteen Audaxes, Four Gordons and nine Oxfords and four Blenheims of 84 Squadron, escorted by no fewer than thirteen Gladiators, mounted a large raid on Raschid and systematically destroyed the Iraqi Air Force base.

Falluja, 22 May 1941

The night of 21 and 22 May was extremely hot and there was no moon.
The 2nd Battalion of the 6th Infantry Brigade failed to reach its rendezvous, and Hasan, after waiting for a fruitless hour and a half, decided to attack at 02.30 with only the 1st Battalion.

Although alerted by the glare of trucks' headlights and a growing rumble from the direction of Baghdad, the defenders were still unprepared for the ferocious mortar barrage that preceded the fast and furious Iraqi assault on the southern and eastern defences. Simultaneously sniping broke out in the town itself

The British forces had been thinned out in preparation for the march on Baghdad, and only two companies of the King's Own and a platoon of Levies manned the town defences.

Lt Chris Hodgson of the King's Own, commanding the first outpost to be reached by the Iraqis, led a counter-attack with a haversack full of grenades, and was killed within minutes, and the outer defences were quickly overrun.

By three o'clock in the morning the Iraqis had penetrated the north-eastern edge of the town and forced C Company, which was suffering heavy casualties, to withdraw from their trenches into buildings astride the main street. David Reese and Lt Ben King were seriously wounded and CSM Maguire was killed. D Company felt the full force of the attack, and was overwhelmed and forced to fall back to the river bank towards the vital bridge, pursued by two of the FIAT light tanks. At the bridge, the Levy platoon's anti-tank gunner, Corporal Marcus Odisho, stood up and fired his Boys rifle from the shoulder, stopping one of the tanks at seventy-five yards and forcing the other to retreat. The rifle was not designed to be fired standing up from the shoulder, and the gunner was knocked flat on his back by the recoil, suffering heavy bruising.

The Iraqis were now very close to the eastern edge of Falluja, and the situation was becoming serious. Graham counter-attacked with one platoon from the bridgehead. One of the platoon commanders, RAB100 Baijan Peeku, led the attack, coming under heavy and he and half of his platoon became casualties, although they did succeed in driving back the Iraqis.

Kingstone received an urgent order from Clark an hour later to go down to Falluja and take personal command of the battle.

At dawn Everett led a platoon of C Company with fixed bayonets against dug-in Iraqi positions, managing to push the Iraqis temporarily out of the town. They came under heavy sniper fire that wounded several men, including Everett, who continued to direct the King's Own from a stretcher.

A new Iraqi attack was mounted at the south-eastern outskirts of the town with infantry and two additional tanks against a heavily outnumbered C Company, which was holding on by the skin of its teeth.

Just after nine Kingstone arrived and found himself in the middle of a ferocious battle with hand-to-hand, house-to-house combat, with an outnumbered King's Own and Levies, who were running out of both ammunition and water, and facing the arrival of fresh enemy troops in the form of the 2nd Battalion of the Iraqi 6th Infantry Brigade.

Miraculously the sole radio still worked. Kingstone first called for reinforcements from Kingcol, and C Squadron of the Household Cavalry and A and D Companies of the 1st Essex camped at Lake Habbaniya left for Falluja. The second call was to Savile to get the Air Striking Force into the air to ground-attack both the Iraqi reinforcements and the enemy strongpoints in Falluja.

Hammond's Bund was still breached, and the reinforcements, having arrived in trucks, had to dismount, strip and wade the six hundred yards across the bund, piling their arms, ammunition and clothing, and those who could not swim, on top of rafts of old oil drums and planks made up by the Madras Sappers.

In parties of ten to fifteen, it took over two hours to get C Squadron of the Household Cavalry and the 1st Essexes across. They then had to hump their equipment, including their heavy Boys anti-tank rifles, their Hotchkiss machine-guns and their rifles and ammunition, another seven miles on foot into Falluja, wading through floodwaters, sometimes chest deep, holding their arms and ammunition over their heads. Capt Morgan Jones of the Cavalry moved up and down the column with words of encouragement, and relieved men of their loads.

A troop of 25-pounders from 237 Battery arrived at the bund and began shelling the Iraqi positions from across the river to give support to the King's Own and the Levies fighting in Falluja.

The reinforcements were thrown into the battle as soon as they arrived. Sniping had become a problem, and the British were taking heavy casualties. The Iraqis developed a habit of wearing *gallabeahs* over their uniforms, making it difficult to distinguish soldiers from civilians, which resulted in a number of ambushes. Kingstone called in the mayor and told him to get the entire population of the town into the Mosque within half an hour. Any civilian seen outside would then be shot. This had a major impact in reducing the level of civilian involvement in the battle.

Despite the additional reinforcements, retaking the town was a long and difficult job, as the Iraqis had dug themselves into trenches and had placed machine-guns on the flat roof-tops commanding the main streets and their approaches.

A Company, under Maj Robert James, was ordered into the attack. A platoon under Lt Terry Muirhead was sent to clear the right-hand side of the main road, and a further platoon was ordered to contain the

Iraqis south of the main road, while the remaining platoon was to guard Iraqi prisoners, conduct anti-sniping patrols and keep the road clear for the evacuation of British wounded and for replenishment of ammunition.

Muirhead soon ran into trouble at the eastern end of Falluja from strong Iraqi fire from trenches and two houses on the north side of the main road, where machine-guns had been placed on flat roof-tops giving an excellent field of fire. James, using his last remaining reserves, his company headquarters platoon, had to destroy the Iraqi machine-gun positions to get to Muirhead. Leading the platoon across the main road under heavy fire, James moved them into an alley leading towards the machine-guns. However, progress was slow as they had to clear each house as they went forward. About fifty yards short of their objective, a light machine-gun opened fire from a window in the alley, severely wounding Private Sibbold. After firing back into the window, the platoon took cover in the house opposite, only to find it full of Iraqi soldiers, but after some fierce hand-to-hand combat they managed to clear the premises. From the roof of the house they engaged the Iraqi machine-guns that were pinning Muirhead down with sustained rifle fire, until the Iraqis retreated, leaving their dead and wounded. After they had poured more fire into the windows of houses occupied by the Iraqis, a white flag was put out of one of the windows and the whole Iraqi force in those houses surrendered.

With daylight the Air Striking Force mounted fifty-six sorties over Falluja, supporting the Army. They found and attacked an Iraqi convoy of some forty vehicles in the open on its way to Falluja, and damaged over twenty. One of the trucks, loaded with gun cotton to demolish the bridge, exploded in a spectacular fireball after a direct hit from an Oxford. RAB100 Peeku returned to the fray with six recently recruited Levies, and captured a Bren gun after a fire-fight with some Iraqis. Setting up in a house, they engaged a large group of Iraqi soldiers and their vehicles. Peeku continued firing the Bren gun until it became too hot to continue. After borrowing a replacement barrel from the King's Own, and supported by a Levy mortar section, Peeku took more than a hundred Iraqi prisoners. The wounded Peeku was awarded the Military Cross for his bravery at Falluja.

An Audax, piloted by Flg Off Dremas of the Royal Hellenic Air Force, was shot down but managed to land between the Iraqi and British positions. His air gunner, AC Peter Pike, dismounted his Lewis gun, and with two drums of ammunition the pair fought their way back to the British lines. Several Levies joined them, and together they made their way back to the rear under fire from snipers. Dremas spoke no

English, so Pike took charge of the party, which now included a number of Levies wounded by snipers.

Two Audaxes on reconnaissance were intercepted and attacked by Iraqi Nisrs, but, although badly damaged, were able to glide down and land. The two pilots and one gunner left the dead gunner and managed to get clear of the aircraft before they were strafed and destroyed on the ground. They were befriended by a local sheikh, but while they were having coffee, an Iraqi policeman burst in and shot them out of hand, killing one pilot. The gunner feigned dead and was later taken to hospital. The other pilot was surrounded by Iraqi *fellahs* who were going to take him prisoner. However, someone in the crowd hit the pilot on the head with a wooden stave, killing him.

Following a prolonged house-to-house battle, the two Essex companies and the Levies finally managed to clear Falluja, and by six o'clock that evening all the Iraqis in the town had surrendered, been wounded or killed, or had fled.

The Iraqis had come very near to retaking Falluja and blowing the bridge, and only the tough defence, the rapid reinforcements and the Air Striking Force had averted a major disaster. Nevertheless, the British had suffered fifty casualties, including seventeen dead and twenty-nine wounded. All but three of the King's Own officers were either killed or wounded.

The Iraqi 6th Infantry Brigade suffered considerable casualties, including eleven officers and 237 men killed or wounded, and around one hundred taken prisoner.

The Iraqis had found that urban cover was an antidote to the striking power of the RAF. A number of Iraqi soldiers had changed their khaki uniforms for civilian clothes, and those caught were shot. As a precaution 1,300 civilians were expelled from Falluja to prevent further sniping.

Everett was evacuated to Habbaniya by launch and ambulance, and after an operation at the base hospital was flown to Shaiba later that day to await a hospital ship for India. Keith May of the Essexes was given temporary command of the King's Own in Falluja.

Mosul

In keeping with the strategy to attack the *Luftwaffe*'s bases, two hit-and-run raids were mounted on Mosul. Two long-range Hurricanes strafed the airfield, claiming two aircraft destroyed, but one, piloted by Flt Lt Sir Robert MacRobert, failed to return. At dusk Flg Off Lane-Sansome in a 203 Squadron Blenheim bombed the airfield in near-darkness, setting one aircraft on fire.

While two He 111s did attack Habbaniya, no support was given to the 6th Infantry Brigade at Falluja. Effective air support for the Iraqis at Falluja could well have turned the counter-attack into a success.

Habbaniya

Dudgeon had suggested that, in the absence of accurate maps, he would fly along the Falluja–Baghdad route and take a series of line-overlap photos of the road and up to a mile on either side. By drawing an arbitrary grid on the photo strip with numbers and letters it would suffice for the advance.

At 10,000 feet in an Oxford, necessary for the camera and lenses to give the correct footprint, Dudgeon began to fly dead straight and level for the next twenty-five minutes.

In a clear blue sky in a flimsy plywood aircraft painted bright 'trainer' yellow, with light being reflected off its curved Plexiglass windscreen and rear gun cupola, Dudgeon began to feel extremely visible and very vulnerable.

The one good thing was that Frankie was safe back at Habbaniya. With no Iraqi shelling to frighten the dog, Dudgeon had started to leave Frankie behind. However, the dachshund had become used to flying and was beginning to resent being taken off his 'flying duties'.

As soon as he was told by his observer that the last photo had been taken, Dudgeon rolled the Oxford onto its back and pulled the stick back to drag the nose into a near-vertical dive. At about 4,000 feet there was a tremendous explosion, which he initially thought was cannon fire, but he soon realized it was the implosion of the Plexiglass bomb aimer's nose-window, which had fragmented when the Oxford exceeded its design limits. Pulling out just above the desert, Dudgeon got back to Habbaniya as fast as he could.

Baghdad, 23 May 1941

With the failure of the Falluja counter-attack, the road to Baghdad was now wide open to the British. al Sabbagh lost no time in demanding that Zaki form a military council to arrange for the defence of the capital. The meeting was held in the early hours in the same window-less conference room in the Citadel that had served for planning the Falluja counter-attack. Instead of a chill, an air of despondency hung over the room, as many of the participants perceived that this was the final phase of the revolt.

al Sabbagh, as C-in-C Western Command, took charge of the pre-

parations for the defence of Baghdad. 'I have recalled Colonel Nur el
Din Mahmud from Basra, and he will oversee the construction of
our civil defences. We will form two defensive positions,' he indicated
on the large wall map, 'one in the north and one in the south. These
cover the only access routes to the city. From the west Lake Aqargouf
forms an effective barrier between our two positions.

'Our defences will be built in depth behind anti-tank ditches. I want
you', he gestured to the two leaders of the paramilitary *Futuwwah* and
the *Kataib al Shabab* youth movements, 'to mobilize the youth, the
workers and the religious organizations to start immediately digging
these ditches. They must be fifteen feet wide and six feet deep. In the
northern sector the ditch is to be four miles long, stretching from
the right bank of the Tigris north of Khadimain here,' he pointed to the
map, 'to the Aqargouf marshes. In the south the ditch is to be six miles
long, extending from where the Tigris bends, near al Dorah, to the
Aqargouf marshes. This needs to be started immediately, and you
should go now to put this into operation.'

After they had left, al Sabbagh turned to the remaining participants.
'Colonel Raghib, I want you to take your 9th Infantry Battalion, the 1st
and 9th Desert Artillery Brigades and the remnants of the Mechanized
Force to defend our northern sector. Colonel Jahid, take your 4th
Infantry Brigade, the reorganized 3rd Infantry Brigade under
Lieutenant-Colonel Bapo and Colonel Yamani's 5th Desert Artillery to
the southern sector.

'We will have a mobile reserve comprising the Cavalry Brigade and
Colonel Hasan's reorganized 6th Infantry Brigade. One of the Cavalry
regiments I want on the east bank of the Tigris, opposite Khadimain,
to prevent any move towards Baghdad from this direction. We have
little time and much to do. Please prepare your positions.'

Istanbulat

A detachment of the Arab Legion plus two RAF armoured cars and a
detachment of Royal Engineers were ferried across the Euphrates at Sin
El Dhibban and drove north to cut the Baghdad–Mosul railway at
Istanbulat, some six miles south of Samara.

Legion scouts found that the Iraqis were sending reinforcements and
ammunition to the Iraqi battalion holding up Habforce at Ramadi by
first going north up to Meshahida and then, a short distance north of
the station, turning west across the desert.

On their return from their successful raid, the Legion lay up on the
track to Ramadi for some time, and was able to ambush a party of

Iraqis, capturing two cars, a captain and six other ranks, and gaining some useful intelligence.

Rhodes

Eleven CR42 fighters of the *155 Squadriglia* of the *3 Gruppo*, accompanied by a Savoia Machetti SM 79 under the command of *Capitano* Francesco Sforza, landed at Gaddura a little after noon. Flying from Valona and Athens, they were on their way to Kirkuk via Aleppo to support the Iraqis.

Although the *Regia Aeronautica* had been ready for a number of days to send reinforcements, the Vichy French were extremely hostile to having the Italians land in Syria. It had finally taken a phone call from Ciano to Ribbentrop to put pressure on the Vichy French to help the Italians stage through Aleppo.

Berlin

Hitler finally gave in to Ribbentrop, agreeing that an operation in Iraq would tie down British forces, weakening their position on the Western front in Europe, and issued *Fuhrer* Directive 30:

> *The Arab liberation movement in the Middle East is our natural ally against England. In this connection, the rising in Iraq has special importance. It strengthens beyond the boundary of Iraq forces hostile to England in the Middle East, disrupts English communications and ties down English troops and shipping space at the expense of other theatres of war. I have therefore decided to advance developments in the Middle East by giving assistance to Iraq. Whether and how the English position between the Mediterranean and Persian Gulf, in connection with an offensive against the Suez Canal, shall later be definitely defeated is to be decided only after Barbarossa.*

While the Directive placed only limited tasks on the OKW and postponed a final decision on Middle East strategy, it did not curtail German activity. In a separate act, Hitler created *Sonderstab F* under *Luftwaffe General der Flieger* Hellmuth Felmy, based at Athens-Tatoi airport, to lead German support for Iraq.

Campaniya, 24 May 1941

British Intelligence had established that the Germans were supplying the Iraqis with weapons using the railway line from Aleppo to Mosul and decided to cut the link. Early in the morning a 216 Squadron Valentia, piloted by Flt Lt Bartlett flew in from Heliopolis in Egypt with Maj David Collins and picked up a party of Sappers and explosives at Habbaniya. The Valentia flew to a point in northern Syria and landed near Campaniya, where the Aleppo–Mosul line crossed a high viaduct. The Sappers, under the direction of Collins, placed charges and demolished the viaduct, cutting the railway line. As Bartlett swung the Valentia round to take off, a Vichy armoured car arrived. Although it fired at the plane, Bartlett got into the air and made a safe return to Habbaniya.

Habbaniya

The Iraqi Army's almost successful counter-attack had delayed the move on Baghdad and raised concern in Clark's mind about the adequacy of the force at his disposal, compared with the strength of the enemy.

He was further unnerved by a patrol action that day which underlined just how weak his forces really were. D Company of the Essexes sent out a fighting patrol from Falluja, and less than a mile away from the town had been vigorously attacked by a larger body of Iraqi troops. Although the Essexes did manage to inflict some casualties, the enemy was too strong and they were forced to withdraw.

Many Iraqi units were still intact, with their troops showing fight, and water obstacles and new anti-tank ditches had been revealed by air reconnaissance. The continued presence of the *Luftwaffe* and the continued heavy fighting between Habforce and the Iraqi 1st Infantry Brigade at Ramadi in his rear made Clark wonder privately if he had gone too far with too little.

Baghdad

The Mufti sat forward in his chair to emphasize to Gabrielli his dissatisfaction with the situation. 'In spite of the good prospects for a revolt in the rest of the Arab world, this is only of limited value if our uprising here in Iraq, which is the key to the whole situation, should fail. What worries me most is not so much the military situation but the political situation. There is no lack of pessimists, many of whom are endeavouring covertly and in the open to sabotage the efforts of myself and Rashid Ali. Even the cabinet includes some individuals who hold that if the Axis powers do not render immediate and substantial assistance it might be better to negotiate with the British. I believe that the next fourteen days will be decisive. If we are unable to last through this period it will be necessary to give in. The aircraft that have arrived were insufficient and we need more, as well as war matériel as proof of Axis solidarity.

'If Iraq should fall in the coming days, the anti-British movement throughout the Middle East would succumb to British arms or British gold and intrigues. I realize that you can cope with this, but it would then be necessary to reconquer each step you have lost by force of arms without being able to rely on Arab goodwill.'

Gabrielli signalled his conversation with the Mufti to Rome later that evening, causing Mussolini to call in the German Military Attaché to clarify whether the Axis should furnish effective or merely symbolic assistance.

Early in the evening the families of Rashid Ali and Naji Shawkat left Baghdad by train for Kirkuk.

25 May 1941

B Squadron of the Household Cavalry and two RAF armoured cars under Lt Gerard Leigh had moved into position west of Ramadi across the Ramadi–Falluja road late the previous evening to prevent Iraqi troops from escaping from RAF bombing.

Early that morning, over a hundred of Fawzi al Qawujki's truck-borne irregulars attacked the squadron. The two armoured cars became bogged down in the sand and had to be abandoned to the Iraqis when B Squadron was forced to withdraw in the face of overwhelming odds. One of the armoured cars was later recovered by a troop of A Squadron with an RAF tender under Lt Valerian Wellesley.

Three Heinkels raided Habbaniya using delayed-action bombs which cut water mains leading to the civil cantonment. This was followed by a strafing attack by five of *ZG76*'s 110s.

Three Blenheims of 84 Squadron bombed Mosul, while three more dropped leaflets on Iraqi troops to the north and west of Falluja.

The Miners and Sappers, aided by Iraqi prisoners, had finally realized the futility of trying to bridge the gap in Hammond's Bund with shovelfuls of earth and sand. Calmer heads had prevailed, and they eventually solved the problem of the seventy-five-yard gap in the bund by placing pontoons at either end and constructing a raft which could be pulled to back and forth between them with a wire hawser.

Aleppo

The *Regia Aeronautica*'s CR42 *Falco* fighters and the supporting SM 79 *Sparviero* rigged-out as a transport for the ground-crews arrived at Aleppo from Gaddura in the late afternoon, and prepared to overnight at the airfield before flying west out to Kirkuk via Mosul early the next morning.

Iraq, 26 May 1941

Two Blenheims, one piloted by Flg Off Lane-Sansome of 203 Squadron and the other flown by Flg Off Goudge of 84 Squadron, made a low-level strafing attack on Kirkuk airfield at dawn, but found no German aircraft on the ground.

In preparation for the assault on Baghdad, Dudgeon flew a photo-reconnaissance mission between Baghdad and Khan Nuqta, some seventeen miles east of Falluja, and then constructed a photo-mosaic map for use by de Chair.

The Arab Legion again sallied forth in the night to the north. Ten Legion trucks and a detachment of Royal Engineers set out from Habbaniya across the Sin el Dhibban ferry at dusk and headed north to Samarra to blow the railway lines. This time they encountered an Iraqi mechanized patrol in seven cars. In a short, sharp skirmish the Iraqis lost three killed, a large number of wounded and one taken prisoner. The British suffered no losses, and pursued the Iraqis to the banks of the Tigris.

Intelligence gained from the prisoners indicated that great consternation had been caused by the raid on Istanbulat, the Iraqis previously believing that the British forces were concentrated to the west of the Euphrates. The Iraqi patrol had been hastily formed to defend the sector, and was made up of a mixed Army and police force in two armed trucks and five civilian vehicles. The Iraqis seemed to have limited motor transport, relying on commandeered vehicles, which created a lot of ill will among the car owners.

Kirkuk, 27 May 1941

The *Regia Aeronautica* flew into Kirkuk in the late afternoon after a brief stop in Mosul, and began to prepare for immediate offensive operations. Fortuitously the Italians had landed half an hour after the departure of two 84 Squadron Blenheims which had bombed and strafed Kirkuk airfield.

North of Baghdad

Leaving at dusk, Ferguson's northern column crossed the Euphrates by the Sin el Dhibban ferry and, guided across the desert by the Arab Legion, circumvented floods, broken bridges and bunds, to arrive some six miles north of Baghdad by midnight, where they bivouacked for the night.

Much was made later of the fact that the Iraq defences guarding the city were not yet in place in the north and that Ferguson could have driven right into the centre of Baghdad unopposed and seized the city by surprise. However, it is difficult to see how Ferguson could have held a city of over 400,000 with just 700 men.

Falluja

At Hammond's Bund Kingstone and the southern column's vehicles and equipment began to arrive at dusk for the crossing. The 25-pounders and their ammunition limbers were the first to arrive. However, the guns had to be manhandled across, and the gun troop alone consumed three and a half hours. It had been decided to complete the crossings by 04.00 and disperse the vehicles which had not been able to get across, to avoid providing daylight targets for the *Luftwaffe*. All the supply lorries had to be driven away from the bridgehead and wait to cross the following evening.

Baghdad

When Gabrielli met Rashid Ali early that evening he found a very embittered man.

'I do not think that we can do anything to save the situation in Iraq. German aid has been rapid but meagre, and I fear that Iraq has been used as a pawn by a Germany that does not wish to commit herself wholeheartedly. I also expected more from Italy.'

Falluja, 28 May 1941

After reveille at three in the morning, followed by breakfast half an hour later, Kingstone's southern column loaded up to leave Falluja. It was chilly, and men everywhere were walking around in greatcoats, which they only discarded once the sun came up.

The armoured cars left first, followed by the trucks of C Squadron of the Household Cavalry, and then A and D Companies of the 1st Essex with the brigade support vehicles bringing up the rear. Although there was a metalled road marked by a line of telephone poles, the column spread out across a wide front to minimize targets in case of an air attack.

Twenty-five miles later, just after five o'clock, the southern column topped a rise and was confronted by the fort at Khan Nuqta, a large, square, cream-washed, plaster building. Air reconnaissance had shown a large number of one-man air raid shelters on both flanks of the fort, indicating the possibility that the column could be facing Iraqi strength of up to a battalion.

C Squadron dismounted from its trucks and worked its way around to the north of the fort. By seven in the morning the fort, together with an Iraqi battalion headquarters and around fifty prisoners, was captured. Interrogating the officers, they found that the Iraqis had dug wide trenches along the Baghdad road at irregular intervals; they had then opened the Abu Ghraib Regulator, flooding the road for about a mile; they were relying on these hidden obstacles to impede the column's advance. Armed with this information, 'Cheeky Chappie' the engineer and his men set to work to bridge the underwater trenches with ten-foot steel ramps.

Brigade Headquarters had moved a little way up the road to a set of low, white buildings set in a small grove of oleander trees, complete with a rudimentary garden. Rummaging around, de Chair discovered a working telephone switchboard which was still connected by circuit to the telephone system of the whole area. When the phone rang de Chair called over his driver and interpreter, Reading, a Christian Palestinian, to answer the call.

'Where have you been, I have been trying to raise you?' Reading told de Chair, covering the mouthpiece.

'Tell them that we are surrounded by the British: that they have tanks and that the tanks are already across the flooding.'

Reading duly spoke to the operator in an excited voice, causing consternation at the other end.

de Chair decided not to spread any more deception. Finding Kingstone, Maj Ian Spence, Kingstone's special liaison officer, Capt Dick Shuster, the signals officer, and Grant-Lawson, de Chair gave them the good news.

The rest of the morning was spent intercepting Iraqi messages.

The battalion commander of the 3rd Division came on the line to tell his headquarters that he had 'just escaped from Khan Nuqta with twelve men and I am hiding at Qasr Milh.' A patrol was ordered out by the 3rd Division Headquarters to report on the presence of British tanks, and later in the morning, with de Chair scarcely believing what he heard, it replied, 'The British have at least fifty tanks, and fifteen are already across the floods.' A distraught artillery officer came on the line crying that he was 'shelling the British and I am engaging a formation of five British tanks.' At this point a stern voice from Headquarters admonished him to 'Stand firm!' to which the agonized gunner replied, 'Can't you hear the firing?'

The battalion commander ejected from Khan Nuqta came back on the line asking for reinforcements to stabilize the retreat. 'I don't mind about Khan Nuqta, what about Baghdad if the British have tanks?'

'Don't worry about Baghdad,' came the Headquarters reply, 'we have dug a ditch around Baghdad that will stop any tank.'

Later the 3rd Division Headquarters and the 3rd Battalion at Khadimain asked where the two companies of the 1st Battalion requested to join the Brigade Colonel at Qasr Milh were.

'They started out all right,' came the reply, 'but when the British aircraft approached they dispersed to the villages.'

Around two o'clock in the afternoon the telephone line went dead.

The intercepted telephone messages had provided the southern column with an almost complete picture of the Iraqi order of battle in its sector. By mounting a highly effective deception operation with a non-existent British tank force it had compelled the Iraqis to retreat to their second line of defence on the Abu Ghraib Canal.

Later in the afternoon the column moved on, cautiously entering the water, which now covered the tarmac road, and carefully searching out the pair of steel ramps that Cheeky Chappie's men had laid, bridging each of the trenches.

The column passed through the water barrier, but on reaching a line of sand hills the leading troop came under heavy fire, two men were wounded and four trucks full of troops were stranded on a straight road with ditches on either side, taking fire. Unable to manoeuvre the trucks, Maj Rupert Hardy dismounted the troopers and advanced across open desert without cover. The three troops who carried out the action moved by section rushes under continuous long-range machine-gun fire, and eventually reached the sand hills. Using their Vickers guns, they forced the Iraqis to retreat to a small village. The column, with its exhausted men, ended the day scattered along a low ridge facing the Abu Ghraib Canal, some twelve miles from the centre of Baghdad.

Things had not gone as well for the northern column.

At first Ferguson advanced without incident to a railway crossing about three miles north of Taji station. The RAF armoured cars met enemy armoured cars and some light tanks near the station, but after an exchange of fire the Iraqis retired.

After a brief fire fight the northern column took Taji station and exchanged fire. When Ferguson was about 200 yards short of the station, the Iraqis stopped firing, and as the troopers rushed forward to the station four car-loads of Iraqi troops and police drew rapidly away from the back of the fort protecting the station, enabling the northern column to take Taji station without casualties.

However, the advance was held up three miles further on as they took heavy fire from a line of sand hills. When they turned south along the railway they began to encounter heavy shell and machine-gun fire from the village of Khadimain which killed Trooper Shone and wounded five other cavalrymen. Ordered to recover Shone's body, Valerian Wellesley's troop was pinned down by accurate Iraqi fire, and Wellesley ordered Corporal of Horse Maxted to lead the fall-back. Maxted, all six foot three, stood up, brushed the sand off his uniform and marched erect with his rifle at the short tail across a hundred yards of open desert to the safety of a ridge while bullets kicked up the sand around him.

Fearful of an attack from the rear, the Arab Legion provided a protective screen against reinforcements from Mosul which could pin the northern column into the narrow strip of land between the Aqargouf marshes and the Tigris.

The Arab Legion had fared well, cutting the railway track and the telephone lines on both sides of Meshahida station. The massive two-storey loop-holed fort protecting the station was garrisoned by around thirty Iraqi soldiers and eight police. Although the Iraqis were armed with Vickers machine-guns and put down heavy fire, the Legion suffered no casualties. During the evening a Legion patrol north of Taji station wounded and captured the Mutasserif of Baghdad, Jellal Beg Khalid, who had been on a visit to Samarra. He confirmed that the advance of the northern column via Meshahida was a complete surprise, as all the defences had focused on the British advance on Baghdad from Falluja.

As darkness fell Ferguson decided to bivouac in a square leaguer with fighting patrols out in front throughout the night. A very tired and weary northern column slept in its trucks.

The intensity of fire from Khadimain made Ferguson think that his column might be facing a full Iraqi brigade. He began to wonder if it would be possible, even with all the luck in the world, for his few trucks of cavalry troopers, a machine-gun troop and three 25-pounders to break through the strong enemy position and take Baghdad. Adding to his problem was the arrival of a regiment of Iraqi cavalry on the east bank of the Tigris opposite Taji. Desultory bursts of fire were exchanged across the river throughout the afternoon between the Iraqis and a picket of the Arab Legion on the west bank.

Despite the progress of the southern column, there were still strong pockets of Iraqi resistance to the north and east of Falluja, and consolidating the British position against continuous sniping and skirmish and an extremely mobile enemy, more 'hide and seek' than regular combat, was proving to be very difficult.

Two platoons of the Essexes, together with a Levy machine-gun section under Keith May, fought a major engagement against an entrenched Iraqi force with well-protected flanks which held an oasis by the Abu Ghraib Regulator. The objective was to close the regulator and control the floodwater over the Baghdad road. A heavy air attack and a barrage from a 25-pounder section failed to shift the well-dug-in Iraqis. The British attack was countered by heavy machine-gun and artillery fire from Iraqi reinforcements, which caused a number of British casualties. A second British attack, led by Major Kelly, tried a limited advance under cover of an artillery barrage, hoping that the Iraqis would retreat. But the Iraqis, reinforced by additional machine-guns and light artillery, caused a number of British casualties, including Kelly, who was seriously wounded. During the evening the Essexes and the Levies withdrew.

Mosul

Junck surveyed the battered airfield and the hulks of his aircraft dotted around the perimeter. The crew chiefs had done a magnificent job in keeping his command airworthy. But there was a limit to how much you can cannibalize damaged aircraft to keep others in the air. The lack of spare parts and supplies, the hostile climate, poor-quality fuel and lubricants, together with the relentless British air raids on his base, meant that there was now little left to fight with.

Sonderkommando Junck was reduced to just two Heinkel bombers and four 50 kg bombs and one Ju 52/3m transport. Junck had lost fourteen Messerchmitt 110s and five Heinkel 111s – an unacceptable loss rate of 95%. Junck had reluctantly signalled Felmy at Athens-Tatoi that his command was no longer operational, and requested immediate air evacuation.

Junck also managed to reach Harry Rother, and asked him to fly in to Mosul at daybreak the next day with the two Junkers 90s and the two Junkers 52/3ms which were sitting on the ground at Aleppo, to pick up the rest of the ground-crews, the *Flak* section and his command group.

He then called a meeting with the flying and ground officers under his command in the only part of the administration building still intact.

The tired and lined faces, mostly sporting beards, looked back at him in their stained and dirty mix of tropical and European summer uniforms. They showed both the immense strain that *Sonderkommando Junck* had been forced to operate under and the poor way in which they had been equipped and supported.

'The situation is as follows. We only have three operational aircraft and virtually no supplies. There are vague promises to send reinforcements, but Student's operation in Crete has taken precedence. I have no choice but to evacuate to avoid our capture. The situation is no reflection on your efforts. You have all performed above and beyond the call of duty under the most difficult of circumstances, and I have been privileged to serve with you. I want you to convey that message to your men. I have notified Berlin and Athens, and I have asked Rother, who is in Aleppo, to get here at first light to help ship us out.

'Miki [to *Hauptmann* Michael Hull, his Administrative Officer], I want you to have the ground-crews rip out the radio station in our remaining *Tante Ju*. We will need this to get our people out of here. We also need to strip the two Heinkels of all non-essential equipment as these are also needed as transports. We have little fuel. You will have to get the ground-crews to drain the tanks of all the damaged aircraft so that we have enough aviation spirit in our three flyable aircraft to get us to Aleppo.

'Finally, you and your men will take only what you can wear. Everything else, including our equipment and all papers, are to be burnt before dawn so that we can evacuate as quickly as possible.'

In late afternoon the third and final shipment of arms and ammunition from Syria arrived in Mosul. Like the second shipment of 26 May, this delivery had been delayed by the destruction of the viaduct outside Tel Kotchek. This had necessitated laboriously unloading the equipment and munitions onto a motley collection of trucks and then driving them across the border to be reloaded onto trains bound for Mosul. Both shipments joined the first delivery in warehouses in Mosul and remained there throughout the conflict.

Baghdad

The Supreme Defence Council met in the windowless, chilly, conference room in the Citadel which was now becoming depressingly familiar to many of the participants.

In addition to the *Golden Square* – al Shabbagh, Salman, Said and Shabib – and senior military figures like Zaki, they were joined by the replacement Regent, Sharif Sharaf. The Mufti, Rashid Ali, also attended, with the Minister of Defence Naji Shawkat, the Finance Minister Naji al Suwaidi and three other cabinet ministers –Yunis Sabawi, Ali Mahmud and Musa Shabandar.

A downcast al Sabbagh took the floor. 'Following the failure of the siege of Habbaniya and the collapse of the Falluja front, our situation is very grave. The Army is rapidly running out of ammunition. The number of British troops facing us is growing by the hour. They are being reinforced by air and by ground from Palestine, and their Army has finally broken out of Basra and is moving north to support their tanks facing Baghdad. They have also enlisted the help of the Arab Legion, and the Jordanians are in Iraq in force.'

'What about the Germans?' asked Shawkat.

'They sent a small, inadequate air force which has now largely been destroyed by the British. The British have also attacked them in Syria, cutting off the German lifeline. The Germans have begun a major operation in Crete and have no more planes to share with us.'

'What happened to the arms that they sent to Mosul from Syria?' asked the replacement Regent, Sharif Sharaf.

'Those arms were French. Their equipment and even their calibres are different from those of the British arms that we use. Their ammunition does not fit our weapons and we have no time to train our soldiers to use different types of weapons.'

'And the Italians?' questioned Said.

'Fewer than twenty planes arrived in Kirkuk in the last few days. Too little, too late.'

'What do you suggest?' the Mufti asked.

'I propose that we withdraw to Kirkuk and establish a new front, using the Diyalah river as a defence line. By withdrawing we can make Baghdad an open city and save the capital from destruction. Kirkuk not only offers us a number of natural defence lines but from there we control Iraq's oil and we can move easily into Turkey and Persia, both neutral, as is necessary.'

'How is Baghdad to be administered?' Yunis Sabawi enquired.

'A Committee for Internal Security is to be formed, consisting of the Mayor of Baghdad, the Director-General of Police and some Army officers who will remain', replied al Sabbagh.

The proposals were endorsed by the replacement Regent, the Defence Council, the military leaders and the cabinet, who lost little time in leaving the meeting to prepare for the move to Kirkuk.

Later that evening Rashid Ali met Suwaidi and Zaki, and they agreed to move the Treasury to Kirkuk in an armed police vehicle, accompanied by the Finance Minister and the Chief-of-Staff.

Grobba had fallen victim to the rumours that were now flying around Baghdad concerning the vast strength of the British forces and their imminent capture of Baghdad. In his daily radio message to *the Auswartiges Amt*, Grobba reported that the British forces were now only a few miles from Baghdad with more than a hundred tanks. He also added, maliciously, that the air support had been completely mishandled by Junck, who had provided almost no support for the Iraqi Army and had been virtually destroyed by a poorly armed British Air Force flying biplanes. *Sonderkommando Junck*, which now had only two bombers in flyable condition, was a spent force. Concerned that the Iraqis would capitulate, he advised the *Auswartiges Amt* that he was preparing to transfer his mission from the capital to Mosul.

Baghdad, 29 May 1941

At two o'clock in the morning Ferguson was woken by a hail of machine-gun bullets from four Iraqi trucks which had come down the main road and opened fire at the northern column's camp at point-blank range. However, accurate counter-fire from an A Squadron machine-gun emplacement knocked out the trucks. After the engagement Ferguson found that he had become the proud owner of a slightly damaged Ford V8 truck, which he used to replace his Haifa taxi, now on its last legs.

Just after dawn, A Squadron took the line of sand hills which had held up its advance on the previous day, and the column again moved forward to the Khadimain brick works. The sand hills had been a covering position of the main Iraqi defence system, and while B Squadron carried on the advance it came up against the main position at Khadimain station, and was held up for five hours by heavy shell fire, which killed one man and wounded five others.

Al Khadimain was one of the most important mosques in Iraq, a factor which seemed to have contributed to the Iraqis' fierce defence – in contrast to the weak defences encountered by the southern column. The flanks of Khadimain were protected by the Tigris on one side and by the virtually impassable Aqargouf marshes on the other. With an Iraqi brigade in place in well-defended positions supported by heavy artillery, it was beyond the power of two dismounted cavalry squadrons, supported by one troop of machine-guns and one troop of 25-pounders, to take. The possibility of collateral damage to the holy shrine ruled out bombing by the Air Striking Force. That evening the northern column returned to its bivouac at Taji station, and although probing patrols were sent out which revealed the strength of the Iraqis, and a further attempt was made the next morning to capture the station, the northern column made no further progress until the armistice was signed.

The southern column moved on towards Baghdad, reaching a twenty-yard-wide canal with a breached road and a bridge which had been blown by the retreating Iraqis. Still entrenched across the canal, the Iraqi heavy machine-gun fire made an immediate crossing impossible. After several hours of sustained fire from the 25-pounders, 2/Lt Grimley led two sections across the damaged bridge, followed by Muirhead and his platoon, to secure the bridgehead

Kingstone sent for 'Cheeky Chappie', who, after surveying the damage, requested a signal to Habbaniya for all the forward bridging equipment available. There was nothing to do except sit and wait.

The Air Striking Force actively sought out and then bombed and strafed Iraqi positions on the outskirts of Baghdad to support the southern column, not only against the Iraqi Army, but also to harry the Zoba tribe, which had thrown in its lot with the revolutionaries, and some *Futuwwah* irregulars who were mobilizing against the British.

At 10.00 three Audaxes escorted by two Gladiators were bombing across the eastern bank of the Abu Ghraib Canal where the Iraqis were strongly entrenched, when they were intercepted by two Italian *Falco*s from Kirkuk flown by *Tenente* De Merich and *Sottotenente* Valentini.

After an attacking pass at one of the Gladiators, both *Falco*s lined up on an Audax flown by Flt Lt Ian Webster. The attack left his gunner, Sgt Alex Payne, slightly wounded, and with smoke pouring out of the engine Webster crash-landed as close to the British lines at Falluja as he could.

Freddie Wightman, flying one of the Gladiators, dived from above, and half-rolled, putting himself behind one of the CR42s. As the *Falco* turned, Wightman kept turning inside, keeping his sights on the CR42 until the range closed to 100 yards. After three short bursts, black smoke poured from Valentini's engine and the *Falco* began to disintegrate. Valentini pulled the nose up to roll inverted, and simply dropped out of the cockpit after popping his seat-belt and harness. De Merich, now facing two Gladiators, decided to fight another day, and headed back to Kirkuk, while Valentini's parachute opened up and he drifted down to the Abu Ghraib Canal.

de Chair was sitting in his car writing up Kingcol's war diary when his driver shouted to him. Scrambling out of the car, de Chair saw one of the planes begin to fall and a white parachute detaching itself. A few minutes later the aircraft hit the ground about two miles away. Almost in slow motion, the parachute with a man underneath followed the plane down and then landed close to the crashed aircraft. de Chair, followed by his driver and Reading, ran towards the wreck until they were brought up short by the Abu Ghraib Canal. Undeterred, de Chair plunged in and swam across to the eastern bank, clambering up to the slope to the wreckage.

There were Iraqi insignia everywhere, but no interesting papers. Looking around he saw a man a few hundred yards away in long trousers, dragging a parachute along the ground. de Chair, drawing his Webley, ran over to confront the man and was startled to receive a Fascist salute and to be addressed in Italian. This was the first inkling the British had of Italian participation in the revolt.

Later that day the Air Striking Force organized a heavy attack on the Italian base at Kirkuk and a raid on the airfield at Baquba. While no damage was done at Kirkuk, two Italian and one Iraqi Air Force aircraft were damaged at Baquba.

The Arab Legion moved towards Meshahida early in the morning to cover the rear of the northern column. The Legion engaged an Iraqi police patrol from Smaicha, which was reconnoitring the rear of the northern column, killing two and capturing five. At this point a train came into view on its way from Meshahida to Taji, carrying Iraqi reinforcements to attack the rear of the British column. Seeing the fire-fight with the Legion, the train went into reverse, heading back towards Meshahida.

Near Falluja the Essexes got into position for a third assault on the Iraqis, who still held their position at the oasis controlling the Abu Ghraib Regulator. A further Air Striking Force raid, bombing the Iraqi positions for an hour, was supported by a sustained bombardment by the 25-pounders. Most of the bombs and much of the artillery fire missed the target through poor spotting. With no impact on the strong Iraqi force, which continued to concentrate heavy, accurate fire on the British positions, it was concluded that they faced at least a full Iraqi battalion, and the attack was called off. Adding insult to injury, the 1st Essexes were then showered with leaflets in Arabic calling on them to surrender.

Rashid Ali called Grobba in the early evening. 'I wanted to advise you of the decisions made by the Supreme Defence Council last night. We intend to defend Baghdad and we will need to have *Luftwaffe* support. Conscious of our situation, we may lose the city. However, we will continue to defend the country step by step. We have decided that we would then concentrate our forces around Kirkuk. Please ask Colonel Junck for his continued support, and I would like you to impress upon your Foreign Minister our need for more aircraft and supplies to continue the fight against our mutual enemy.'

Gabrielli managed to reach Sforza by radio just after four in the afternoon, and advised him to leave Kirkuk in a hurry as the Iraqis were about to capitulate. Sforza's men immediately began to pack up to be able to leave Mosul at daybreak the next morning.

Rashid Ali was just finishing the packing of his papers, and was surprised to receive a call in his office from an agitated Mahmud Salman.

'You should know that the Army leaders decided early this morning to abandon their command posts, and have already left in their cars for Persia.'

'But how can they do this when the Supreme Defence Council has decided to continue the resistance and to establish a new front at Kirkuk?'

'Rashid Ali, I am going to follow my colleagues, and I suggest that you do the same, otherwise you will be left here on your own', replied Salman before he cut the line.

Rashid Ali informed Sharif Sharaf of the situation, and then called Suwaidi and Zaki, who were still at Baquba, to hand over the Treasury to the Governor of Diyalah and then strike out for Persia. He then, together with the Mufti, Gabrielli and the rest of his civilian cabinet, left Baghdad for Persia. Later that day they crossed the border a mile or so south of Quasir e Shirin.

Facing delays in repairing the bridge, the 1st Essexes crossed on foot and advanced for six miles until, with the pontoons finally in place by the late afternoon, the southern column caught up with A and D Companies. The land now changed from desert to a region irrigated by dykes and canals, where the hard, sandy ground was broken by ridges covered with thick green scrub, and lines of gum trees followed the banks of the canals.

Early in the afternoon a further canal bridge was reached, this time unblown, and Robert James quickly cut the wires leading to demolition charges. With Capt Greene left commanding the bridgehead, the advance on Baghdad continued. During mid-afternoon an Iraqi Gladiator strafed the bridge, but was finally driven off by sustained rifle fire from A Company Headquarters.

A and B Squadrons of the Cavalry saw action as their advance guard of two armoured cars came under machine-gun and shell fire. They quickly dismounted from their trucks, and while one troop began to work its way around the Iraqi position in a wide sweep on the right flank, the rest of the squadron advanced up a narrow ditch running alongside the road. They occupied this position throughout the night.

When the light began to fade, the main column turned off the Baghdad road at the Government Agricultural Station and drove along a track to the Experimental Farm which nestled in among some eucalyptus trees. The main part of the southern column, which had bivouacked for the night at the Experimental Farm, found that they had acquired a large number of abandoned chickens, which quickly supplemented their hard rations.

Baghdad, 30 May 1941

This was a confusing day for Grobba. His first signal to the *Auswartiges Amt* at daybreak advised Ribbentrop that the military situation had improved as a result of both Iraqi Army action against the British and their flooding of the approaches to Baghdad. He also confirmed that command of the Iraqi Army and the cabinet were on their way to Kirkuk and were determined to continue the fight, provided that Germany immediately sent military aid.

Kirkuk

At daybreak Sforza's men poured petrol on two damaged *Falco* biplane fighters and on stores and equipment which were no longer needed. As soon as the fires were well alight, some of the ground-crew left in the unit's *Sparviero* transport, while the remaining staff left in two small commandeered buses, heading towards Mosul and the Syrian border, some 150 miles away.

The nine remaining CR42s flew cover for both the *Sparviero* and the buses until they were safely into Syrian territory. This ended the *Regia Aeronautica*'s participation in the Anglo-Iraqi war.

Mosul

The air evacuation of *Sonderkommando Junck* had been delayed by a day. One of the Junkers 90s had been destroyed on the ground at Aleppo by a British raid, and one of the Junkers 52/3ms had become unserviceable.

Rother, flying the remaining Junkers 90, had already made one trip that day from Aleppo. He had flown in at dawn in company with the three-engined Junkers. He had agreed with Junck that the Command Unit and the remaining officers fly out in the *Tante Ju* to Aleppo while he took the remaining ground-crew members and the *Flak* team. This still left a dozen men at Mosul. Rother, in the faster plane, agreed to return from Aleppo to pick up the remaining *Luftwaffe* personnel, who during his absence would systematically destroy all remaining equipment and stores.

After loading up, Rother took off at 05.30, arriving back at Aleppo by 09.00. Unloading and refuelling took an hour, and a shade after ten in the morning he was back in the air heading towards Mosul to pick up the remaining airmen. Before landing, his radio operator, Klaus Meier, advised him that following another heavy RAF raid on Aleppo, Rother should now route himself through Palmyra before flying on to Gaddura.

Due to a slight headwind it was almost 14.00 when Rother touched down at Mosul airport and taxied over to the damaged administration block and swung the tail around so that he could make a fast take-off.

Leaving his co-pilot, Ernst Hauser, at the controls, Rother walked down the sloping floor of the aircraft, opened the door and jumped out. Rather than a dozen or so men waiting for him, there were just two.

'Where the hell are your comrades?' he asked the *Gefreiter*.

'They did not believe that you would return for us, *Herr Hauptmann*. They commandeered two cars and set out for Syria', the tall one said.

'When was this?'

'They argued for a bit after you and *Oberst* Junck flew out, and then they left about 08.30, just after the last British raid.'

'Why did you stay?'

'You said you were coming back for us, *Herr Hauptman*', said the shorter one.

'Well, we are not going to hang around here with the RAF looking for us, so you had better get aboard quickly', Rother said, and climbed up the short ladder into the Junkers, followed by the two young airmen.

At 14.12 the last aircraft of *Sonderkommando Junck* took off from Mosul airfield. The Junkers 90 in its drab camouflage and peeling Royal Iraqi Air Force markings struggled into the hot, overcast sky. The plane made a slow, lazy turn over the airfield and slowly gained height as Rother set course south-west for Palmyra in Syria.

Berlin

Ribbentrop's reply to Grobba advised him that new air units were on the way and would land at Mosul on or around 1 June, and he should brief Rashid Ali and the Iraqis. In the meantime Grobba learned that Rashid Ali, his cabinet and the senior Iraqi military commanders, including the *Golden Square*, had all left for Persia. Given the circumstances, Grobba advised Ribbentrop that he was evacuating his team to Mosul and would resume contact later that day.

Meshahida

With Meshahida station still in the hands of the Iraqis, Ferguson's column was dangerously penned-in by the Iraqi brigade to the south at Khadimain, an unknown number of Iraqis who could be quickly re-inforced by troops by rail from the north at Meshahida, and the natural barriers of the Tigris to the east and the Marsh to the west.

The Arab Legion was tasked with taking the fort at Meshahida, backed up by one 25-pounder and one squadron of the Household Cavalry.

After a heavy bombardment of the fort by the 25-pounder, the garrison fled, dispersing among the neighbouring tribes, where they changed into civilian clothes. While the 25-pounder and the Household Cavalry squadron rejoined the column in front of Khadimain, a detachment of the Legion under Major Lash occupied the fort to cover the rear of the northern column from attack. Lash began to patrol aggressively in the Ramadi–Meshahida–Habbaniya area, keeping it clear of Iraqi military and police forces, intensified subversive activities among the Shammar and other tribes, and maintained the railway-line break near Samarra.

Baghdad

The southern column was now three miles from Baghdad, by the Khir Iron Bridge, facing the Iraqi forward defence line at the Washash Canal, while the northern column was at Khadimain opposite the Iraqi northern defence line, which was some five miles north of the city.

With a combined force of fewer than 1,400 men, eight 25-pounders and four old armoured cars, the British faced an Iraqi Army of well over a division in size which was resolved to defend the sprawling urban capital to the bitter end.

In both sectors the British came under increasingly heavy fire from the Iraqi positions, and replied with strafing and bombing attacks by the Audaxes, Blenheims, Gordons and Oxfords of the Air Striking Force on the northern and southern defence lines, followed by barrages from the 25-pounders.

As dusk began to fall the Audaxes conducted a twelve-minute dive-bombing attack on the Washash Army barracks about a mile behind the Iraqi lines facing Kingstone's southern column.

This last attack, which devastated the barracks, together with the banshee wails from the tails of the 250 lb bombs which had been modified by the engineers at Habbaniya, had a tremendous impact on Iraqi troop morale. This was instrumental in deterring the Iraqi commanders from prolonging the conflict.

Mosul

Arriving at Mosul air base in the early evening, Grobba found a deserted airfield littered with the still-burning hulks of unserviceable and damaged *Luftwaffe* Messerschmitt 110s, Heinkel 111s and Junkers 52s that marked the end of *Sonderkommando Junck*. He signalled Ribbentrop that it was now impossible to land at Mosul due to British bombing, and that as a result of the shortage of high-octane aviation spirit reinforcements would now have to operate out of Syria. With the Syrian border only sixty miles away, and with the capture of Mosul by the British imminent, he and his party would head towards Syria.

Grobba and his small group were on their way, and did not receive Ribbentrop's signal to stay in Mosul until the air reinforcements arrived.

Baghdad

Earlier that day al Sabawi, who had organized an armed force of irregulars from his paramilitary *Futuwwah* and the *Kataib al Shabab* youth, heard of the flight of Rashid Ali, the Mufti and the *Golden Square* to Tehran. He immediately issued a statement that Rashid Ali had named him Military Governor of Baghdad, and that he would prepare for popular resistance against the British.

The Committee for Internal Security quickly denounced his move, divested al Sabawi of all powers and dispatched a joint Army and police force to surround his headquarters at the Council of Ministers, where he was arrested.

Brought in front of the Council, al Sabawi conducted a heated discussion about continuing the resistance. 'We must continue to fight the British. We must win. Only then can we be masters of our own destiny.'

'We have lost against superior forces. There is no point in encouraging the destruction of Baghdad nor in sacrificing more Iraqis', said the Mayor of Baghdad, Arshad al Umari.

'You are all defeatists! All we need is a few more weeks until the Germans and the Italians come in strength. Then we can rout the British and together with our Arab brothers throw them out of the Middle East for good.'

Colonel Nur el din Mahmud looked aross the table at al Sabawi and said, pointedly, 'Your Axis friends have gone and none of your brother Arabs bothered to lift a finger to help us. All we will do is to destroy ourselves. This is the wrong time and the wrong place to continue our fight. If you will not agree then we must consult with all the Army commanders and convene an emergency meeting of the Council of Ministers. Let them see this treachery and decide for themselves!'

'Enough!. We have decided to seek a peace treaty to stop the fighting. You would be better to leave immediately for Tehran.'

A little after eight that evening, the Mayor of Baghdad, together with Colonel Nur el din Mahmud, arrived at the British Embassy to meet Cornwallis. They were kept waiting some twenty minutes while Cornwallis quickly shaved and changed into a formal suit, and arranged to have the last of the Embassy's coffee served. Appearances were everything in the Arab world.

As they were shown into his office, Cornwallis rose and walked over to the two men and gestured that they should sit in the comfortable chairs by the coffee table, and help themselves to coffee.

'How can I help you?' asked Cornwallis, as if the siege of the Embassy had never occurred.

'Ambassador,' began al Umari, 'Rashid Ali, the Mufti and the members of the *Golden Square* have all fled to Persia, and Grobba and Gabrielli and the rest of the Germans and Italians have also left the city. Control of the city has now been assumed by a Committee of Internal Security under my command.'

'Under these conditions the military have elected me to request a cessation of hostilities and to arrange a meeting to negotiate terms', added Colonel Nur el din Mahmud.

'Naturally I will have to discuss this with my colleagues at Habbaniya, and I need access to a telegraph line to communicate with them.'

'I will arrange this immediately', replied al Umari. 'In the meantime could I suggest that our envoys from Baghdad meet with your envoys to negotiate terms?'

'Where do you suggest, and when?'

'At the Khir Iron Bridge over the Washash Canal, where our troops face each other', suggested Mahmud, 'at, say, two o'clock in the morning?'

Kingstone received a message from Clark informing him that Iraqi envoys would arrive at the Iron Bridge at 02.00 to negotiate armistice terms.

Baghdad, 31 May 1941

The meeting had been postponed at the Iraqis' request to four o'clock in the morning.

Even at the height of the summer the desert at night can be a bitterly cold place. On the western bank of the Washash Canal, masked by a ridge, Clark, D'Albiac and Glubb, wearing their greatcoats with upturned collars, stamped their feet to keep warm as they waited for the Iraqi delegation.

The Iraqis had cut all the canal banks in the vicinity, and water was lapping the road in the grey dawn. With waterfowl flapping overhead, the scene, to Glubb, was more reminiscent of the Norfolk Broads than of the City of the Caliphs.

'Cornwallis has recommended that as part of the negotiations we allow the Iraqi Army to keep all their weapons and equipment and let them return to their peacetime locations. He believes that this will help them to keep face by suggesting that the war was against Rashid Ali and his friends, and not the Iraqi people. That would make for simple terms which the Iraqis can agree to quickly. What do you think?' Clark said, turning to Glubb.

'A quick agreement would cover up the fact that we have just carried out a colossal bluff and do not have enough troops to finish off the Iraqi Army. It would also put the Regent in power and get things back to normal as quickly as possible.'

'And you, John?'

'It makes sense. However, I don't think that your troops and my airmen are going to be very happy. The Iraqis will seem to have got off scot-free.'

'Well, that seems to be the word from the Foreign Office, so we will have to go along with their plan, and Kingstone and his men and your pilots will just have to lump it.'

'That's true, but all of this would never have happened if the Foreign Office had done its job in the first place', replied D'Albiac.

Two Iraqi officers, Colonel Ahmed Aquid and Captain Ghazi Daghistani, arrived promptly at four o'clock in a civilian car and walked across the bridge to de Chair and Gerald de Gaury. de Gaury, with a long history of the Middle East, had been appointed *Chargé d'Affaires* to the Regent by the Foreign Office and had flown in to Habbaniya the day before with the Regent and his retinue.

As the two groups came together, de Gaury and Daghistani, who had met on a course at Sandhurst, incongruously greeted each other as old friends.

Clark asked de Chair for some paper, sat down on the grass by the side of the road and wrote on the back of de Chair's telegraph form:

Your Excellency,

AOC and self have met the delegates. I have ordered the advance to stand fast at 04.00 hrs. I have here in my possession the instructions of my C-in-C General Wavell regarding terms. AOC and I would be grateful if you could see your way to come out here for discussion. We will await your instructions.

G. Clark, Major General

Clark looked at Daghestani and said, 'I will keep Colonel Aquid here as a hostage while you take Lt de Chair, Capt Spence and Mr de Gaury to the Embassy. with my message.'

They boarded Daghestani's car and he asked them to blindfold themselves as they passed through the Iraqi defence lines. As they entered the city he told them to remove their blindfolds. They drove quickly through the quiet streets of Baghdad, almost deserted save for groups of patrolling Iraqi soldiers, to the Embassy.

It took some time before Vyvyan Holt, the Oriental Secretary, wearing a plaid dressing-gown, let them in through the wooden postern gate. They found Cornwallis in bed and gave him Clark's message.

'Right, give me half an hour to dress and I will be with you. In the meantime I expect that they will find you some tea at the canteen, which we have here for the people on night guard.'

They left the Ambassador to dress, and Holt showed them down some stairs into the courtyard, through the garden and into the canteen. A buxom lady poured them tea and with tears in her eyes said, 'We have been waiting a long time for this.'

People, who seemed to be sleeping all over the Embassy grounds, began to get up and to crowd around them, sensing that their ordeal was coming to an end.

Cornwallis emerged from the main entrance, wearing an immaculate white tropical-drill suit topped-off by a white topee, and beckoned to de Chair, de Gaury, Spence and Daghestani to join him.

With Cornwallis and Daghestani in the front, and de Chair, de Gaury and Spence squashed in the back of the car, they drove back to the Iron Bridge. This time it took longer to pass through the Iraqi defence lines. After some argument and clicking of rifle bolts, which seemed very ominous to the three blindfolded men in the back, Daghistani was cleared to take them back to the bridge.

On their arrival, a shade before six o'clock in the morning, Cornwallis hurried across to the British side, joining Clark and D'Albiac in the latter's Air Force blue Humber saloon, while the others were left to wander about.

An hour or so later, Clark emerged and called de Chair over to dictate the armistice agreement which the three had worked out in D'Albiac's car. When the draft was shown to Glubb, he embarrassingly pointed out that it did not provide for a cessation of hostilities. After a further session in the back of D'Albiac's car, a final text was dictated on the back of another of de Chair's telegram forms:

> *Whereas representatives of the Iraq Army have sought for an Armistice and in view of the fact that His Highness the Regent Abdul Ilah is on his way to reign over the country, the following terms must be observed by the Iraq Army. The mildness of the terms will be noticed because the British Army has, in fact, no quarrel with the Iraqi people or their Army, but only with the pro-Axis adventurers who were determined to use the Army for their own end:*
>
> *All hostilities between the two armies cease forthwith.*
>
> *The Iraq Army will be permitted to retain all its arms.*
>
> *All British prisoners of war (military, RAF and civilian) to be released forthwith.*
>
> *All enemy (German and Italian) service personnel to be interned and their war material retained by the Iraqi Government pending further instructions.*
>
> *The town and vicinity of Ramadi to be evacuated by the Iraq Army by 12.00 noon on 1st June, 1941.*
>
> *All Iraqi prisoners of war now in British hands to be handed over to the Regent as soon as the terms in paragraphs 3, 4 and 5 are complied with.*

Cornwallis took one copy and returned across the bridge for Daghestani and Aquid to take him to the Citadel to lay the terms before the Committee of Internal Security.

Early in the afternoon, al Umari, together with Brigadier Ismail Namiq, Colonel Hamd Nasrat and Colonel Nur el din Mahmud, came to the Embassy to discuss terms. At first they wished to make some textual alterations, with the intention of making the armistice appear to have been the result of mutual agreement, and not the terms offered by the victor to the vanquished. Cornwallis refused to debate the issue, indicating that he had no authority to amend the terms offered by Clark and D'Albiac. After some discussion, in which Cornwallis was supported by al Umari, the Iraqi officers signed the armistice terms.

As the sun began to go down, the Air Striking Force dropped hurriedly printed leaflets on Iraqi positions at Amara, Diwaniya, Nasiray and al Qurna, setting out the terms of the armistice.

The news of the armistice reached Paul Knabenshue at the United States Legation a few minutes after four in the afternoon.

He looked back on the siege with a mixture of pride and relief.

Pride because he had refused to submit to intimidation. Midway through the siege, the American University in Beirut had expelled all Iraqi students, and in retaliation the Iraqis threatened to arrest and intern him. With no radio he had asked the Iraqis to send a telegram to Washington requesting his replacement. Knowing that the Iraqis would read his message, he banked on Arab pride by informing Cordell Hull not to judge the Iraqis too harshly as they had only temporarily forgotten their well-known manners. The telegram was never sent and the matter was quietly dropped.

Relief because all of his wards, American and British, had come through the ordeal unharmed. The ten women inside had encountered no problems. He was amused when he recalled that the King's attractive English governess, Betty Sulman, came to ask his advice on how to reject four proposals of marriage without offending her suitors.

For Freya at the British Embassy, the end of the of the siege was a time for reflection.

The Colonel, Aquid, who had come the Embassy with Daghestani, was aggressive and quite rude, reaffirming her belief that the Iraqis have the worst manners of all the Arabs.

People like Bill Bailey, who had been seized in the street, the BOAC staff from Lake Habbaniya and British prisoners of war who were brought to the Embassy, came with tales of vicious treatment. Some had been chained up by both hands for the first six days. None had received medical attention, and all shared cells with convicted criminals. Most were thin, looked strained and carried the marks of severe beatings. Reports began to come in of homes systematically looted, then defiled with excrement, and what was not stolen was destroyed. Dr Sinderson, for example, whose house was thoroughly looted, was amazed to see after an interval his wife's dresses appearing at public balls and concerts.

The terms of the agreement seemed to be very lenient, and Freya wondered if not bringing in the Regent with a great show of force seemed to be placating one's enemies rather than encouraging one's friends. The talk around the Embassy was that it was all over. Just seeing the faces of Iraqis, however, brought home the fact to Freya that the revolt had not changed their attitudes. She knew that it was just a question of time before there was another revolt.

Habbaniya

Around noon Savile authorized Paul Holder to secure replacement stocks to resupply Habbaniya with over 100 tons of bombs and 250,000 rounds of ammunition which the RAF had expended during the revolt. He also requested a full set of checks on the remaining Air Striking Force aircraft, most of which were barely flyable after some 1,600 sorties within a month.

Tony Dudgeon's last photo-reconnaissance mission ended just after three. He had been tasked to photograph the Iraqi Army units around Falluja, Ramadi and in front of Baghdad at Khadimain, at the Abu Ghraib Regulator and at the Washash Canal. These were needed to check that the Iraqis were indeed observing the cessation of hostilities and were evacuating their positions and begining to return to barracks. This was also Frankie's last 'operational' mission.

Berlin

To General *Hellmuth Felmy, Athens-Tatoi:*
> *All forces are to gather at Aleppo, They are to stand down until further intentions have been clarified with the French Government in Vichy. Remove all Iraqi insignia. Further orders will follow.*
> *Feldmarschall Wilhelm Keitel*

No further orders were ever sent from Berlin.

Epilogue

The war in Iraq in 1941 was lost by those who hesitated, miscalculated and were misled and won by those who had nothing to lose and who were prepared to take massive gambles.

The Iraqis hesitated at Habbaniya, which they could easily have overrun, passing the initiative to the British. The Germans and Italians hesitated in sending adequate support to Rashid Ali, which allowed an inferior British force to prevail.

The Iraqis miscalculated that the British would resort to negotiation to free their hostages surrounded at Habbaniya and besieged at the Embassy and would not fight. The lack of international political experience of the Iraqi leadership led to unfounded optimism concerning the foreign support that they could expect from other states – particularly Saudi Arabia and Turkey – and they conspicuously failed to mobilize pan-Arab support throughout the Middle East to their cause.

Rashid Ali miscalculated that he could balance the demands of the Mufti, a malevolent zealot, and the nationalists in the *Golden Square* with British needs.

The Germans wrongly assumed that the strength, morale and fighting spirit of the Iraqis was enough to contain the British until their forces could intervene in strength. They sent only a token force, which was poorly prepared and inadequately supported. Hitler made a crucial mistake in thinking that Crete was more valuable strategically than Iraq. For far less than the huge casualties and loss of equipment sustained in Crete the Germans could have comfortably taken Iraq. A great prize which was theirs for the taking at little cost slipped from their grasp.

The Mufti misled the Iraqis by urging them to confront the British for his own ends. A climb-down by the British over Iraq and negotiated changes to the British policy on Palestine would have elevated the Mufti to unassailable leadership of the pan-Arab world. The Iraqi leadership also misled the population. True, many would have gone along with a victory over the British, but the leadership did not have a deep understanding of Iraq's religious and political factions. Many of the Shia tribes and the Kurds were either neutral or against fighting a war which was not their concern or in their interest.

Grobba misled the *Wehrmacht*, the *Abwehr* and the *Auswartiges Amt* on the true strength and capabilities of the Iraqi armed forces. The Germans were economical with the truth about the extent of their commitment, which encouraged the Iraqi leadership to begin hostilities before support was in place, while the Iraqis misled the Germans on their ability to supply high-octane fuel and quality lubricants.

The airmen and soldiers who fought at Habbaniya and went on to take Bahgdad won because they had nothing to lose and everything to gain.

The guiding forces were Churchill and Auchinleck, who saw the strategic implications. Losing Iraq would have had untold consequences. It would have inspired other ultra-nationalists in the region – Zahir Shah and Abdul Majid Khan in Afghanistan, King Farouk and Azil el Misri in Egypt, Subhas Chandra Bose in India and Reza Shah Pahlevi and Bandar Shah in Persia – all of whom had been courting or were being courted by the Germans to revolt.

Losing Iraq would have meant losing the Middle East, Britain's oil supplies in the sterling area and the fight for Roosevelt's support, which in turn meant the battle for American public opinion against the isolationists.

The real heroes at Habbaniya and on the march on Baghdad were the airmen – like Dudgeon, Ling, Hawtrey, Savile, Cleaver, Evans, Casano and Page – and the soldiers, Clark, Kingstone, Roberts, Brawn, Graham, Everett, Ferguson, May and Glubb – who were all prepared to take massive gambles.

While 31 May 1941 was the end of the revolt, in many ways it was the beginning of Iraq's troubles. That night Baghdadis came out onto the streets and, egged on by the *Futuwwah* and other nationalists, killed a large number of Jews in the streets and in their homes. As far as anyone knows, between two and four hundred Jews died, and up to a thousand were injured that night and over the next two days in what came to be known as the *Farhud*.

The streets were full of hatred. Rioting and looting erupted throughout the city by a populace poisoned for years by a fascist education system, radio propaganda and the problems in Palestine. Humiliated by their defeat, they went looking for scapegoats, and selected the Jews and anyone who tried to help them.

The Iraqi police and the Army were either part of the *Farhud* or turned a blind eye, and the 1,500 British soldiers camped outside the city were powerless to protect the Jews from the rage of a city of 400,000.

The Regent arrived in the city the next day and put together a cabinet that would support him. His overriding objective was to hunt down and execute or dismiss and humiliate any officers even vaguely connected with the revolt, in order to protect the royal family.

However, the Regent had lost the loyalty of many Iraqis, and his actions merely created hatred for the monarchy and pushed nationalism in the Army underground. The wave of executions, arrests, trials and dismissals had a deep and lasting effect on the Iraqis. The atmosphere of fear that this created bred a deep resentment against the Regent, the royal family, Nuri al Said and the British. al Sabbagh's memoirs, written during his imprisonment in Turkey and published posthumously, inspired a generation of nationalists within the Iraqi armed forces.

This poisonous environment provided a breeding-ground for revenge. Many of the young Army officers dismissed by the Regent came back to haunt him – Ahmad Hassan al Bakr, for example, later became President of Iraq. Young officers who were cadets in the Iraqi Military Academy in 1941 were involved in the bloody coups of Abdul Karem Kassem in 1958 and Abdul Salam Arif in 1966, and they supported the Baath Party coup in 1968 and Saddam Hussein's rise to power in 1979.

The *Farhud* was the beginning of the end for the 2,600-year-old Baghdad Jewish community, one of the oldest and richest in the world, and one which had brought great cultural achievements and wealth to Iraq. The final nail in the coffin was the Arab-Jewish war of 1948 and the humbling performance of the Iraq Army. From then on the Jewish community was systematically humiliated and their property confiscated. Arrests, trials and even executions became commonplace. By 1951 virtually all the remaining Jews, some 120,000, had been airlifted, or had been smuggled, out of Iraq carrying a few possessions. They, and the great families like the Khadhouries and the Sassoons, made countries like Britain and America wealthier with their talents.

Despite the huge strategic significance of the war in Iraq in 1941, very little is known about what actually happened. In some respects this is understandable. From the British perspective the war being fought in the North Atlantic to protect Britain's food, oil and munitions from Doenitz's Wolfpacks and the Condors, Rommel's successes in the Western Desert, the loss of Crete and the follow-on campaign in Syria dominated the public consciousness.

Also helping to deflect attention was inter-service rivalry. D'Albiac's 'definitive' report, written second-hand after the battle for Habbaniya and the capture of Baghdad, rightly praises the RAF but contains little mention of the role of the Army. With a split command, no soldier of any stature and a diverse set of units, the role of the Army remains largely in the historical archives of the participating regiments.

From the German and Italian perspectives the lack of attention is also understandable, as few wish to dwell on their misfortunes.

Using any yardstick but the war in Europe, the strategic issues were exceptional. Those thirty-one days in Iraq in May 1941 produced extraordinary acts of courage and incredible improvisations in the air and on land, which rivalled anything in Europe and later in the Far East. The tactical lessons learned by the British were to become immensely valuable. Air resupply and air-landing troops behind enemy lines under fire soon became the norm. Montgomery's use of the Desert Air Force from late 1942 and the 2nd Tactical Air Force in 1944–45 to support ground troops from Normandy through to the North German Plain vindicated the use of combined operations.

A faraway place with unfamiliar people and unpronounceable names, and a steady stream of fresh disasters and setbacks, drove the victory in Iraq in 1941 from the news within a matter of days. There has been no official recognition or honours given to anyone on either side, and few, if any, who participated in this epic struggle are alive today.

Sadly the memory of a battle that, if lost, could quite possibly have changed the course of the war and the world has just faded away, like the participants, and has become just another very small, overlooked footnote in history.

Appendix

What Happened to . . . ?

People follow very different paths to their future, and their pasts are largely poor guides to their later lives.

The characters in *Hitler's Gulf War* are no exception. A few went on to bigger and better things – for some this was the crowning point of their lives – while many others just faded into obscurity. Some had long and productive lives into their 90s while others had their lives cruelly taken from them.

Here are the post-1941 biographies of the key participants that I have been able to trace.

Otto Abetz, the German Ambassador to Vichy France, left Paris ahead of the Allied invasion in 1944. He was captured in the Black Forest in 1945 by the US Army and was sentenced in 1949 by a French court to twenty years' hard labour for his part in the deportation of French Jews to the death camps. He was released in 1954 from Loos prison, and died in a car accident near Langenfeld on the Cologne-Ruhr Autobahn in May 1958. He was 55 years old.

Prince Abdul Ilah pursued and punished all those officers who had mutinied against the Kingdom in 1941. Death, imprisonment, and loss of status and pensions created a great hatred for the Regent. Saddam Hussein, although a child at the time, was touched personally by the events of 1941. His uncle, Khayrallah Tulfah, was an officer who had participated in the war and whose career was ruined by the Regent. Following the Kassem coup in 1958, the Regent's mutilated body was symbolically hung up at the gate of the Ministry of Defence at the spot where the Regent had had Salah ed Din al Sabbagh hanged in 1945. The Regent was 46 years old.

Yacob Khoshaba Aboona of the RAF Levies went on to serve in Basra and Palestine, and was awarded the MBE. At the disbandment of the Levies in 1955 and the handover to the Iraqi government, Aboona was the senior serving Levy officer. Following his release from military service, he moved to Baghdad and started his own business. He emigrated to the United States in 1981 and died in Skokie, Illinois, in 1984, aged 84.

John D'Albiac was appointed to command 2 Group at the end of 1942, followed by the 2nd Tactical Air Force in Europe. At the end of the war as an air marshal he was knighted. He became the first Commandant of London's Heathrow airport. He retired in 1961 after serving for ten years as Deputy Chairman of the Air Transport Advisory Council. D'Albiac died aged 69 in Beaconsfield in August 1969.

Butch, Casano's devoted black-and-white mongrel, was by his master's side everywhere, from action in Vichy-controlled Syria into the hallowed ground of the Long Bar at Shepheard's Hotel in Cairo, where dogs, except Butch, were not allowed. Butch was killed by the same burst of enemy fire that wounded Casano in the Western Desert. Such was his fame that Butch's demise was reported in the *Egyptian Gazette.*

John George Walters Clark went on to command in the Syrian Campaign which followed the fall of Baghdad. He briefly commanded the 10th Armoured Division in North Africa and then held administrative posts in the Mediterranean and led missions to the Netherlands and Greece. Clark retired from the Army with the honorary title of Lieutenant-General in 1946, and died after a brief illness in 1948 at the age of 56.

Dudley Wrangel Clarke remained in the Mediterranean theatre with A Force for the rest of the war. Clarke was one of the most influential soldiers of the Second World War. He thought up the name SAS for a phantom army in North Africa which became a reality, and gave Wild Bill Donovan the name 'Rangers' for US Commando forces. Clarke was the ideas man behind a number of other successful deceptions, such as 'The Man that Never Was' and 'I was Monty's Double', both of which were made into successful films. Clarke was arrested in Madrid in full drag in October 1941, in circumstances which have never been explained, while on a secret mission to Spain. He retired as a brigadier, and was appointed Head of Public Opinion Research for the Conservative Central Office, where he served from 1948 until his retirement in 1952. In the early 1950s the Australian Secret Intelligence Service used Clarke to produce a report on methods to combat communist subversion in South-East Asia using propaganda, economic warfare and covert operations. He later became a director of Securicor. Clarke died at the age of 75 in 1974.

Michael Peter 'Cass' Casano continued to command No. 2 Armoured Car Company RAF, and played a very active role with Habforce in the invasion of Vichy-controlled Syria, for which he was awarded the Military Cross for his inspiring and courageous leadership. He was badly wounded by the same burst of enemy fire in North Africa that killed Butch. At Glubb Pasha's request, Casano was transferred to command the Arab Legion's armoured-car force, and he remained in Transjordan for the rest of the war, marrying the daughter of a White Russian general.

Casano was granted a permanent commission in 1945 in administration, serving in Germany, Malta and the UK. Retiring from the RAF in 1958, he became a driving instructor. He died in August 2006 at the age of 93.

Somerset de Chair was wounded in the Syrian campaign in late 1941 and invalided out of the Army. He was in and out of parliament several times, became a shrewd collector of antiques and paintings, bought a succession of stately homes and was a prolific writer. Married four times, de Chair died in Antigua at 83 in January 1995.

Gian Galeazzo Ciano, Mussolini's Foreign Minister and son-in-law, began to lobby for Italy's withdrawal from the conflict following the Axis defeat in North Africa, the Allied landings in Sicily and the *Wehrmacht*'s setbacks in the East.

He was arrested by Mussolini's Italian Social Republic police for treason. Under intense German pressure he was tried and executed by firing squad in Verona in January 1944.

Richard 'Dicky' Cleaver went on to fly Hurricanes with 216 Squadron in Ceylon, achieving a second victory – this time against the Japanese. As a supernumerary squadron leader, Dicky joined 611 Squadron in the summer of 1944. He died when his Spitfire inexplicably crashed into the sea in June that year off the Normandy coast. He was 25 years old.

Kinahan Cornwallis remained British Ambassador in Baghdad until his retirement in 1945. He was then appointed Chairman of the influential Middle East Committee of the Foreign Office and became a Director of the British Bank of the Middle East. Cornwallis died in June 1959 in Basingstoke at the age of 76.

Ghazi Muhammad Fadhil Daghistani, the captain escorting de Gaury and de Chair to the Embassy, remained in the Iraqi Army, and in 1952 was appointed Military Attaché in London. In 1957 he was promoted major-general, but when the monarchy was overthrown in 1958 Daghistani was arrested and sentenced to death by a military court. His sentence was subsequently commuted to three years' imprisonment, and in 1960 he was released and came to live in London, where he died in 1966, aged 56.

Henri-Ferdinand Dentz, the Military Governor of Vichy Syria, was evacuated to France at the end of the Syrian campaign in late 1941 as part of an agreement with the Vichy French. At the end of the war he was arrested, tried and convicted of treason by the French government and sentenced to death. De Gaulle commuted the sentence to life imprisonment. Dentz died in Fresnes jail in December 1945 at the age of 64.

John Patrick Domvile, the Air Liaison Officer in the British Military Mission to Iraq, who was caught at the Embassy siege, was promoted to wing commander in 1942. He resigned his commission in September 1945, retiring as a group captain. He later held a teaching post at the Royal Military Academy, Sandhurst. On a visit to Baghdad in 1958, he was caught up in the Revolution, and was forced to flee for his life. His possessions and money due to him were confiscated, and no repayment was ever made.

William Joseph Donovan went on to found the Office of Strategic Service (OSS) in 1942. After Roosevelt's death in 1945 his personal connexion with the President was broken and his position weakened as a Republican in a Democratic administration; he returned to his Wall Street law firm – Donovan, Leisure, Newton & Irvine. His last official duty was serving as special assistant to Chief Prosecutor Telford Taylor at the Nuremberg War Crimes Trials.

Donovan was the only American to have received all four of the United States' highest awards – the Medal of Honor, the Distinguished Service Cross, the Distinguished Service Medal and the National Security Medal.

Donovan died in early 1959 at the age of 76, and is buried in Arlington National Cemetery. When he heard the news, President Eisenhower remarked, 'What a man! We have lost the last hero.'

Martin Drewes, the leading fighter pilot in 4/ZG 76, later became an '*Experte*' in the night-fighter role over Germany. He ran up an impressive score of forty-nine victories, mainly against RAF Lancasters, and ended the war as *Gruppen Kommander 111/NJG 3*, being awarded the Knight's Cross with Oak Leaves. At the end of the war he emigrated to Brazil, first working as a pilot and then as a businessman.

Tony Dudgeon, despite his unconventional approach to authority, retired from the RAF as an air vice-marshal in 1968. He spent the next ten years as head of McKinsey in Paris. He fought tenaciously to have battle honours awarded to No. 4 Flying Training School for its contribution to the war. This was continuously rejected with the argument that the Flying School was a non-operational unit. Dudgeon died in Paris in July 2004 aged 89. His son is a wing commander in the RAF.

William Henry Dunwoodie left Habbaniya with 94 Squadron on 31 May and flew to Amman, forming part of X Flight, which took part in the conflict with the Vichy French in Syria. He was awarded a DFM in 1941, was commissioned as a pilot officer in 1943 and was a flight lieutenant on his discharge from the RAF in 1946.

Robert Anthony Eden, who tried unsuccessfully to persuade al Suwaidi, the Iraqi Foreign Minister, to have al Hashimi replace the officers of the *Golden Square*, remained in politics after the war. He was knighted in 1954, and succeeded Winston Churchill as Prime Minister in 1955. However, his famous diplomatic flair failed him. His conduct of the 1956 Suez Crisis proved disastrous, leading to the end of a Britain as the most important player in the Middle East, to the country's demise as a superpower, and to his own continuous health problems. Eden retired in 1957, ostensibly for health reasons. He was ennobled as the Earl Of Avon in 1961, and died in Salisbury in 1977, at the age of 79.

Edward Newbey Everett (-Heath) spent a year recovering from wounds he sustained at Falluja. He rejoined the King's Own Royal Regiment in the Western Desert and was captured at Sollum in 1942. A POW for the rest of the war, he had a number of attempted escapes and a considerable period of 'freedom' to his credit. He was promoted colonel in 1950 and retired from the Army in 1952. He died in Camberley aged 74 in November 1976.

Hellmuth Felmy remained in Athens following the disbandment of *Sonderstab F*, and became Commandant of German forces in southern Greece. He was captured by the US Army in May 1945 in Germany, and was tried in 1948 at Nuremberg for war crimes involving reprisal killings in the Balkans while Commandant of southern Greece. He received a sentence of fifteen years, but was released in 1951 after serving only thirty-four months. Felmy died in December 1965, aged 80. His son, Hansjoerg, became a leading German actor.

Andrew Henry Ferguson, who led Kingcol's northern column, remaind in the Life Guards until his retirement. His son Ronald followed the long family tradition of service in the regiment. Ferguson's granddaughter, Sarah, was briefly married to Prince Andrew, Duke of York. Andrew Ferguson died aged 67 in 1966.

Frankie, the dachshund, the veteran of over thirty 'unofficial' bombing missions, accompanied Tony Dudgeon to Cairo in June 1941. One evening at around midnight at the southern end of Gezira Island, Frankie was hit by a passing car, which did not stop. Frankie died of his internal injuries two days later.

Rashid Ali al Gailani, the Iraqi Prime Minister, fled first to Persia during the evening of 29 May 1941, and then to Berlin, where he cooperated with the Germans.

At the end of the war he lived in exile in Saudi Arabia, returning to Iraq in 1958 following the revolution overthrowing the monarchy. In December 1958 he was implicated in a plot against Abdul Karem Kassem, and was sentenced to death for treason and plotting against the regime. His sentence was commuted to life in prison, and he was released by special amnesty in 1961.

Rashid Ali settled in Beirut, where he died in August 1965 at the age of 73. Even though he lived in the same city as Haj Amin for a number of years, it is not believed that they met.

Gerald de Gaury, Chargé d'Affaires at the Regent Abdul Ilah's court in exile, rejoined the Army, and as a lieutenant-colonel raised and commanded the Druze Cavalry, which took part in the Syrian campaign. Further assignments in the Middle East continued, and he travelled extensively into the early 1960s, maintaining his friendship with the ruling families of Saudi Arabia and Kuwait. de Gaury published twelve books on his journeys in the Middle East and biographies of its rulers. He died in Brighton in mid-January 1984.

John Bagot Glubb, commanding the Arab Legion, was devoted to the Hashemite dynasty, the people of Jordan and the Arab cause throughout the rest of his life. Despite his loyalty, he was discourteously sacked as head of the Arab Legion in 1956, and given two hours to leave Jordan, arriving in England with £5 in his pocket and little more in the bank. Although he was knighted, the British government washed its hands of Glubb, offering no employment or asking for advice from a man many believed to be far greater than T.E. Lawrence. He supported his family through lecturing and writing nineteen books. The Pasha died in March 1986 at the age of 88.

Alistair Graham, of the Levies, was awarded the Military Cross for his part in the battle for Falluja. He returned to the Green Howards and took part in the Normandy landings, and was in action in north-western Europe. He was promoted major in 1948 and retired in 1961. Graham died after a long illness at the age of 60 in 1975.

Hans-Ulrich Granow, who flew to Baghdad with Grobba, re-entered the German Foreign Service after the war and served as Ambassador in Malaya, South Africa and Sweden. He died at his post in Stockholm in March 1963 of a heart attack. He was 62 years of age.

Nigel St George Gribbon was wounded at Felluja and remained in Iraq through 1942. His subsequent career took him through staff colleges in Canada, India and with the RAF, operational tours with the Parachute Brigade, the King's Own and 161 Brigade, and in intelligence roles. He retired from the Army in 1972 as a major-general, with a last posting as Assistant Chief of Staff (Intelligence) with SHAPE. His post-Army career combined high-profile private sector and public service appointments. He died in Sussex aged 91 in early 2009.

Fritz Konrad Ferdinand Grobba, after making his way back to Berlin, became embroiled in a feud between Rashid Ali and the Mufti for leadership of the 'Arab Cause'. Unwisely Grobba chose the 'politician' over the 'fanatical idealist' whom the SS supported, believing that the Mufti had greater influence across the Arab world. Grobba was outmanoeuvred by the far more influential and ruthless SS, who had him dismissed in 1943 and sent to France to analyse documents. Grobba was pensioned in 1944 and joined the Saxon government in Dresden before being appointed Public Prosecutor for Meiningen. Following his capture by the Russian Occupying Forces, who believed him to be a spy, he spent ten years in captivity.

On his return to Germany, Grobba cooperated with the CIA, and, it is claimed, during his capitivity in Russia with the KGB, providing his network of contacts in the Middle East. He later made several trips to Iraq, Lebanon, Saudi Arabia and Syria, promoting a German-Arab Society based in Bonn. Grobba published his memoirs in 1967 and died at the age of 87 in Bad Godesburg in September 1973.

Jacques Guerard returned to Vichy and became Secretary-General to Prime Minister Pierre Laval. He fled to Spain ahead of the Allies in 1944 and was condemned to death *in absentia*. He returned voluntarily in 1955, and by the time of his trial in 1958 the French government had lost its appetitie for revenge and he was handed out a five-year suspended sentence. He died in 1977.

Habbaniya. Control of the air base reverted to Iraq in May 1955, but it was still used extensively by the RAF. Kassem's bloody revolution in July 1958 made a continued RAF presence untenable. The RAF ensign was finally lowered on 31 May 1959. The Iraqi Air Force took over Habbaniya, but abandoned the air base after the 1991 Gulf War.

Today Habbaniya lies derelict. The cast-iron road signs are still there, but the English text on top has been covered in black paint and the Arab script on the bottom is highlighted in white. In all RAF stations the curbs along the streets are painted white: in Habbaniya the colour has long since gone. Now they are all faded, chipped and scuffed.

The officers' mess, where Ling and Dudgeon met to plan the rebellion against stupidity, is rather forlorn, and deserves a coat of paint, like most of the buildings. The two-storey administration block with its inner balcony encloses a grass quadrangle. The grass has long since gone, and through neglect the roots of the trees at each coner of the quadrangle have been allowed to damage the structure. The Iraqis had no interest in tennis: weeds and bushes now sprout up through the courts. Incongruously there are a number of wooden VHF aerials dotted around the camp, all of which seem to have storks' nests perched on their tops.

When the US Marines took over Habbaniya in 2003 they found a terrible mess. The building that once housed the St George's Anglican church had been turned into a mosque, the Astra cinema sported a mural of Saddam Hussein, and the 290 graves where those who had sacrificed their lives in the defence of Habbaniya, at Falluja and in the march on Baghdad lie buried were neglected and vandalized.

A group of servicemen from the US Army, Air Force, Marines and Navy, together with some British, Nepalese and Philippino civilians, formed a volunteer work-party to clean up the graveyard.

Remembrance Day services have been held at Habbaniya since 2005, and in 2008, at a ceremony attended by the British Ambassador to Iraq and the top US Marine general in Iraq, the cemetery was rededicated, a ceremonial wreath was laid and two minutes of silence were observed.

John Gosset Hawtrey remained in the RAF and took a number of staff postings, including command of RAF stations in the UK and overseas. Early in 1952, following a promotion to air vice-marshal, he was appointed AOC Air Headquarters Iraq. Hawtrey died on holiday in San Remo, Italy, at the age of 53 in 1954.

Otto-Werner von Hentig, Head of the Political Department responsible for the Middle East at the German Foreign Office, joined the Foreign Service of the post-war German government and served as Ambassador to Indonesia in 1952–53. On his retirement from the Foreign Service, he was a personal adviser to the Saudi Royal Family for almost two years. Von Hentig died in August 1984 in Norway.

Paul Davie Holder had a successful career in the RAF which took him in and out of operations with Bomber, Coastal and Transport Commands and staff postings in the UK and overseas. He was promoted to air marshal and knighted in 1965, retiring from the RAF in 1968. He died aged 89 in November 2001.

Adrian Holman, Cornwallis's deputy, later served in Tehran, Algiers, Paris and Bucharest, becoming Ambassador in Cuba in 1952. He retired from the Foreign Service with a knighthood in 1954, and died in Hampshire in 1974 at the age of 79.

Vyvyan Holt, the Oriental Secretary at the Embassy, remained in post until 1944, when he transferred to the Embassy in Tehran as Oriental Counsellor. He was posted as Minister to the British Legation in Seoul in 1949. Believing in Diplomatic Immunity, he stayed at his post when the North Koreans invaded in 1950. He was detained and taken on a death march to Chung-Gang-jin. Holt was harshly treated, contracted pneumonia and was probably saved by the intervention of George Blake, the SIS agent who converted to Marxism and subsequently became a double agent for the KGB.

He was released in 1953, and took up his final post as Minister in El Salvador in 1954, retiring from the Foreign Service in 1956, when he was knighted. Holt died in 1960, aged 64, his harsh treatment by the North Koreans probably having precipitated his early death.

Cordell Hull, the longest-serving Secretary of State, retained his position to late 1944, eleven years after his appointment, until he resigned because of failing health.

He was the underlying force and architect behind the creation of the United Nations, and was awarded the Nobel Prize for 'cofounding the United Nations' in 1945.

Hull died in 1955 and is buried in the Washington National Cathedral.

Haj Amin al Husayni escaped on the evening of 29 May 1941 first to Persia, and then to Italy and Germany. He helped to organize a Bosnian Muslim *Waffen SS* unit in the Balkans and Arab saboteurs for action in the Middle East, and he broadcast radio propaganda on behalf of the Germans. Haj Amin was denied residence in Switzerland at the end of the war and fled to Paris. He escaped house arrest in Paris in 1946, and using false papers to travel to Cairo on an American aircraft he obtained asylum in Egypt, where he became one of the sponsors of the 1948 Arab–Israeli war. Haj-Amin set up a Palestinian government for eight days in Gaza in 1948, before the final collapse of the Arab armies and the annexation of the West Bank by Jordan. The Mufti was reputed to have been involved in the assassination of King Abdullah of Jordan in 1951. He was made a scapegoat for the Arab losses in 1948 and was marginalized by moderate Arab groups as well as extreme Palestinian organizations.

Haj Amin settled in Beirut in 1959 and died there, an embittered man, in July 1974, at the age of 77. His wish to be buried in Jerusalem was refused by the Israelis, and his tomb lies in a corner of the Palestinian 'Martyrs' Cemetery' in West Beirut.

Robert James, of the 1st Batallion Essex Regiment, was awarded the DSO for his actions at Falluja. Promoted lieutenant-colonel, he transferred to command the 5th Batallion East Yorkshire Regiment, and fought in Tunisia and Sicily, winning two more DSOs. He was given a staff appointment, but volunteered to rejoin the 5th Battalion to take part in the Normandy landings. James was killed at Amayre by a German shell in early August 1944.

Hans Jeschonnek was promoted to *Generaloberst* in 1942. Hitler grew increasingly critical of the *Luftwaffe*, and Goering abandoned Jeschonnek to his fate. The last straws were the massive RAF raid on Hamburg and, less than a month later, another RAF raid which devastated Peenemunde. Facing Hitler's wrath and his own recent personal tragedy with the deaths of his father, brother and brother-in-law, he committed suicide at the Fuhrer's Wolfschanze Headquarters at Rastenburg in East Prussia in August 1943. Jeschonnek was 53 years old.

Werner Junck. Misled by Grobba, Jeschonnek had Junck court-martialled on his return to Germany. Junck was cleared, and his offers to resign his commission were rejected. Junck later distinguished himself as commander of *Jagdkorps II*, and he retired as a *Generalleutnant* in 1944. Junck died aged 81 in July 1976 in Munich.

James Joseph Kingstone, who commanded Kingcol, went on to command 30th Armoured Corps. He became ADC to King George VI in 1944, and although he retired from the Army in 1945 he remained Colonel of the Queen's Bays until 1954. He was made Deputy Lord Lieutenant of Wiltshire in 1953 and died in Warminster in 1966 at the age of 74.

Paul Knabenshue, the American Consul-General, contracted tetanus in Baghdad and died at his post in February 1942 at the age of 56. His Irish-born wife, Olive, wanted to return to Ireland but was refused permission by the Irish government, which said that she was an American citizen, despite never having lived in or visited the United

States.

The Regent, Abdul Ilah, remembering how the Knabenshues had saved his life, granted Olive a pension large enough for her to live comfortably in Baghdad until the end of the war, when she could travel safely home.

RAF Levies remained, guarding RAF installations in the Middle East throughout the Second World War. Some joined a Levy parachute company which later served with distinction in Albania, Greece, Italy and Yugoslavia. The Levies were disbanded in Iraq in May 1955. A few decided to stay in Iraq, joined the Iraqi Army and became Iraqi nationals, but most Assyrians emigrated to Britain, Australia, Syria and the United States, which all host Iraqi Christians of different persuasions.

Christopher 'Larry' William Mitchell Ling was awarded the DFC in November 1945 and retired from the RAF as a group captain in June 1946.

Eitel Frederich Rodiger von Manteuffel, Junck's staff officer on Rhodes, later served on the staff of the OKL, then commanded Airbase 4/XIII and, on promotion to *Generalmajor* in 1944, led the German Mission to Rumania.He was captured by the Russians in Rumania in late 1944, and liberated in 1950. Von Manteuffel died in Germany in 1984, aged 88.

Raymund John Maunsell remained in Cairo until 1944 when he moved to a counter-intelligence post at SHAEF. On leaving the Army in 1948 as a brigadier, he directed Unilever's Information Department until his retirement in 1963. Maunsell died in 1976 at the age of 73.

Keith 'Steve' May of the 1st Battalion Essex Regiment was promoted lieutenant-colonel and captured at Deir el Shein in Cyrenaica in May 1942. He spent the rest of the war as a POW in Italy and Germany, with a number of escape attempts to his credit

Ernest 'Mel' Melluish left Habbaniya in 1942 as a corporal, taking up duties as an armourer with Bomber Command at Waterbeech. He was scheduled for night duty, and swapped this with his best friend to take out his future wife. While a Lancaster was being bombed-up one of the bombs detonated, killing his friend. This stayed with Mel for the rest of his life. He demobilized in 1945 and worked as an agricultural, and later a heavy goods, mechanic. Mel died aged 81 in Norfolk in 2002.

Benito Mussolini was imprisoned in Gran Sasso in northen Italy following the overthrow of his Fascist regime in September 1943 and a switch in the new administration's alliegiance to the Allies. Spectacularly rescued by Otto Skorzeny on Hitler's orders, he became head of a German puppet government – the Italian Social Republic – in northern Italy.

Mussolini's past eventually caught up with him, and he was captured and executed by partisans on the banks of Lake Como with his mistress Claretta Petacci. Subsequently their bodies were hung upside-down from a girder in the forecourt of a Milan garage in April 1945.

John Joseph Joffre Page, the commander of No. 1 Armoured Car Company RAF at Habbaniya, became a liaison officer with Montgomery's staff, and rose to the rank of group captain, commanding RAF Halton before being demobilized in 1946.

He rejoined the oil industry, working with Iraq Petroleum in Palestine, Syria and the Gulf until his retirement in 1972. He then held a number of chairmanships and was knighted in 1979. He died in February 2006 aged 91.

Franz von Papen, the German Ambassador to Turkey, was acquitted at the Nuremberg War Crimes Trials of crimes against humanity, but was found guilty of political immorality, which was not a punishable offence. On release he was immediately rearrested by the German authorities in their de-Nazification programme, and was released in the late 1940s. Von Papen tried, unsuccessfully, to restart his political career in the 1950s. He wrote a number of books and retired to a castle in Upper Swabia. Von Papen died in Germany in May 1969 at the age of 89.

Baijan Peeku, who was wounded and won the Military Cross at Falluja, together with fellow Military Cross winner Stephan Nessan, represented the RAF Levies in the June 1946 Victory Parade in London. He died aged 88 in Sydney, Australia, in 1984.

James Maitland Nicholson Pike, Flight Commander of 203 Squadron, went on to command 185, 220 and 248 Squadrons. He joined the RAF Staff College as a wing commander in 1945, went on to command RAF bases at St Mawgan, Kinloss, Malta and Gibraltar as a group captain, and finished his service career as an air commodore in Intelligence in 1969. After his retirement he worked for the Ministry of Defence until 1978. Pike died in March 1999 at the age of 83.

Fawzi al Qawujki, Haj Amin's military aide and a colonel in the Iraqi Army in charge of irregular warfare, made a fighting retreat across the border to Syria. He was later wounded in the Syrian campaign and airlifted out by the Germans He married a German whom he met while hospitalized in 1942 in Berlin, and earned the enmity of the Mufti, who denounced him as a British spy when he supported

Rashid Ali. In 1947 he returned to Tripoli via Paris after six years in exile in Germany. He served as field commander of the Arab Liberation Army during the Arab–Israeli war of 1948, fighting alongside his old adversary, Glubb Pasha, and emerged as a rival to Haj Amin. His experience as a successful guerrilla leader was ineffective on the battlefield, and his forces were driven out of Palestine into Lebanon in October 1948. al Qawujki died in Beirut in 1977 at the age of 87.

Rudolf Rahn, Ribbentrop's emissary, served later in the war as Reich plenipotentiary in Tunisia, Hungary and Italy. He conducted himself like a relatively discreet viceroy, focusing more on collaborating than on coercing, believing that a more subtle approach would provide greater benefits. Rahn died in Germany aged 75 in 1975.

David Raziel, of the Haganah, was buried in the military cemetery at Habbaniya on 19 May 1941. In 1952 his sister, Esther, contacted the Military Attaché at the British Embassy in Tel Aviv to find out what had happened to her brother. SIME records in Cairo had been destroyed, and it took some time to find his place of burial. His sister requested that the body be returned to Israel. In 1955 David Raziel's remains were exhumed from the Habbaniya cemetery and transferred to Cyprus. In 1961 he was reburied in Jerusalem at the Mount Herzle Military Cemetery.

Joachim von Ribbentrop, the German Foreign Minister, lost Hitler's favour following the 20 July 1944 bomb plot, when it was discovered that a number of those involved came from the *Auswartiges Amt*. The end of the war came just as Hitler was about to replace him with Artur Seyss-Inquart. Nevertheless, Ribbentrop remained a fanatical Nazi and a vociferous anti-Semite. He was tried and convicted by the Nuremberg Military Tribunal of crimes against humanity, and executed in October 1946.

Ouvry Linfield Roberts served in a number of staff positions in the Middle East and Ceylon until August 1943, when he was given command of the 23rd Indian Division. The 23rd was one of the divisions of 4th Corps which defended Imphal against the Japanese. Encircled, the 23rd fought a bitter battle for three months until the Japanese were forced to abandon their attack on India and fell back into Burma with heavy casualties. Roberts ended the war as Quartermaster-General, was knighted and later served as ADC-General to the Queen. Following a successful business career in Canada, he died at 87 in March 1986 at his home in Buckinghamshire.

Yunis al Sabawi, the most pro-Axis member of Rashid Ali's cabinet, and founder of the fascist *Futuwwah* movement, fled to Persia. He was brought back to Baghdad, tried and executed in 1942.

Salah ed Din al Sabbagh, a leading member of the *Golden Square*, who commanded the 3rd Iraqi Division, escaped to Persia on 29 May 1941. He later crossed the border into Turkey, dressed as a Dervish, and was arrested. He was extradited to Iraq and executed in 1945. During his imprisonment in Turkey he wrote his memoirs and thoughts about the thirty-one-day war, which were published posthumously. al Sabbagh's work inspired future nationalists like Abdul Karim Kassem, who was a young officer in 1941, and Saddam Hussein.

Fahmi Said, the member of the *Golden Square* who commanded the mechanized forces besieging Habbaniya, fled to Persia on 29 May. He was later extradited to Iraq and executed in 1942.

Nuri al Said served as Prime Minister of Iraq fourteen times. His support for Britain over the Suez crisis in 1956 severely weakened his position with the nationalists. A military junta led by Abdul Karem Kassem, who was a junior officer in the Iraqi Army in 1941, seized power in August 1958. The King and the Regent were assassinated at the palace, ending the Hashemite monarchy in Iraq, and Nuri was caught trying to escape in a Baghdad street the next day, disguised as a woman. He was killed on the spot. The mob mutilated his body.

Mahmud Salman, one of the four Colonels of the *Golden Square* who commanded the Royal Iraqi Air Force, fled to Persia but was extradited and executed with his co-conspirators in 1942.

Walter Archer Bourchier Savile retired from the RAF as a group captain in May 1944 and died aged 90 in June 1988.

Kamil Shabib, Commander of the 1st Iraqi Division and a member of the *Golden Square*, fled to Persia on 29 May 1941 with his colleagues. He was extradited from Persia and tried and executed in Iraq in 1944.

Naji Shawkat, Minister of Defence in Rashid Ali's cabinet in 1941, was captured by the British in Italy in July 1945 and handed over to the Iraqis to serve a five-year term of imprisonment. Shawkat died in Baghdad in 1979.

Glynn Silyn-Roberts retired from the RAF in November 1961 as an air vice-marshal, and died at the age of 77 in September 1983.

Harry Chapman 'Sinbad' Sinderson remained in Baghdad, continuing his many roles as physician to the Royal Family and Household, adviser to the Iraqi Ministry of Social Affairs, and as Dean and

Emeritus Professor of Medicine in the Royal College of Medicine, which he had founded. In 1943 he and his wife created Noah's Ark, a welfare centre for Allied servicemen in Baghdad, of whom a million received a welcome in three years. He also introduced the Red Crescent and the Save the Children Fund to Iraq.

Sinderson was knighted on his retirement in 1946, and he continued to serve people through the Order of St John and local and national charities. He died aged 83 in November 1974.

Harry George Smart, evacuated from his command at RAF Habbaniya, was subsequently appointed AOC No. 17 Operational Training Group, and his promotion to air vice-marshal was confirmed in 1943. He retired from the RAF in September 1945. He emigrated to South Africa, and died at Simonstown in Cape Province in 1966, at the age of 75.

Leslie Ernest Smith left Habbaniya at the end of May with 94 Squadron, and was commissioned in August 1941 as a pilot officer. In 1943, as a flight commander in 609 Squadron, flying Hawker Typhoons on 'Rhubarbs' across the Channel, he was forced to ditch off Deal in Kent after his aircraft sustained heavy flak damage over Brussels. Smith was awarded a DFC in 1944 and was a flight lieutenant on his discharge from the RAF in 1947.

Freya Stark continued her work with the Ministry of Information until the end of the War. Sent to the United States in 1943 to lecture on the dangers of imposing a Zionist state in Palestine, she received a bruising reception which stayed with her for the rest of her life. In 1945 Freya left public service, and in 1947 married Stewart Perowne, the Public Relations Attaché at the British Embassy in Baghdad during the siege. She accompanied Perowne on postings to Barbados and Libya, but they separated in 1952.

Freya continued to travel, with memorable visits to Afghanistan, India and Nepal. She was a true eccentric, who wore Dior in the wilder reaches of Asia and Arabic dress in London. Her will of iron, infinite patience and remarkable powers of persuasion helped her to overcome her lack of money and worldly advantage to become a widely read and admired explorer, photographer and author, who was courted by generals, intellectuals, politicians and royalty. She was made a Dame Commander by Queen Elizabeth II in 1972. Freya died at the ripe old age of 100 at her home in Asolo, Italy, in May 1993.

Betty Sulman (Morrison) remained the King's Governess until 1942, when she married John Morrison, a British intelligence officer, in Baghdad. After the war Morrison, a classicist, returned to a successful academic career. Betty championed the phonic method of reading, helping many children and adults with learning disabilities to read. Betty had five children and remained very active until her death in Cambridge in 2003 at the age of 94.

Naji al Suwaidi died in South Africa in 1942 during his deportation to Baghdad to face trial for treason.

Tawfiq al Suwaidi became Prime Minister of Iraq in 1946 and again in 1950. He died in Beirut in 1968.

George Guy Waterhouse, head of the British Military Mission in Iraq, retired in 1941, only to be recalled later that year. He served until 1945 as OC North-West District, finally retiring as a major-general. He died in 1975 aged 89.

Archibald Wavell was dismissed by Churchill in June 1941 and sent as C-in-C India, a relative backwater. His appointment coincided with the Japanese declaration of war, and he was made Supreme Commander of Allied Forces in South-East Asia just in time to oversee the British defeats in Burma, Malaya and Singapore, which Churchill saw as failures by Wavell, Now a field marshal, Wavell was offered another 'backwater' post, Viceroy of India, which he held from 1943 to 1947. He died in London in May 1950.

Ernst von Weizsacher, Secretary of State at the German Foreign Office, was appointed Ambassador to the Vatican in 1943. He was convicted by the Nuremberg Military Tribunal of crimes against humanity and sentenced to seven years. He was released in 1950 after serving eighteen months. He died in Germany in 1951 shortly after completing his memoirs. His son, Richard, became President of the Federal Republic of Germany in 1984.

Arthur Valerian Wellesley served throughout the war, winning a Military Cross in 1941. Promoted lieutenant-colonel after the war, he commanded, in turn, the Royal Horse Guards, the Household Cavalry, 22nd Armoured Brigade and the RAC 1st (British) Corps. Prior to his retirement in 1967 he served for three years as Defence Attache in Madrid. He succeeded his father as the 8th Duke of Wellington in 1972, was on the board of several companies and has remained active taking a leading role in many local and national associations and charities, and in animal welfare.

William Taylor Forest Wightman, with three victories flying Gladiators, was taken off flying duties after Habbaniya. He was promoted to wing commander in 1945 and to group captain in 1951. He retired from the RAF in late 1958 and died at the age of 80 in November 1989.

Henry Maitland Wilson led the successful Syrian Campaign against the

Vichy French later in 1941, and in 1943 was appointed C-in-C Middle East. Despite a disastrous campaign in the Dodecanese, he became Supreme Allied Commander Mediterranean after Eisenhower. In 1945 Wilson was appointed a field marshal and was ennobled, taking the title of Baron Wilson of Libya. He finished his Army career as the Senior British Military Representative in Washington DC. Wilson died in Oxfordshire at 83 at the end of December 1964.

Ernst Woermann, Under-Secretary of State at the German Foreign Office, was convicted at the Nuremberg Military Tribunal of crimes against humanity, and was sentenced to seven years' imprisonment, which was later reduced to five years. He was released in 1951. Woermann died in Heidelberg in 1979 at the age of 91.

Amin Zaki (Sulaiman), the Iraqi Chief-of-Staff, fled to Persia on the night of 30 May 1941. He was returned to Iraq and sentenced to death in 1942, which was later commuted to life imprisonment.

Bibliography

Hitler's Gulf War has been based on a wide selection of books, articles, official documents and academic work.

The large number of works used to research this book are based on two issues. First I wanted to go beyond the purely physical aspects of the conflict to look at the people and the decisions that they made. I also drew widely on personal reminiscences in the air, on the battlefield, at the Embassy and at the various locations featured in *Hitler's Gulf War*. This was to help to explore, explain and put into context the factors driving the events which led up to those thirty-one days in May 1941, and the actions of Germany, Italy, Iraq and the United States, in addition to those of Great Britain, as well as the attitudes and experiences of those personally involved. All of these influenced the conflict and its outcome.

Secondly, virtually everyone involved is no longer alive, which means relying on published information. However, anything written about events which occurred almost seventy years ago comes with a set of inbuilt problems. Time has a subjective influence on the accuracy and the context of information. Works written at the time or shortly afterwards capture the detail and are sharply focused, although they tend to miss out on the wider perspective and are often written for purpose. Those written sometime later have greater perspective and see things in context, although they suffer from self-justification and important lapses of memory. Then there are those that reinterpret the information and those that confuse people, places and fact.

Nothing is black and white, it is merely shades of grey. I have therefore used as wide a variety of sources as possible in an attempt to avoid the most obvious pitfalls and to iron out the inconsistencies.

I have also been very fortunate to tap into the rich vein of Iraqi academic material. This not only gives more dimension but provides both the context in which decisions were made and a new level of detail of combat from the Iraqi perspective. Here are some of the numerous books and other literature worth reading on the subject, which I have used as references for this book:

Books

Aaronson, S., *Hitler, the Allies & the Jews*, Cambridge University Press, Cambridge, 2004

Allen, M., *Arabs*, Continuum, London, 2006

Al-Marashi, A. and Salama, S., *Iraq's Armed Forces: An Analytical History*, Routledge, London, 2008

Antonius, G., *The Arab Awakening*, Hamish Hamilton, London, 1938

Arthur, M., *Lost Voices of the Royal Air Force*, Hodder, London, 1993

Avon, The Earl of, *The Eden Memoirs: The Reckoning*, Cassell, London, 1965

Benjamin, M., *Last days of Babylon*, Bloomsbury, London, 2007

Birdwood, B., *Nuri al Said: A Study in Arab Leadership*, Cassell, London, 1959

Black, E., *Banking on Baghdad*, Wiley, London, 2004

Bloch, M., *Ribbentrop*, Crown, New York, 1992

Buckley, C., *Five Ventures*, HMSO, London, 1977

Bullock, A. (Introd.),*The Ribbentrop Memoirs*, Weidenfeld & Nicholoson, London, 1954

Burnett, A. (Ed.), *Iraq Defence Intelligence, Vol. 3 (1933–1941)*, Cambridge Archive Editions, Slough, 2005

Candler, E., *The Long Road to Baghdad, Vol. 1*, Cassell, London, 1919

Catherwood, C., *Winston's Folly: Imperialsm and the Creation of Modern Iraq*, Constable, London, 2004

Central Office of Information, *Paiforce: The Story of the Persia and Iraq Command, 1941–1946*, London, 1948

Chaillot, C., *The Syrian Orthodox Church of Antioch and all the East*, Inter-Orthodox Dialogue, Geneva, 1995

de Chair, S., *The Golden Carpet*, Faber & Faber, London, 1943
Morning Glory, Cassell, London, 1994

Churchill, W.S., *The Second World War*, Vol. III, 'The Grand Alliance', Houghton Mifflin, Boston, 1950

Ciano, G., *Diary 1937–1943*, Enigma Books, New York, 2002

Cole, W.S., *Roosevelt and the Isolationists 1939–1945*, University of Nebraska Press, Lincoln, 1983

Cooper, A., *Cairo in the War 1939–1945*, Hamish Hamilton, London, 1989

Cowper, J.M., *The King's Own*, Vol. 3, 1914–1950, Gale & Polden, Aldershot, 1957

Dahl, Roald, *Going Solo*, Puffin, London, 1988

Dann, U. (Ed.), *The Great Powers in the Middle East 1919–1939*, Holmes & Meier, Teaneck, 1988

Doenecke, J.D., *The Battle Against Intervention 1939–1941*, Krieger, Malabar, 1997

Dodge, T., *Inventing Iraq*, Hurst & Co., London, 2003

Dudgeon, A.G., *Hidden Victory*, Airlife, Shrewsbury, 1991
The War That Never Was, Tempus, Stroud, 2000

El-Sohl, R., *Britain's Two Iraq Wars*, Ithaca Press, Reading, 1996

Epelag, Z., *The Grand Mufti*, Taylor & Francis, London, 1963

Everett-Heath, E.N. and Westworth, J.R., *The Flying Fourth*, KORR Museum, Lancaster, 2005

Felmy, H. and Warlimont, W., *German Exploitation of Arab Nationalist Movements in World War II*, Hailer, St Peterburg, 2007

Fisk, R., *The Great War for Civilization: The Conquest of the Middle East*, Fourth Estate, London, 2005

de Gaury, G., *Three Kings in Baghdad*, Hutchinson, London, 1961

Geniese, J.F., *Freya Stark*, Chatto & Windus, London, 1999

Glubb, J., *The Story of the Arab Legion*, Hodder & Stoughton, London, 1948

Green, H., *King's Own Royal Regiment*, Leo Cooper, London, 1972

Grobba, F., *Maenner und Machte im Orient*, Musterschmidt, Gottingen, 1967

Gundelach, K., *Kampgeschwader 'General Wever' 4*, Motorbuch Verlag, Stuttgart, 1978

Die Deutsche Luftwaffe im Mittelmeer 1940–45, Band 1: 1940–1942, Verlag Peter D. Lang, Frankfurt-am-Main, 1981

Gunter, J., *Inside Asia*, Harper, London, 1942

Haddad, G., *Revolutions and Military Rule in the Middle East*, Vol. 1, Speller, New York, 1971

Halbert, C., *Il Duce*, Little, Brown, Boston, 1962

Halpern, M., *The Politics of Social Change in the Middle East & North Africa*, Princeton University Press, Princeton, 1963

von Hentig, W.O., *Mein Leben eine Dienstreise*, Vandenhoeck & Ruprecht, Gottingen, 1962

Hildebrand, K., *The Foreign Policy of the Third Reich*, University of California Press, Berkeley, 1970

Hill, Roderic, *The Baghdad Airmail*, Nonsuch, 2005

Hinsley, F.H. et al. *British Intelligence in the Second World War, Vol. 1*, HMSO, London, 1979

Hirszowicz, L., *The Third Reich and the Arab East*, Routledge & Keegan Paul, London, 1966

Holt, T., *The Deceivers*, Weidenfeld & Nicolson, London, 2004

Hooton, E.R., *Eagle in Flames*, Arms & Armour Press, London, 1997

Hopwood, D., *Tales of Empire*, I.B. Taurus, London, 1989

Horne, E., *A Job Well Done*, The Anchor Press, London, 1982

Ingram, E. (Ed.), *National & International Politics in the Middle East*, Frank Cass, London, 1986

Jbara, T., *Palestinian Leader Hajj Amin Al-Husayni, Mufti of Jerusalem*, Kingston Press, Princeton, 1985

Kadduri, M., *Independent Iraq*, Oxford University Press, London, 1960

Kattan, N., *Farewell Babylon*, Souvenir Press, London, 2007

Karsh, E., *The Arab-Israeli War 1948*, Osprey, Oxford, 2002

Kedourie, E., *The Chatham House Version and Other Middle Eastern Studies*, Frank Cass, London, 1970
    Arab Political Memoirs and Other Studies, Frank Cass, London, 1974

Kelidar, A. (Ed.), *The Integration of Modern Iraq*, Croom Helm, London, 1979

Kershaw, I., *Fateful Choices*, Allen Lane, London, 2007

Kirk, G., *The Middle East in the War*, Oxford University Press, Oxford, 1952

Kolinsky, M., *Britain's War in the Middle East*, MacMillan, London, 1999

Langer. W. and Gleason, S.E., *The Undeclared War 1940–1941*, Little Brown, London, 1953

Lukitz, L., *A Quest in the Middle East: Gertrude Bell and the making of Modern Iraq*, I.B. Taurus, London, 2006

Lunt, J.D., *Imperial Sunset: Frontier Soldiering in the 20th Century*, Madonald Futura, London, 1981

Lyman, R., *Iraq 1941*, Osprey, Oxford, 2006
    First Victory, Constable & Robinson, London, 2006

Mackenzie, C., *Eastern Epic Vo.l 1*, Chatto & Windus, London, 1951

Martin, T.A., *The Essex Regiment*, Essex Regiment Association, Brentwood, 1951

Matter, P., *The Mufti of Jerusalem*, Cambridge University Press, Cambridge, 1988

Meir-Glitzenstein, E., *Zionism in an Arab Country: Jews in Iraq in the 1940s*, Routledge, London, 2004

Mockler, A., *Our Enemies The French*, Leo Cooper, London, 1976

Muggeridge, M. (Ed.), *Ciano's Diplomatic Papers*, Odhams, London, 1948

Mure, D., *Practice to Deceive*, William Kimber, London, 1977

Nettleton, S. (Ed.), *Social Forces in Middle East*, Fisher, New York, 1955

Nightingale, P.R., *The East Yorkshire Regiment in the War of 1939–45*, Mr Pye (Books), Goole,1998

Omissi, D., *Air Power and Colonial Control*, University of Manchester Press, 1990

Pearce, F., *Under the Red Eagle*, Woodfield, Bognor Regis, 2004

Pearlman, M., *The Mufti of Jerusalem*, Gollanz, London, 1947

Pelly-Fry, J., *Heavenly Days*, Crecy Books, 1994

Playfair, I.S.O., *History of the Second World War*, Vol. 2, HMSO, London, 1956

Priestland, J. (Ed.), *Records of Iraq, Vol. 8, Politics and the Palace*

(1936–1941) and *Vol. 9, The Second World War (1941–1945)*, Cambridge Archive Editions, Slough,2001

Rahn, R., *Ruheloses Leben: Aufzeichnungen und Erinnerungen*, Diederichs Verlag, Dusseldorf, 1949

Ranfurly, H., *To War with Whitaker*, Mandarin, 1995

Rankin. N., *Churchill's Wizards*, Faber & Faber, London, 2008

Rassam, S., *Christianity in Iraq*, Gracewings, London, 2004

Raugh, H.E., *Wavell in the Middle East, 1939–41*, Brassey, 1993

Ross, A.E. (Ed.), *Through Eyes of Blue*, Airlife, Shrewsbury, 2002

Schechtman, J.B., *The Mufti and the Fuhrer*, Thomas Yoseloff, New York, 1965

Schofield, J., *Wavell*, John Murray, London, 2006

Schreiber, G., Stegman, B., and Vogel, D., *Germany and the Second World War*, Clarendon Press, Oxford, 1991

Schroder, B., *Deutschland und der Mittlere Ostern in Zweiter Weltkreig*, Musterschmidt Verlag, Gottingen, 1975

Schwanitz, W.G., *Germany and the Middle East*, Marcus Weiner, Princeton, 2004

Shams, I. (Ed.), *Iraq: Its History, People & Politics*, Humanity Books, London, 2003

Simpson, C., *Blowback*, Weidenfeld & Nicholson, London, 1988

Smith, D.M., *Mussolini's Roman Empire*, Longman, London, 1976

Shores, C., *Dust Clouds in the Middle East*, Grub Street, London, 1996

Silverfarb, D., *Britain's Informal Empire in the Middle East: A Case Study of Iraq 1929–1941*, Oxford University Press, 1997

Simon, R.S., *Iraq between the Two World Wars*, Columbia University Press, New York, 1986

Sinderson, H.C., *Ten Thousand and One Nights: Memories of the Sherifian Dynasty*, Hodder & Stoughton, London, 1973

Sluglett P.J. and Steer, I., *British in Iraq 1914–1932: Contriving King & Country*, Columbia University Press, New York, 2007

Spears, E., *Fulfilment of a Mission*, Leo Cooper, London, 1977

Stark, F., *Baghdad Sketches*, John Murray, London, 1937
Dust in the Lion's Paw, Century, London, 1985

Sweet-Escott, B., *Baker Street Irregular*, Methuen, London, 1976

Tarbush, M.A., *The Role of the Military in Politics: A Case Study of Iraq to 1941*, K. Paul International, London, 1982

Tedder, Lord, *With Prejudice*, Cassell, London, 1966

Tillman, H., *Deutschlands Araberpolitik in Zweiten Weltkreig*, Deutsche Verlag fur Wissenschaft, Berlin, 1965

Trigg, J., *Hitler's Jihadis*, The History Press, Stroud, 2008

Tripp, C., *A History of Iraq*, Cambridge University Press, Cambridge, 2000

Warner, G., *Iraq & Syria*, University of Delaware Press, Newark, 1974
von Weizsacher, E., *Memoirs*, Victor Gollanz, London, 1951
White-Spunner, B. *Horse Guards*, Macmillan, London, 2006
Wilson, Lord, *Eight Years Overseas*, Hutchinson, London, 1950
Wyndham, H., *The Household Cavalry at War*, Gale & Polden, Aldershot, 1952

Magazines and Journals

(*A selection of those articles found to be of most use*)

Arsenian, S., Wartime Propaganda in the Middle East, *Middle East Journal*, Vol. II, 1948
Atherton, L., SOE: Operations in the Middle East, *PRO Publications*, 1997
Cohen, H.J., The Anti-Jewish Farhud in Baghdad 1941, *Middle Eastern Studies*, Vol. 3, No. 1, October 1966
Dawn, C.E., The Formation of Pan-Arab Ideology in the Interwar Years, *Int. Journal of Middle East Studies*, Vol. 20, No. 1, February 1988
Deringil, S., The Preservation of Turkey's Neutrality During the Second World War, *Middle Eastern Studies*, Vol. 18, No. 1, February 1988
Dietrich, R., German relations with Iraq, *Middle Eastern Studies*, Vol. 41, No. 4, July 2005
Documents – German Ideas on Iraq 1937–1938, *The Middle East Journal*, Vol. 12, No. 2, Spring 1958
Dovey, H.O., The Middle East Intelligence Centre, *Intelligence & National Security*, Vol. 4, No. 4, October 1989
The Eighth Assignment 1941–1942, *Intelligence & National Security*, Vol. 11, No. 4, October 1996
Graham, A., The Iraq Levies at Habbaniya, *The Army Quarterly*, Vol. XLIV, 1942
Heller, M., Politics and the Military in Iraq and Jordan, *Armed Forces & Society*, Vol. 4, No. 1, November 1977
Hilgruber, A., England's Place in Hitler's Plans for World Domination, *Journal of Contemporary History*, Vol. 9, No. 9, January 1974
Isaacs, H.D., Sir Harry Sinderson Pasha (1891–1974), *British Society For Middle Eastern Studies Bulletin*, Vol. 2, No. 1, 1975
Kedourie E., Wavell and Iraq, *Middle Eastern Studies*, Vol. 11, July 1966
Kelidar, A., Iraq: The Search for Stability, *Middle East Review*, Vol. 11, No. 4, Summer 1979
Kelly, S., A Succession of Crises: SOE in the Middle East, 1940–45, *Intelligence & National Security*, Vol. 20, No. 1, March 2005

Khadduri, M., General Nuri's flirtations with the Axis Powers, *Middle East Journal*, Vol. XVI, 1962

De Luca, A.R., Der Grossmufti in Berlin: The Politics of Collaboration, *Int. Journal of Middle East Studies*, Vol. 10, No. 1, 1988

MacDonald, C.A., Radio Bari, *Middle Eastern Studies*, Vol. 13, 1977

Marmorstein, M., Review of Fritz Grobba's Memoirs, *Middle Eastern Studies*, Vol. 5, No. 3, October 1969

Mattar, P., Al-Husayni and Iraq's Quest for Independence 1939–1941, *Arab Studies Quarterly*, Vol. 6, No. 4, 1984

Maunsell and Mure, *Intelligence & National Security*, Vol. 8, No. 1, January 1993

Murphy, J.F., The March on Baghdad, *Military Heritage*, August 2000

Nafi, B.M., The Arabs and the Axis 1933–1940, *Arab Studies Quarterly*, Spring 1997

Nevo, J., Al-Hajj Amin and the British in World War II, *Middle Eastern Studies*, Vol. 20, No. 1, January 1984

Nicosia, F., Arab Nationalism & National Socialist Germany 1933–1939, *Int. Journal of Middle East Studies*, Vol. 12, 1980

Ogilvy, D., Airspeed Oxford, *General Aviation*, April, 2007

The Last of a Line, *The Aeroplane*, January 2008

Parsons, L., Soldiering for Arab Nationalism: Fawzi al-Qawuqji in Palestine, *Journal of Palestinian Studies*, Vol. 36, No. 4, 2007

Pool, D.C., Light on Nazi Foreign Policy, *Foreign Affairs*, Vol. 25, 1946

Porch. D., The Other Gulf War, British Intervention in Iraq 1941, *JFQ*, Issue 35

Price, A., Messerschmitt Bf 110, *The Aeroplane*, August 2007

Al-Qazzaz, A., The Iraq-British War of 1941: A Review Article, *Int. Journal of Middle East Studies*, Vol. 7, No. 4, 1976

Schwanitz, W.G., The Jinee and the Magic Bottle, *Interdisciplinary Journal of Middle Eastern Studies*, Vols X & XI

Stratton, M.B., British Railways & Motor Roads in the Middle East 1930–1940, *Economic Geography*, Vol. 20, No. 2, April 1944

Sulzberger, D.L., German Preparations in the Middle East, *Foreign Affairs*, Vol. 20, 1942

Thorpe, J.A., The US and the 1940–1941 Iraqi Crisis, *Middle East Journal*, Vol. 25, 1979

Williams, M., Mussolini's Secret War in the Mediterranean and the Middle East, *Intelligence & National Security*, Vol. 22, No. 6, December 2007

Yisraeli, D., The Third Reich and Palestine, *Middle East Studies*, Vol. 7, 1971

Archival Sources

Cabinet, CAB 106
Air Ministry, AIR 23, 40 & 41
Foreign Office, FO 370, 371 & 406
Security Service, KV 5/34, 5/35 & 5/40
War Office, WO 208
SOE, HS 3/198

PhD Theses

Al-Jamail, K., Nationalism in Iraq 1936–1941: Rashid Ali and Foreign
    Involvement, University of Keele, 1978
Flacker, E., Fritz Grobba and Germany's Middle East Policy 1933–1942,
    University of London, 1998
Hamdi, W.M.S., Rashid Ali Al-Gailani and the Nationalist Movement in Iraq
    1939–1941: A Political and Military Study of the British campaign in Iraq
    and the National Revolution of May 1941, University of Birmingham, 1986
Tarbush, M., The role of the Military in Politics: A Case Study of Iraq from
    1936–1941, University of Oxford, 1977

Internet Sources

www.assyrianlevies.com
Assyrian RAF Levies: The Battle for Habbaniya

www.csus.edu/indiv/s/scottjc/introduction.htm
Iraqi Coup, 1941

www.generals.dk/
Generals of World War II

www.geocities.com/acrawfordO/revo1t.html
The Iraqi Revolt

www.Habbaniya. org

RAF Habbaniya Association
www.latimesblogs.latimes.com/babylonbeyond/2008/12/fifty-years-aft.html
Rededication of the Habbaniya Cemetery

www.lasecondaguerramondiale.it/iraq.html
La Rivolta dell'Iraq

www.michael-reimer.com/CFS2/CFS2 Profiles/MTO AXIS Iraq.html
Iraqi and Axis aircraft in the fight for Habbaniya

www.mogggy.org/iraq/iraq.htm
Allied, Iraqi and Axis aircraft used in Iraq, 1941

www.mideastweb.org/iraqaxiscoup.htm
Iraq Coup Attempt of 1941: the Mufti and the Farhud

www.piltonenbunker.de/nachtjaeger/Luftwaffe/Drewes Martin.htm
Martin Drewes

www.rafarmouredcarsassociation.com
RAF Armoured Car Company Association

www.surfcity.kund.dalnet.se
Biplane fighter aces of World War II

Index